The Ontology of Psychology

In this volume Brakel raises questions about conventions in the study of mind in three disciplines—psychoanalysis, philosophy of mind, and experimental philosophy. She illuminates new understandings of the mind through interdisciplinary challenges to views long accepted.

Here she proposes a view of psychoanalysis as a treatment that owes its successes largely to its *biological* nature—biological in its capacity to best approximate the extinction of problems arising owing to aversive conditioning. She also discusses whether "the mental" can have any real ontological standing, advancing a new form of reductive physicalism—diachronic conjunctive token physicalism (DiCoToP)—which not only provides an understanding of mind/brain properties synchronically but can also be sufficient to address human-sized epistemological considerations that require a diachronic view. She then notes the positive implications of her account for psychiatry and psychoanalysis. Finally, she investigates the uses and abuses of consistency, both in method and content, in the several domains of interest: empirical research, psychoanalysis, thought experiments, and experimental philosophy.

In essence, Brakel articulates different sets of challenges pertaining to: (a) ancient dilemmas such as the mind/body problem; (b) long-standing debates about the nature of therapeutic action in psychoanalysis; and (c) new core questions arising in the relatively young discipline of experimental philosophy.

Linda A.W. Brakel is an adjunct associate professor in the Department of Psychiatry at the University of Michigan Medical School, a faculty research associate in the Department of Philosophy at the University of Michigan, and a faculty member of the Michigan Psychoanalytic Institute.

Routledge Studies in Contemporary Philosophy

For a full list of titles in this series, please visit www.routledge.com

18 **The Force of Argument**
Essays in Honor of Timothy Smiley
Jonathan Lear and Alex Oliver

19 **Autonomy and Liberalism**
Ben Colburn

20 **Habermas and Literary Rationality**
David L. Colclasure

21 **Rawls, Citizenship, and Education**
M. Victoria Costa

22 **Objectivity and the Language-Dependence of Thought**
A Transcendental Defence of Universal Lingualism
Christian Barth

23 **Habermas and Rawls**
Disputing the Political
Edited by James Gordon Finlayson and Fabian Freyenhagen

24 **Philosophical Delusion and Its Therapy**
Outline of a Philosophical Revolution
Eugen Fischer

25 **Epistemology and the Regress Problem**
Scott F. Aikin

26 **Civil Society in Liberal Democracy**
Mark Jensen

27 **The Politics of Logic**
Badiou, Wittgenstein, and the Consequences of Formalism
Paul M. Livingston

28 **Pluralism and Liberal Politics**
Robert B. Talisse

29 **Kant and Education**
Interpretations and Commentary
Edited by Klas Roth and Chris W. Surprenant

30 **Feminism, Psychoanalysis, and Maternal Subjectivity**
Alison Stone

31 **Civility in Politics and Education**
Edited by Deborah S. Mower and Wade L. Robison

32 **Philosophical Inquiry into Pregnancy, Childbirth, and Mothering**
Maternal Subjects
Edited by Sheila Lintott and Maureen Sander-Staudt

33 **Authenticity as an Ethical Ideal**
Somogy Varga

34 The Philosophy of Curiosity
Ilhan Inan

35 Self-Realization and Justice
A Liberal-Perfectionist Defense of the Right to Freedom from Employment
Julia Maskivker

36 Narrative Identity, Autonomy, and Mortality
From Frankfurt and MacIntyre to Kierkegaard
John J. Davenport

37 Contemporary Feminist Pragmatism
Edited by Maurice Hamington and Celia Bardwell-Jones

38 Morality, Self Knowledge, and Human Suffering
An Essay on the Loss of Confidence in the World
Josep Corbi

39 Contrastivism in Philosophy
Edited by Martijn Blaauw

40 Aesthetics After Metaphysics
From Mimesis to Metaphor
Miguel de Beistegui

41 Foundations of Freedom
Welfare-Based Arguments Against Paternalism
Simon R. Clarke

42 Pittsburgh School of Philosophy
Sellars, McDowell, Brandom
Chauncey Maher

43 Reference and Structure in the Philosophy of Language
A Defense of the Russellian Orthodoxy
Arthur Sullivan

44 Civic Virtue and the Sovereignty of Evil
Derek Edyvane

45 Philosophy of Language and Webs of Information
Heimir Geirsson

46 Disagreement and Skepticism
Edited by Diego E. Machuca

47 Philosophy in Schools
An Introduction for Philosophers and Teachers
Edited by Sara Goering, Nicholas J. Shudak, and Thomas E. Wartenberg

48 A Philosophy of Material Culture
Action, Function, and Mind
Beth Preston

49 A Philosophy of the Screenplay
Ted Nannicelli

50 Race, Philosophy, and Film
Edited by Mary K. Bloodsworth-Lugo and Dan Flory

51 Knowledge, Virtue, and Action
Essays on Putting Epistemic Virtues to Work
Edited by Tim Henning and David P. Schweikard

52 The Ontology of Psychology
Questioning Foundations in the Philosophy of Mind
Linda A.W. Brakel

The Ontology of Psychology

Questioning Foundations in the Philosophy of Mind

Linda A.W. Brakel

Routledge
Taylor & Francis Group
LONDON AND NEW YORK

First published 2013
by Routledge

2 Park Square, Milton Park, Abingdon, Oxon OX14 4RN
711 Third Avenue, New York, NY 10017, USA

Routledge is an imprint of the Taylor & Francis Group, an informa business

First issued in paperback 2016

Library of Congress Cataloging-in-Publication Data

Brakel, Linda A. W.
The ontology of psychology : questioning foundations in the philosophy of mind / by Linda A.W. Brakel. — 1 [edition].
pages cm. — (Routledge studies in contemporary philosophy ; 52)
Includes bibliographical references and index.
1. Psychoanalysis and philosophy. 2. Psychology and philosophy.
3. Ontology. I. Title.
BF175.4.P45B727 2013
150.1—dc23
2013002679

ISBN: 978-0-415-63562-2 (hbk)
ISBN: 978-1-138-20963-3 (pbk)

Typeset in Sabon
by Apex CoVantage, LLC

To my brother Rob.

And to Arthur, who still makes it all worthwhile.

Contents

PART V
Conclusion

Figure

Acknowledgments

Rights and Permissions

For permission to reprint Figure 4.1, I thank Sage Publications. This figure was originally in the following article:

Medin, D., Goldstone, R., & Gentner, D. (1990). Similarities involving attributes and relations: Judgments of similarity and difference are not inverses. *Psychological Science, 1*, 64–69, copyright © 1990 by Sage Publications. The figure is on page 66 and is reprinted by permission of Sage Publications.

I also thank *Frontiers in Psychology* for permission to reprint with revision an article originally published there. This appears as Chapter Two herein. The original citation is:

Brakel, L.A.W. (2011). Extinction phenomena: A biologic account of how and why psychoanalysis works. *Frontiers in Psychology/Neuropsychoanalysis and Psychoanalysis, 2*, article 223, 1–12.

General

There are many people to whom I owe thanks regarding the publication of this book. Among them are several people from Routledge, philosophy division. I thank my editor, Felisa N. Salvago-Keyes, who had the fortitude to go forth with this unconventional volume, and three anonymous reviewers who offered detailed critical comments that I found quite helpful. On the emotional and intellectual sides (which actually for me are not very separate), I thank Randolph M. Nesse and the entire Nesse Lab Group (a division of the Program for Evolution and Human Adaptation at the University of Michigan). This group supports and encourages wide-ranging and interdisciplinary works in diverse areas. Both for an inspiring body of empirical experiments and for taking my research ideas seriously I want to acknowledge Douglas L. Medin. Also, I thank J. David Velleman for recognizing my love for philosophy and recommending my independent work therein. And last and most, I thank my husband Arthur, for being first reader (and tough critic), intriguing if sometimes contentious interlocutor, and so much more.

Part I
Introduction

1 Introduction

This is an academic book, one published in the philosophy division of Routledge. I am proud of its placement here; I sought it, and, indeed, for the great majority of the book, I intend to adhere to the standard format and content befitting such an endeavor. However, because I believe my best (and rather) unique contributions can be made only as an interdisciplinary thinker, I will take the liberty of first approaching this introductory chapter as a psychoanalyst so as to offer a highly subjective and rather personal account of this volume's subject matter.

This book grew out of several experiences of what I shall call epistemological queasiness. The following examples will, I hope, serve to describe, if not fully explain, this phenomenon. The first example concerns my work as a clinical psychoanalyst. Over time I have found myself growing uncomfortable with certain trends in modern-day practice: (1) the burgeoning use of the telephone and Skype visual computerized technology to conduct sessions when patient and analyst are not able to meet in person, and (2) the reduction of sessions from four or five times weekly to once a week. The emergence of these two measures has been attributed to reality constraints on time and money, especially time and money deemed worthy of spending on psychoanalysis in twenty-first-century life. Since these trends were often practiced by the most progressive of psychoanalysts, and since my own self-view does not admit of cleaving to the traditional, I felt uncomfortable with my discomfort and thus motivated to understand just what was so irksome about these seeming improvements, aimed as they are at expanding psychoanalysis to far-off countries and maybe even to a younger demographic. I address this particular uneasiness about psychoanalysis in Chapter Two.

My next example of epistemological discomfort is quite different. While reading in many areas, all broadly considered branches of academic psychology or psychiatry, I experienced a sudden and acute onset of actual epistemological disorientation—I felt a paroxysmal loss of understanding of just what it *is* that actually constitutes the psychological realm. In other words, I became aware that I could no longer answer the questions: (1) What is it that is *psychological*? (2) What is *the mental*? Perhaps triggered most directly by the current emphasis in psychiatry and neuroscience on correlational studies—colorfully mapping various behaviors and their associated neurochemical changes (including those brought about by intervening stimuli, e.g., psychopharmacological agents and experimental tasks) onto particular brain areas—my epistemic qualms also owe much of their severity to the methodological predominance of quantitative measurements of observable phenomena (including, but not limited to, behavior), in biological, cognitive, and social psychology experiments.

While I understand that changes such as these *are* objectively measureable and therefore (as an empiricist) cheer their use, and while I also understand that the advances involved in brain imaging are remarkable and must be utilized, the downside of such technology-based studies should not be overlooked. Psychology, the realm of the mental, seems to be disappearing as we center our focus on one or both of the following: (1) The highly complex brain goings-on which are the causal foundations of any psychology; (2) the physical and behavioral manifestations of psychology—psychology's observable instantiations. In short, in a pithy phrase (for which I regrettably cannot take credit), psychology seems to be losing its mind! Recognition of this state of affairs as possibly true was the direct precipitant of Chapter Three, in which I undertake a lengthy investigation of classic mind/body solutions with the aim of finding some small steadier place for psychology and the mental realm.

The final instance of epistemological queasiness, which I explore in Chapter Four, is really a composite of many smaller examples and is perhaps the trickiest. It concerns the use of consistency in empirical science generally as well as in thought experiments, experimental philosophy, and psychoanalysis. The first bout of my distress regarding this matter occurred while reviewing various experimental philosophy studies. It became increasingly clear that consistency could be used in a variety of inconsistent ways to both rule in desired exciting/surprising findings and rule out dull or counterproductive ones. But, of course, this sort of epistemic queasiness is not a discrete time-limited and domain-specific malaise. Misguided appeals to consistency occur in empirical experiments, thought experiments, and psychoanalytic theory no less than they do in experimental philosophy. Further, the abuses of consistency, as well as successful uses, appear almost everywhere one looks for them, and probably exist at least as often when one does not.

Because the above is true, of course, for my work too, I must be careful in what I say in this introduction concerning the overarching themes of the book. Indeed, rather than say "careful," I should have said "truthful." Thus, much as I would like to claim that my epistemological queasiness, despite being registered in such diverse domains, nonetheless has a singular and important conceptual source; and, more importantly, though I would like to say that this sense of unease points the way to a unifying and striking discovery in the four domains of interest, I cannot, in good faith, make these claims. Moreover, although I would like to present the entire project of this book as a well-integrated program, I cannot do this either. Even to artificially construct one that would be as persuasive as it was smooth is not possible. For, in being my best psychoanalytic self, and my best academic self as well, truthfulness trumps everything, including strong desire and what has become the academy's standard aggrandizing style. So I will now proceed to present the admittedly much more modest achievements herein.

GENERAL CONSIDERATIONS

The more general advantages of the volume result from a thoroughly interdisciplinary approach to all the material examined—an approach that, because of my own variegated background, I cannot help but take. The central assumption of a method such as this holds that from within the center of one domain, questions and difficulties obvious to interdisciplinary "outsiders" are not even recognized as problematic. This is not to say that deeper, narrower concerns should not occupy those in the mainstream; they should. But gadflies, working tangentially are necessary too. For this volume the questioning curiosity of the clinical psychoanalyst provides the prototype gadfly model. Analysts feel a version of epistemological queasiness many times each workday: whenever some account is either too facile or found to be subtly incoherent, and more generally when a person's life fits together coherently but is felt by that person to be "not good." Thus, based on the underlying assumptions of psychoanalysis,[1] analysts can realistically offer to patients not only that the underlying meanings of particular situations can be better understood but also that a *better, consistent* life—a life that subjectively makes more sense to the subject living it—can be worked toward and realized. However, with respect to the issues addressed and then challenged in this volume, unfortunately, no such expansively sanguine promise of "better" or even "more coherent" theory is warranted. Instead, arising from my epistemological queasiness, the following is what I can (and do) realistically offer:

1. I demonstrate how states of puzzlement may lead to formulating serious questions and challenges.
2. I review and discuss several standard solutions, according them their strengths and pointing out their weaknesses.
3. I show that, for some puzzles, new and better alternative answers can be derived. The new answers, although they do not provide or promise grand or sweeping changes, do contribute small steps toward better understanding.

With these expectations in mind, let me turn now to the plan of the book. I will introduce individually the three parts of the book's main body. Each of the three parts has one chapter. These three chapters along with this introductory chapter and a final summary/conclusion chapter complete the entire volume.

PART TWO/CHAPTER TWO

Part Two, following directly after this introductory chapter, is called "Biological Psychology," and it consists of a single chapter, Chapter Two, "Extinction Phenomena: A Biologic Perspective on How and Why Psychoanalysis Works."

In this chapter I make the rather bold claim that psychoanalysis actually works, and does so fundamentally on a biological basis. I present and argue for the view that the effectiveness of classical analysis is predicated on its *biological* potency—focusing not on the currently popular biology of neuroscience, but instead on the biology of conditioning. My argument draws heavily on very recent biological research literature advancing a new view on the extinction of aversively conditioned stimuli. Namely, the current research findings convincingly demonstrate that complete extinction is *never* possible. However, extinction can be best approximated by deconditioning[2] in a great many different contexts. From here I affirm that, paradoxical as it might seem, only the most classical psychoanalytic technique can work. Why? Because only classical psychoanalysis—patient reclining on a couch for several sessions per week—can regularly deliver the multiplicity of deconditioning contexts necessary to best approximate extinction. How? Through the development of a sufficient variety of intense transference experiences, something classical analytic technique is uniquely able to facilitate.

The chapter opens with an explanation of conditioning—particularly aversive or fear conditioning. Next I illustrate how aversive conditioning can play a central role in much psychopathology, offering a paradigm case example. From here, extinction is described with a particular emphasis on the current research literature, which is unequivocal in propounding the great importance of multiple contexts for any chance of deconditioning. The last section of Chapter Two characterizes and explains important features of classical psychoanalytic technique, including use of the couch, and the concept of transference, particularly with respect to how it is that intense and myriad transference experiences can serve as the multiple deconditioning contexts needed to approximate extinction.

PART THREE/CHAPTER THREE

Part Three is called "Psychological Biology" and also consists of a single chapter, Chapter Three, "The Ontology of Psychology." Starting with genuine puzzlement about what is "psychological" and what constitutes "the mental," and after a lengthy (and I hope even-handed) investigation of the mind/body problem, I propose a modest, but new, partial solution to this ancient/modern problem. In summary form, here is a preview: I embrace a Token Physicalist position and then propose that, in considering the ontology of the mental, one must take into account both the synchronic view—the phenomena of interest at a particular time point—and the diachronic view—the phenomena of interest over time.[3] From a *synchronic* view—at a single particular time point (time t_1)—the *brain/biologic underpinnings* of any event/state/property considered "mental" *are* what is *causally sufficient* for the event/state/property. Given this causal efficacy (sufficiency) of the underlying brain goings-on synchronically, at any specified time point (time t_n), the mental-ness of any mental event/state/property is rendered not only causally irrelevant but ontologically irrelevant.[4] However, *diachronically*—over time (time $t_1 \rightarrow$ time $t_2 \rightarrow$ time t_n)—particularly as any mental event/state/property can be (and is) multiply realized by various physical instantiations, the *mental* event/state/property *is causally relevant* and has real ontologic standing.

This account rests on both:

1. The philosophical concept of multiple realization, particularly as it has received convergent support from recent work in the neurosciences on "biological degeneracy." Biological degeneracy (a species of redundancy) demonstrates that, even within a single individual, various *different* neuronal assemblies underpin what is regarded as the same mental state.
2. Considerations of mereological composites—specifically that, despite gradual shifts, sometimes leading to a total alteration in the materials constituting an entity, the entity is nevertheless regarded as "the same entity," these underlying compositional changes notwithstanding.

It is from the background of these two concepts that the new account—Diachronic Conjunctive Token Physicalism, or DiCoToP—outlined briefly above is proposed, potentially offering a small advance in the understanding of mind/body relations. And yet however pleasing, or even convincing, this small potential step toward a new understanding of a piece of the mind/body problem might be, I must remind the reader (and especially I must remind myself) that any progress this represents is indeed small. The explanatory gap—that between the physical neuronal causal foundations of the mental on the one side and the psychological effects seen in consciousness, qualia, intentions, and mental contents on the other—remains as perplexingly and exasperatingly large as ever.

Although I've led with the broad conclusions of this chapter, the chapter actually proceeds according to the following detailed organizational sequence: I begin by exploring some very interesting arguments for dualism. But then, reasons for endorsing physicalism and supervenience are given. Next, I discuss both the advantages and disadvantages of nonreductive physicalism, taking up the major problems and arguments, which include: (1) emergence and epiphenomenalism, (2) the problem with mental (and downward) causation, (3) the Exclusion Argument, (4) the argument derived from determinates/determinables, and (5) the Generalization Argument. Following this discussion, reductive physicalism is likewise reviewed with respect to its advantages and disadvantages, with both type and token reductive (identity) physicalism examined. In these sections, multiple realization and its brain structure/neuronal counterpart, biological degeneracy, figure prominently. It becomes clear that, while multiple realization and biological degeneracy present serious problems for type identity, they provide important assets for token identity, thus leading the way to my particular take on token physicalism.

PART FOUR/CHAPTER FOUR

Part Four is titled "Uses and Abuses of Consistency." Like the sections before it, this section is made up of a single chapter, Chapter Four, "The Uses and Abuses of Consistency in Thought Experiments, Empirical Research, Experimental Philosophy, and Psychoanalysis." Also like the earlier chapters, Chapter Four arose in response to my own sense of epistemological unease. In this case, I experienced a growing epistemic squirminess as I realized that a great many of the reported experiments I came across seemed at once *too* well fashioned, almost perfectly formed, and yet capable of delivering too many exciting, surprising findings. Further, my discomfort was heightened rather than assuaged by observing this phenomenon across the four domains of interest, as if a certain sort of polished regularity yielding striking results represented the current-day overarching norm in all academic endeavors.

But, indeed, although the motivation for this chapter is like that of the others, there is something quite unique and a bit disquieting about Chapter Four. This chapter, unlike the others, impels one toward examining one's own work with a greater critical sense than is usual, insisting on a less-than-comfortable scrutiny of this very volume. Thus, while I do have the impulse in this introductory chapter to characterize Chapter Four, and the volume as a whole, as providing a fresh and original and yet coherent, consistent view—an account important and illuminating in its unitary approach to four cognate disciplines—I must follow my own recommendations, present the more modest but more realistic accomplishments herein, and be satisfied.

In Chapter Four I assert that consistency is always among the fundamental elements organizing human endeavors, recognizing, too, that consistency as a concept takes many (and sometimes inconsistent) forms. The opening sections of the chapter explore the many and necessary uses of consistency in empirical research, thought experiments, experimental philosophy, and psychoanalysis. Then, in the sections that follow, I introduce the rather paradoxical notion of "abuses of consistency." Here specific examples from empirical research, experimental philosophy, psychoanalysis, and thought experiments reveal several types of serious consistency-based problems, all of which seem to be motivated by highlighting, and therefore making more influential, the findings observed and reported.

But striking results cannot be the norm. Moreover, more modest but accurate findings should suffice, and they do. Thus, this chapter endeavors to provide not just a critique of seemingly consistency-based "important" and flashy results but also a positive account for findings that are more routine and less dramatic. This takes place in two stages. First, I diagnose an abuse-of-consistency problem in many of the solutions given to the seminal thought experiment puzzle: the Trolley Case and its many offshoots. Namely, I suggest that a plethora of *false* (but consistent) parallels are routinely constructed. In the second stage, I offer a curative treatment—the method of intervening stepwise cases. Here I show how better parallels can be derived. The end results are clearly less exciting—they are no longer striking, but they are more realistic. The same could be said for the contributions of Chapter Four.

PART FIVE/CHAPTER FIVE

The volume ends with Chapter Five, "Summary and Conclusions." In this chapter I will restate and evaluate the main goal of the book—to question certain foundations in studies of the mind, with challenges arising from an interdisciplinary perspective. I suggest that it is only by pursuing mental studies outside the bounds of a single discipline that one can appreciate certain sorts of serious problems—problems that otherwise either go unrecognized within any single discipline or fall between the boundaries of two or more. With this in mind, in the summary and conclusions chapter, I review each of the chapters in the body of the book by first restating the nature of the particular issues giving rise to the problems; next articulating the questions that were posed and the challenges that were raised; and finally evaluating the new understandings and solutions proposed, recognizing their limitations but at the same time appreciating that even modest realistic gains are indeed gains—wins rather than losses.

REFERENCES

Brakel, L.A.W. (2009). *Philosophy, psychoanalysis, and the a-rational mind.* Oxford: Oxford University Press.

Kim, J. (1993). *Supervenience and mind.* Cambridge, UK: Cambridge University Press.
Kim, J. (1998). *Mind in a physical world.* Cambridge, MA: MIT Press.
Kim, J. (2005). *Physicalism or something near enough.* Princeton, NJ: Princeton University Press.
Kim, J. (2010). *Essays in the metaphysics of mind.* Oxford: Oxford University Press.

Part II

Biological Psychology

2 Extinction Phenomena

A Biologic Perspective on How and Why Psychoanalysis Works

INTRODUCTION

Increasingly over the past decade, psychoanalysts have shown a willingness to believe that various aspects of psychoanalytic technique, heretofore viewed as important, if not essential, can be altered or actually even dispensed with entirely without substantially compromising treatment effects. This new flexibility is due to a variety of reasons. For example, as a consequence of strained economic circumstances, modern-day busy schedules, and competition both from pharmacological treatments and cognitive-behavioral therapies requiring less time, the frequency of sessions per week in the typical psychoanalysis has decreased. This is so clearly the trend that some training institutions even permit thrice-weekly analyses to count both for the psychoanalyses that candidates conduct and for their own required treatments (their so-called training analyses). Although most view this as less than ideal, patients and analysts have coped with the consequent decrease in intensity.

Another recent change is that psychoanalyses (or portions thereof) now sometimes take place largely by telephone or over the Internet with Skype software enabling visual contact to accompany auditory communication. The increased mobility of analysands (often necessitated by their careers) and major technological advances contribute to this change, and it is too early to evaluate the effects.[1]

Related to this last alteration in psychoanalytic technique, but far predating it, are questions about the use of the psychoanalytic couch.[2] Never really deemed essential to psychoanalytic treatments, analysts have considered the couch to be *useful* in allowing both patients and analysts to associate more freely. Certainly without the social conventions and regulators of everyday conversations (including eye contact and nodding), when patients are on the couch, both patients and analysts experience far fewer constraints. And yet (as will be discussed below), in the analytic treatment of children, adolescents, and even some adults, the couch has been regarded by some as optional at best, and even detrimental. This last position seems to have gained some strength as anecdotal reports of patients feeling alienated on the couch grow, especially as the frequency of sessions per week diminishes. This last is not that surprising—for whatever else, each session can at least provide an opportunity for human contact.

Paradoxically, despite these recent trends, I want to make an argument favoring aspects of classical psychoanalytic technique—in particular, the couch—as essential in effecting changes in psychopathology. More surprisingly, I want to make this argument on a *biological* basis. Further, I shall propose that psychoanalysis, with the *biologically potent* classical techniques in place, can produce changes over and above those that rival treatments can deliver. Note here that I am not holding that the particular features of classical analytic techniques that I will discuss are definitionally essential. No one of these features alone, nor any combination thereof, is constitutive of psychoanalysis. Rather, I claim that frequency, physical presence of patient and analyst, and especially the couch are essential for the capacity of patients to establish varied and deeply experienced transferences, and that these in turn are necessary for the lasting *biologically mediated* improvements in psychopathology that psychoanalysis can uniquely offer.

Note that my view implies that treatments (including cognitive-behavioral therapy, various psychotherapies, and even nonclassical psychoanalyses), to the extent that they rely *solely* on changes effected through higher-level psychological processes, cannot be as effective as classical psychoanalysis. Why? Because these treatments are predicated *only* on distinctly human learning systems involving rationality-based learning and an autobiographical memory system rather than allowing the simultaneous functioning of diverse unconscious (irrational and a-rational) transferences constituting the biological underpinnings that I will begin to describe below.[3]

The *biological model* upon which I draw in formulating these claims involves neither brain chemistry nor neuroanatomy (at least not primarily). Rather, I turn to the *biology of conditioning*, specifically that of conditioned fear responses and extinction learning, to construct the case. The argument will take shape as follows: In the first section I describe the basic concepts of conditioning, including fear conditioning. In the section to follow I suggest that various sorts of psychopathologies in fact result (at least in part) from complex conditioning. Continuing my account, the next section provides an outline of recent developments in the understanding of extinction phenomena. Finally, in the last section I propose that psychoanalyses, particularly those using classic psychoanalytic techniques, can better provide the procedures (or analogues thereof) currently thought to be necessary to best approximate successful extinction. In this final section I will make the claim that in understanding the processes of conditioned learning and extinction, one can have a new biological perspective on explaining how and why psychoanalysis can (and does) work.

CONDITIONING PARADIGMS

Conditioning, both in its classical Pavlovian form and of the instrumental or operant type, is a robust and widespread biological phenomenon. Functioning in living organisms ranging from those that are quite simple (e.g., the sea slug, aplysia [see Walters, Carew, and Kandel, 1979])[4] to those that are very complicated (e.g., human beings), conditioning is perhaps the most basic form of learning. Both types of conditioning essentially involve associative learning.

The basic paradigm for classical conditioning can be readily seen in Pavlov's (1927) famous work with dogs. A hungry dog salivates when food is presented. The food, an unconditioned stimulus (US), will bring about salivating, the biological unconditioned response (UR), quite spontaneously. Now add trials in which a ringing bell just precedes the presentation of food. The bell is a conditioned stimulus (CS) paired with the food (US). After some number of trials, the mere ringing of the bell (CS) will occasion the dog to salivate—that is, to have the conditioned response (the CR, which is equivalent to the UR), before or even in the absence of food. The bell (CS) has become associated with the food (US) such that salivation (CR) results.

"Operant conditioning," according to conditioning researchers Bouton and Swartzentruber (1991, p. 124), "is a similar process [to classical conditioning] through which organisms learn to associate new behaviors or acts with reinforcers." In operant conditioning (also called instrumental learning), an animal's behavior is shaped not by antecedent stimuli, as in classical conditioning, but instead by the reinforcers (rewarding or punishing in nature) that are experienced as consequences of the behavioral acts (see Bouton and Swartzentruber, 1991, p. 129; Skinner, 1938). Training a dog, for example, involves much instrumental conditioning. Take the basic voice command "sit." When teaching a puppy to sit, the owner positively reinforces as many instances of sitting as possible—at first whenever the puppy sits for whatever puppy reason, and later only after the oral command "sit" has been given. Pigeons likewise demonstrate instrumental conditioning when differential reinforcement leads to differential pecking behaviors. For example, a pigeon will learn to peck the middle key in a series of keys far more than any other key if pecking the middle one has been followed more often by food reward than has pecking the other keys. Similarly, rats can be trained to differentially explore particular areas of their environments based on operant conditioning. They will engage in far more lively exploratory behavior of any portion of the cage in which some sort of positive reinforcement has taken place, spending far more time in that area over nonreinforced areas.

Regarding operant *versus* classical conditioning, Bouton and Swartzentruber (1991, p. 129) point out that, despite decades of textbooks emphasizing the differences, ". . . recent research has established strong parallels between the mechanisms . . ." so much so that "[i]t has become useful to view Pavlovian and operant learning as examples of the same basic learning process: Just as Pavlovian based behavior reflects knowledge of a CS-US association, instrumentally based behavior may reflect knowledge of a response-reinforcer association."

Conditioning of both types can be employed to demonstrate a wide variety of responses in animals and humans. For example, reactions to various chemicals and drugs can be enhanced or inhibited by employing conditioning procedures in many species. Conditioning can also induce and then shape basic learning behaviors, including those involving memory, item discrimination, and categorization. Researchers can also use conditioning to explore how and what animals understand as well as extend animals' capacities to perform tasks that would be unusual in nature—as in pigeons trained via conditioning protocols to: (a) indicate the presence or absence of humans in photos (Herrnstein and Loveland, 1964) and (b) categorize different types of music (Porter and Neuringer, 1984). But, as will be taken up below, conditioning can also result in taste aversions, fears, and phobias.

FEAR CONDITIONING

In the descriptions of both classical and operant conditioning above, all the examples concerned what is termed "appetitive conditioning." Simply put by Martin-Soelch, Linthicum, and Ernst (2007, p. 426): "Appetitive conditioning is the process through which new rewards are learned and acquire their motivational salience." Indeed, the emphasis is on the word *rewards*. Thus, in the operant conditioning paradigms briefly discussed, the rats, pigeons, and puppies all received positive rewards, shaping the behaviors desired by the researchers or dog owner. Eventually, after sufficient association with reward, the behaviors themselves become experienced as desirable. Similarly, after their classical conditioning trials, Pavlov's dogs salivated at the bell alone, because its tone had been paired with, and thereby associatively linked with, the intrinsically rewarding meat.

But "aversive conditioning" is equally important, perhaps more so for our purposes. The motivational salience of negative reinforcers is readily learned—with aversive stimuli ranging from psychological punishments to foot shocks and toxins—all capable of producing conditioned inhibitions, symptoms (such as phobias), anxiety, and fear. Aversive classical conditioning looks much like its appetitive counterpart except that the unconditioned stimulus (US) is highly negative, and the unconditioned response (UR) is that of fear and avoidance. Thus, for example, Ji and Maren (2007, p. 749) report that, when a rat ". . . is exposed to pairing of a neutral conditioned stimulus (CS), such as a tone or light, with an aversive unconditional stimulus (US), such as a foot-shock; this procedure yields a conditioned fear response to the CS [the tone or light]." In operant aversive conditioning, negative (punishing) reinforcers are applied after a particular behavior. This leads to the cessation of the behavior, sometimes abruptly and sometimes more gradually. For instance, returning to the world of dog training, dogs engaged in "counter surfing" (standing up on two legs to obtain food from countertops) can be conditioned to stop these activities after instances of surfing behaviors are greeted by the crashing of cleverly placed pans. This produces a loud aversive negative reinforcer in its own right, as well as dampening the positive pleasure of tasty morsels of food obtained in this manner.

Despite the obvious difference in valence between aversive and appetitive types of conditioning, in much of the literature (see Bouton, 1988, 1993; Bouton and Swartzentruber, 1991; Bouton, Westbrook, Cochran, and Maren, 2006; and Quirk and Mueller, 2008), the structure of the two is found to be so fundamentally analogous that in most matters of interest they are treated together. (I shall take this up in more detail below in the section on "Extinction".) However, at least one group of researchers (Chang, Knapska, Orsini, Rabinak, Zimmerman, and Maren, 2009, p. 5) recognizes something distinctive: "A unique feature of fear memory is that it can be acquired with as little as one exposure and can persist for a lifetime." Along these lines, I speculate that compared with appetitive conditioning, fear conditioning is (1) faster, (2) more readily generalizable, and (3) more difficult to render extinct. My hypothesis is based on evolutionary considerations: It would make evolutionary sense for conditioned fears to take hold more readily and to be more generalizable in many directions than would be the case for appetitive conditioned responses. Add to this that conditioned fears *should* be difficult to supplant with benign memory experiences simply because a false negative would be far more dangerous and ultimately costly than a false positive when dealing with a genuinely aversive stimulus. Indeed, a rustle of grass mistaken for a snake would cost a fleeing animal some energy, but a poisonous snake taken for a rustle of grass could be fatal. Stephen Maren (2011), a neuropsychobiological researcher specializing in fear conditioning, agrees:

> [Regarding] the evolutionary forces that have shaped the two types of learning: Yes, aversive learning is typically much faster and readily generalized. You can go days without food, so the penalties for not rapidly learning about food-predictive stimuli or responses to get food are not as severe as the penalties for failing to anticipate something potentially lethal (predator, speeding car, etc). Learned fear is rather resistant to extinction. I do not know if anyone has systematically compared the two types of learning with respect to reinstatement/recovery/renewal [of the conditioned fear responses], but my gut reaction is that extinction of fear would be more context-specific as the price of broadly generalizing extinction (that something [that was] dangerous, now safe, is really safe everywhere) might be costly.[5]

With this important difference in mind, let me now move to the role of conditioning, particularly but not exclusively aversive fear conditioning, in the development of neurotic psychopathologies of various sorts. After that, a section on extinction will follow.

THE ROLE OF CONDITIONING IN PSYCHOPATHOLOGY

To establish my claim regarding the efficacy of classical psychoanalysis in approximating extinction, I must first demonstrate that conditioning—aversive and appetitive, classical and operant—actually does play an important role in the sort of psychopathologies seen by psychoanalysts. Further, since my claim is so general, I should be able to illustrate it using any and every patient. And so, I will present in detail one patient, Mr. H, whose case does readily exemplify the sorts of psychopathological effects (obvious and subtle) resulting from behaviors and actions as well as beliefs, desires, and fantasies, all occasioned by classical and operant conditioning.

Mr. H came into psychoanalytic treatment when he was in his late forties. A geologist of modest success, the presenting symptom was his feeling depressed and anxious that his marriage was deteriorating. He was the father of three children, all in their teens when he began his analysis. His wife, a nurse by training, had stayed at home (by choice) for more than a decade to raise the children in the fashion that both she and Mr. H thought best. Now, with the children in middle and high school, his wife had returned to work. With that major adjustment, Mrs. H was experiencing a new excitement for life, one that she wanted to share with Mr. H, particularly sexually. But the more Mrs. H wanted him, the more distant Mr. H felt. Once in a while, when he did allow sexual intimacy, he would suffer a wave of great anxiety and then tremendous concern for the integrity of his penis. He would consequently rush through intercourse and/or suffer from premature ejaculation. As we explored this problem, Mr. H associated to other fears he had recently developed, all of which he knew to be irrational and all of which he felt he could manage (unlike the sexual problem). He was afraid of elevators, so he took the stairs. He was afraid of doors slamming on him, so he was very careful, and he always avoided automatic doors. He was afraid of cutting himself on jagged edges of cans, and so his wife always opened these. Doing occasional fieldwork for his job, he found himself in some locations where he became quite unreasonably afraid that he would step into some trap set for animals.

Quite early in the treatment I could (as could any analyst) see a connection among these seemingly disparate fears. Mr. H was afraid that some part of his body would be caught in and damaged by *some dangerous hole and its surrounding parts*—the elevator and its automatic doors, powerful doors in general, rough-edged cans, animal traps with teeth, and finally the vagina.

Did Mr. H also have a fantasy of vagina dentata? Certainly Mr. H suffered from a phobia with symptoms that were spreading and generalizing.

But additional questions arose. How did his phobia develop? Why did he have sexual troubles with his wife now, and not in the preceding years of their marriage? What was the central phobic object from which the other fears generalized? These were not questions that could be asked or answered directly. However, even in the early phase of his analysis, Mr. H discovered several things. The sexual problem with his wife was a function of her increased interest in him. During the many years when she was an exhausted mother and housewife, her sexual interest in Mr. H was minimal. Moreover, whatever sexual activity they had had was always initiated by him. This was true, albeit for different reasons, early in their marriage, too. Mrs. H was at that time young and sexually inhibited as well as uninitiated. She followed Mr. H's lead in all matters sexual. But why was this wonderful midlife change in Mrs. H proving so problematic for Mr. H?

With further analytic work we found some answers, many involving conditioning. First let me describe the aversive classically conditioned event likely central to Mr. H's presenting psychopathology—namely, his sexual anxiety. It occurred when Mr. H was around four years old—in particular, on the day he learned to ride a bicycle with no training wheels. He and his father, who had been helping him master bike riding, came rushing into the house, and the screen door banged noisily. Mr. H remembers feeling "on top of the world." Shouting about his triumph, both Mr. H's mother and the much-loved family dog, a young (but large) German shepherd, ran toward Mr. H and his father. His mother hugged him, seeming to ignore his father. And the excited (and not-yet-well-trained dog) lunged at Mr. H, knocking him over. Mr. H felt the wind knocked out of him; he felt scared; and he reflexively started to flail at the dog, who just as reflexively responded by biting his hand hard, drawing enough blood to increase Mr. H's terror. In fact the wound to Mr. H's hand required a trip to the emergency room and several stitches.

In this episode, we can see the *unconditioned stimuli* (US)—the dog knocking Mr. H over, biting him, injuring him, with the emergency room trip and stitches to follow; the *unconditioned responses* (UR)—the pain, fear, and traumatic anxiety occasioned by these events; and the *conditioned stimuli* (CS)—the happy mother and the eager dog, both positively disposed toward Mr. H and therefore approaching him exuberantly. This part of the episode—the excited interest of the beloved other—was the central feature occasioning the *conditioned response* (CR), a response seen to continue unchanged even so many years later in his pathological reactions to his wife's sexual advances.

But the story does not end here. This aversive conditioning episode with its conditioned stimulus (or stimuli) took place in a multifaceted situation experienced as many contexts. Thus, in addition to the overexcited, too eager, and then biting dog, many other factors comprised the conditioned stimulus and/or its context(s).[6] From the emotional side, there were at least two important feelings. First, there was the wonderful "on top of the world" feeling of triumph associated with the real success of having learned to ride a bike. Then there was another sort of triumph, as Mr. H felt that he was more important to his mother than was his father. There was at least one identifiable physical context too. The door noisily slamming just preceding the incident can be seen in Mr. H's secondary symptoms, particularly his fear of certain doors.

Further, conditioned aversive stimuli tend to generalize. In other words, stimuli related to the CS (those similar to the original in terms of category, or even those closely connected in time or space) can also be expected to give rise to the conditioned response. In fact this was the case for Mr. H. We can note the generalization of the phobic stimuli producing his fearful (phobic) reactions: he became afraid of all sorts of elements resembling the dog's mouth—the teeth of the animal trap and the jagged can; the strong, jawlike doors of the elevator; inexorable automatic doors; and the primary fear of his wife's vaginal musculature.[7,8]

Of course, one might ask the following question: Why did Mr. H develop the precise form of phobia from which he suffered and not a fear of dogs, or doctors, or emergency rooms, or blood? A complex question that I cannot answer, there is, however, more to say about the specific symptoms he *did* develop—more about his particular phobias and the role of conditioning in his psychopathology. Some relevant additional information concerns his parents, their relationship to him, and their relationship to each another. As Mr. H's psychoanalysis progressed, it became increasingly clear that his mother and father both contributed (without conscious intent) to the aversive conditioning crystallized by the excited dog/stitches episode. His mother was domineering, warm, loud, and overbearing, while his father was quiet, kind, and unassuming. Especially when Mr. H was in high school, he had worries (which were at the same time unconscious unacceptable wishes) that his mother thought more highly of Mr. H than of his father and that she preferred him (her son) over her own husband. Therefore, when his mother actively encouraged him in his athletic and scholarly endeavors (becoming like the CS, the overeager and excited dog), Mr. H withdrew from her and became distant, much as he did decades later with his newly passionate wife. Moreover, especially as he measured himself against his father, who, as it happened, was enduring some business losses during Mr. H's adolescence, Mr. H inhibited his own high school achievements. Thus we see that his mother's implicit (and natural) attempts at appetitive operant conditioning, aimed toward increasing Mr. H's involvement with her and at heightening his success in school and sports, actually functioned as operant aversive conditioning. Given his unconscious feelings of guilt at his perceived victory over his father, both with respect to his mother and with respect to his high school endeavors, and given Mr. H's consequent need to curtail himself in both domains, his mother's encouragement functioned as aversive stimuli—operant shapers inhibiting Mr. H's behaviors.

Finally, to form a more complete picture of Mr. H's complex psychopathology, we must return to an important contextual aspect of the aversive conditioning event. Remember that emotionally Mr. H was feeling "on top of the world," triumphant, both over his father and, perhaps more importantly, because of his real life accomplishment—he could now ride a bicycle. Through the course of the psychoanalysis, then, we became aware of a chronic painful symptom from which Mr. H suffered almost his whole life, a symptom as debilitating as his sexual problem and also traceable ultimately to the context of the aversive conditioning. Whenever Mr. H experienced himself as about to be tremendously successful—that is, whenever an important real-life success about which he would likely feel "on top of the world" and triumphant loomed ahead—Mr. H would inhibit his success, kill his victory.

Thus, to take things in reverse chronological order, Mr. H was only moderately successful as a geologist. Many others in his company had more prestige and earned more money. In graduate school, he had given some thought to obtaining a PhD and opening possibilities for a more high-profile university career or for more lucrative employment than that for which he settled. His plans evanesced however, as his grades dropped precipitously just as he began the application process. He left school with a terminal master's degree. He was a B+ student at college; and in high school, despite a strong start, his grades plummeted in his junior year as he and his classmates contemplated college applications. (Note the similarity to his graduate school career.) Mr. H's participation in sports and the arts followed a similar pattern. He enjoyed his school's theatrical productions, but when he was offered a significant role, he became anxious and declined. Similarly, when told that he was one of a few students named to compete for first chair violin, Mr. H remembered that his audition piece was critiqued as "workman-like and wooden, without much feeling." He didn't even win second chair. Finally, in little league from an early age, Mr. H's baseball prowess also always seemed to fade whenever it seemed possible that he could become a truly outstanding player. Functioning as a lifelong defense against the "on top of the world" context of the conditioned stimulus, a CS that would inexorably lead to the conditioned fear response, Mr. H (unconsciously) arranged things to make sure that his achievements were moderate at best.

Although the majority of psychoanalytic cases may not have an aversively conditioned response event that is so striking, most do involve various combinations of the more subtle sort of conditionings, classical and operant, aversive and appetitive just reported in the case of Mr. H.[9] We will return to Mr. H in discussing psychoanalytic techniques with respect to best approximating extinction of aversively conditioned stimuli. But first I must address in some detail the process of extinction itself, with particular emphasis on recent research developments. And so, I turn to this next.

EXTINCTION

It is widely recognized by modern conditioning researchers[10] that, although "fear conditioning . . . can generalize very well across contexts" (Bouton, 1988, p. 143), Chang et al. (2009, p. 1) forcefully remind us that ". . . unlike fear conditioning, extinction is highly context specific . . . [it is in fact] a new learning process, . . . [in which] the fear reduction results from inhibition rather than erasure of the original fear memory." In other words, according to Bouton et al. (2006, p. 352): "Extinction depends . . . on new learning that is specific to the context in which it is learned." That this is true not only for laboratory animals but also for human fear extinction in both laboratory and clinical settings has also been widely established.[11]

The implications of this are important theoretically and also more practically toward devising better treatments for several human psychopathologies such as post-traumatic stress disorder, phobias, and a variety of anxiety disorders including panic attack. Naturally it had been logical to assume that by presenting the conditioned stimulus (CS) without the unconditioned stimulus (US), and therefore without the conditioned response (CR), that extinction would be achieved and that the pairing of the CS with the US would be unlearned. For it was in fact the case that after Pavlov's dogs were exposed to many bell tones without the meat quickly following, the bell (CS) no longer evoked the salivating response (CR). Similarly for aversive classical conditioning, Quirk (2002, p. 402) reports: "Conditioned fear responses to a tone paired with footshocks rapidly extinguish when the tone is presented in the absence of the shock." And indeed, fear responses (like other conditioned responses) will diminish significantly after exposure to the CS alone. However, the spontaneous recovery of extinguished responses was also observed, this as early as 1927, as reported by Pavlov. This was, according to Bouton (1988, p. 81), despite the fact that it ". . . has often been convenient to assume that extinction involves the destruction of the original CS-US association . . ." What is in fact the case is that the bond between CS and CR is not destroyed "even after extensive extinction training." Add to this that fear and other aversively conditioned responses are extinguished with more difficulty than other conditioned responses, while they reappear more easily, and we can begin to appreciate some of the problems encountered in the exposure therapies for human fear psychopathologies.

To understand these difficulties better, and before we can return to the main theme of this project—how psychoanalysis can work precisely because it supplies what is needed for more effective extinction—I must provide a detailed account of the problems with extinction, discussing both the specific types of aversive conditioned response reappearance that occur despite extinction training and the general finding of the rigid context dependency of the extinction process. Therefore, I turn now to descriptions of *renewal*, *spontaneous recovery*, *reinstatement*, and *rapid reacquisition* of the aversive conditioned responses, followed by a discussion of contexts, given their importance in attempting to extinguish aversively conditioned responses.

RENEWAL

The renewal effect (i.e., the renewal of the formerly extinguished conditioned response) is the effect in which the context dependency of extinction is best demonstrated. Renewal effects occur whenever the extinction trials for a conditioned stimulus are delivered in contexts different from the areas in which any later tests of the CS-CR independence are held. For example, suppose that a rat undergoes aversive conditioning as follows:

1. In Cage A, a specific tone (CS) is paired with a foot shock (US) to produce the conditioned fear response of freezing (UR/CR) to that tone alone.
2. At a later time, after this conditioned fear is well established, the extinction trials are set up to take place in Cage B. Here the tone (CS) is presented alone without the foot shock (US) until the conditioned fear is behaviorally extinguished—that is, until the tone no longer gives rise to the freezing fear response (CR).
3. Next, at some time after this extinguishing of the conditioned fear response, the tests of the extinction are arranged. These tests entail presenting the same tone (CS) alone without the foot shock (US) in several different contexts:

    a. Cage A, the site of the original fear conditioning
    b. Cage B, where extinction took place
    c. Cage C, a new area.

Here are the results: Only when testing occurs in Cage B does the extinction remain. If testing occurs in Cage A, the site of the initial pairings of tone and foot shock, the CS (tone) again yields CR (freezing)—in other words, the conditioned fear is renewed. More critically, if testing occurs in some new place, Cage C, the conditioned fear response is also renewed. Only in the specific context of Cage B is the independence of CS-CR maintained; only Cage B can be considered a "safe-here" context.[12]

The renewal effect is very robust. It has been demonstrated in appetitive as well as aversive conditioning in both classical and operant forms. Further, renewal has been shown not only with laboratory animal subjects but also with people both in the laboratory and the clinic (see notes 10 and 11 for references). As Ji and Maren (2007, p. 751) point out, there have been many attempts to deal with renewal, each involving some way to deal with the fact that ". . . the excitatory CS-US association established during conditioning is not context-specific and generalizes in all test contexts. In contrast, the inhibitory CS-'no US' association established during extinction is [highly] context-specific." They suggest (p. 751) that it might be the case that activation of the CS-no US association *always* "... requires simultaneous presence of the CS and the extinction context."

SPONTANEOUS RECOVERY

Noted quite early by Pavlov (1927), spontaneous recovery of a conditioned response assumed to have been extinguished is now thought by most modern researchers to be a subtype of renewal. Here the very passage of time provides "a functional change in context" (Bouton et al., 2006, p. 354) such that when tests of CS-CR independence occur somewhat after the extinction trials, the conditioned stimuli (CSs) presented alone are no longer experienced as part of the extinction contexts and consequently no longer considered "safe now." This is the case even when testing takes place in the same physical context as the "successful" extinction trials (see also Ji and Maren, 2007, p. 751). Like renewal, this effect is robust and widespread.

REINSTATEMENT

In reinstatement an extinguished conditioned response can be easily reestablished. The subject is exposed to the unconditioned stimulus (US) without the conditioned stimulus (CS) in a new context, a context in which there will be a later test of independence of the conditioned stimulus (CS) from the conditioned response (CR). Thought to be an example of contextual conditioning, the association of the unconditioned stimulus with the unconditioned response (US with UR) in some new specific context promotes the link between the heretofore extinguished conditioned response to the conditioned stimulus (CR with CS) whenever the old conditioned stimulus is introduced into the new context. This is complicated, so let me illustrate this first schematically and then with two concrete examples. Take a subject whose conditioned response has been extinguished in context A:

1. The old unconditioned stimulus (US) is presented alone without the conditioned stimulus (CS) in a new context, Context B, giving rise to the unconditioned response (UR) and the association *Context B-US/UR*.
2. Later, the old conditioned stimulus (CS) alone, not paired with the unconditioned stimulus (US), is presented in new Context B. Although the conditioned stimulus (CS) is not now and has never been paired with the unconditioned stimulus (US) at Context B, after some number of presentations of the conditioned stimulus, the conditioned response (CR) does take place! How?

3. Although the US and the CS are each presented alone at Context B, and these distinct presentations are separated in time, at Context B the associations *Context B-US/UR* and *Context B-CS* have each been formed. This yields the compound association *Context B-CS-US/UR*. In other words, *at Context B* there is an associative link between the conditioned stimulus and the unconditioned stimulus and its unconditioned response (CS-US/UR), and therefore a link *at Context B* between the conditioned stimulus and the conditioned response (CS-CR). All of this means that Context B has itself in effect been conditioned, producing *at Context B* a *return of CS-CR* (Bouton, 1993, p. 82; Bouton et al., 2006, p. 353; Ji and Maren, 2007, p. 752).

Again, and more succinctly, what we have in reinstatement is essentially the conditioning of a context itself (here Context B) as a site for reestablishing CS-UR/CR. Thus, at Context B, the conditioned stimulus produces the conditioned response, even though here at Context B the conditioned stimulus was never paired directly with the unconditioned stimulus (no direct US-CS)![13]

Now to make it clearer, let's use two concrete examples to illustrate. First, return to Pavlov's dogs. Suppose a dog is conditioned so that a bell's tone (CS), which had been paired with meat (US), can now itself elicit salivation (CS-UR/CR). In the next step this conditioning is extinguished to the point that salivation no longer follows the tone (CS) alone. Reinstatement can be produced in a few easy steps. First deliver the dog and the meat (US) to a new location, a particular kennel, Kennel A. Of course the dog will salivate (UR). Then remove the dog from Kennel A. After some period of time, return the dog to Kennel A and sound the bell (CS). The dog will salivate (CR), often on the first trial, despite this conditioned response having been extinguished.

The same reinstatement pattern applies with aversive conditioning. Take a rat that has undergone successful extinction trials of a conditioned freeze reaction to a tone (CS) alone that had been paired with a foot shock (US). The rat's fear response will become reinstated if this rat: (1) is placed in an area, Cage B, and receives foot shocks alone (US), and then (2) some time later is returned to Cage B, where the tone alone (CS without US [foot shock]) is sounded.

RAPID REACQUISITION

The phenomenon of rapid reacquisition provides additional evidence that extinction learning—that is, the association CS-no US—does not erase the original conditioned learning (the association CS-US). In situations where rapid reacquisition occurs, the original conditioned response, despite having been rendered behaviorally extinct, emerges extremely quickly, after just one new pairing (or only a few new pairings) of the CS with the US (Bouton et al., 2006, p. 353).

Attempting to deal with the rapid reacquisition problem (as well as reinstatement) Bouton and his colleagues (2006, p. 353) propose a paradoxical technique that involves adding a few aversive conditioning trials along with the many trials of extinction. Indeed, this is a counterintuitive plan, because the experience of intermittent pairings of a few CS-US trials interspersed with many CS-no US trials would seem to strengthen the conditioned response, much as behaviors intermittently reinforced are more resistant to extinguishing. But the researchers explain (p. 353) that this procedure could "make a recent conditioning trial a part of the [overall] extinction context . . . and thus less likely to retrieve conditioning (as opposed to the [desired] extinction) . . . during reacquisition." They continue with the explanation as follows: given that the extinction trials are in great preponderance, the subject *should* be able to tolerate the occasional aversive US-CS pairings. Bouton reports (p. 353) having in fact tested this method, claiming that in work of his own, "reacquisition was less rapid following an extinction procedure that included occasional trials when the CS was paired with the US."[14]

CONTEXTS

The difficulty in achieving lasting extinction, seen in four types of conditioned response reappearances, demonstrates how dependent extinction is upon context. Therefore, it is important to understand what can constitute a context. Certainly there are the physical surroundings in which the conditioning events take place; rooms, cages, or kennels are perhaps the most obvious. Less obvious, but no less physical, are the materials out of which the conditioned stimuli themselves are constructed. These also contribute to the highly particular nature of contexts. For example, take the case reported in Vervliet et al. (2005), in which particular geometric figures were paired with shocks so that the figures became the conditioned stimulus (CS). Extinction trials were highly context specific to the particular size and shape of the figure presented. In other words, the successful extinguishing of the aversive conditioning achieved in initial extinction trials was not preserved in later trials when the size and/or shape of the figure varied perceptibly from those used earlier. On the basis of this finding, it is quite likely that textures and colors in the visual domain, and pitch and decibel level in the auditory realm—actually whatever characteristics can be perceived by a subject—contribute significantly to the constitution of specific conditioning and extinction contexts.

In addition to these physical contexts, there are temporal contexts, as was discussed above regarding the phenomenon of spontaneous recovery. Further, even more subtle contexts also exist. Bouton and Swartzentruber

(1991, p. 132), for instance, "encourage a more expanded definition of context," holding that "nearly *any* stimulus in the background [of a conditioning event] can potentially play the role of context and control performance in extinction."

Finally, there are state contexts—that is, state-dependent learning phenomena, which include state-dependent conditioning and extinction. There are many drugs, including alcohol, some tranquilizers, and stress hormones like adrenocorticotropin, for instance, all of which induce specific state contexts. Thus, extinction of a conditioned fear achieved under the influence of alcohol will not hold up when the subject is no longer in an inebriated state (see Bouton et al., 2006, pp. 354–355; Bouton and Swartzentruber, 1991, pp. 132–133). Related to this, and even more interesting, are findings that various emotional states including stress can themselves have contextual effects. If a particular emotion accompanies the conditioning of a response, even after extinction, according to Bouton and Swartzentruber (1991, p. 135), ". . . encountering an extinguished CS in combination with that emotion could cause a renewal of responding after extinction has occurred. Such a mechanism could account for why phobias and anxiety disorders are sometimes precipitated by stress."

Given the many types of contexts and the dependence of extinction upon contexts, the next section will consider some suggestions conditioning researchers have offered, as well as actual attempts they have made, to better achieve (or at least more nearly approximate) extinction.

SEVERAL APPROACHES TO EXTINCTION, ALL INVOLVING MANY CONTEXTS

Since conditioned fear responses causally contribute to many human psychopathologies, including phobias and various anxiety disorders, it is an important clinical goal to improve techniques to facilitate extinction. But this goal is difficult to achieve—and understandably so, given the modern research findings establishing that the CS-US associations causing conditioned fear responses are never abolished. True, many studies have shown also that these CS-US associations can recede, but only through the formation of new memories of CS-no US (i.e., safe CSs), accomplished by a great number of extinction trials in a variety of different contexts. According to Mystkowski and Mineka (2007, p. 218), given this state of affairs, clinical researchers have logically considered ". . . that one way to decrease the effects of contextual change on enhancing the return of fear would be to conduct exposure therapy in multiple contexts so that extinction memories can be cued by multiple contexts."[15] These same authors note, however, that the results of such interventions have been "inconsistent" at best, even in animal models, and therefore conclude that extinction trials in multiple contexts are no panacea (p. 218).

Hermans et al. (2006, p. 362) suggested a mode of treatment designed to circumvent these difficulties. They report that "... the presence of the therapist during exposure to anxiety-provoking cues can act as a conditioned inhibitor [of the conditioned fear response] ('when the therapist is present, nothing bad will happen')." But these authors predict that this type of intervention too would only meet with minimal success. "The presence of the therapist may lead to rapid symptom reduction, but a return of anxiety may occur when the client subsequently confronts the stimuli alone" (p. 362).

Addressing these dilemmas, Bouton and colleagues recommended "treatments that 'bridge' connections between the extinction context and potential relapse contexts," noting that this sort of intervention "may be more effective at preventing relapse than treatments designed to 'optimize' extinction learning" (Bouton et al., 2006, p. 358). One promising study demonstrating this approach was conducted by Mystkowski, Craske, Echiverri, and Labus (2006) and reported in Mystowski and Mineka (2007, pp. 216–218). In this study of 48 people with spider phobia, half were asked to rehearse mentally the particular treatment context of the extinction trials they had received just prior to entering subsequent test contexts. This was the "bridging" intervention. The other 24 participants in the control group were asked to recall a neutral situation unrelated to the treatment. In the two types of test contexts, those identical to the extinction trials and those that were novel, the participants using mental rehearsal of the treatment contexts as a bridge reported significantly less return of fear on a self-report fear measure. In fact the mental rehearsal subjects tested in novel settings did as well as subjects without the rehearsal instruction who were retested in the original extinction context. This is a quite striking result, as new test settings are new contexts and therefore likely to promote renewal of conditioned fear effects.

Interestingly, other cognitive interventions with human clinical subjects, specifically those involving higher-level judgments, have not proved very successful in extinguishing phobias and other conditioned fear responses. Mystkowski et al. (2002, p. 414), for example, reported on a study they conducted with 63 people with spider phobia in which "... our results did not support the hypothesis that changing perceptions of safety, danger, control, and predictability mediate and/or moderate a contextually influenced return of fear." They concluded: "If the null findings stand up ... they imply that contextually based return of fear is not dependent on or affected by judgments of safety and so forth" (p. 414).

Keeping in mind these problems in achieving extinction—both in studies employing higher-level cognitively mediated processes and in those using straightforward multiple context exposures[16]—and especially in light of the potential *positive* role of imaginative rehearsal in extinction shown in one experiment, we return in the next section to psychoanalysis with two specific questions. First, how does psychoanalysis fare in terms of extinction processes? Second, and more importantly for this project (and perhaps generally), can the success of classical psychoanalysis best be understand in terms of extinction—that is, by recognizing that the standard classic techniques actually can and do provide the multiple contexts necessary for approximating extinction of aversively conditioned responses?

CLASSICAL PSYCHOANALYTIC TECHNIQUE AND EXTINCTION

It is my view that for two interconnected reasons classical psychoanalytic technique is uniquely capable of promoting extinction learning. But before we get to those reasons, some definitional matters are in order. First, what is it that constitutes classical technique? The features that are most often noted include free association, frequency of sessions, and the use of the analytic couch. The patient (the analysand) reclines on a psychoanalytic couch with the analyst sitting behind the patient (out of his or her sight), ideally for around forty-five minutes at least four times per week, typically for a number of years. The analysand freely associates as much as possible—expressing thoughts, feelings, wishes, and desires; recounting dreams, memories, daydreams, and fantasies; discussing all manner of important experiences from the financial to the sexual, from parenting to being parented, from the past and the present, including whatever thoughts, feelings, and fantasies the patient has about the analyst—always trying not to edit his or her thoughts. This attempt to experience and then articulate anything and everything that comes to mind, all without regulation and in the absence of the usual conversational cues and social conventions, facilitates the analysand's imaginative engagement toward the formation of multiple transferences.

Transference experiences are often profoundly felt and can be quite enduring. They are experiences (including beliefs, desires, wishes, and fantasies) about the analyst and analytic situation that are predicated not simply on present-day reality but are amalgams of that reality along with features from the patient's fantasy life and from the patient's past. For example, patients with domineering parents often believe their analysts to be authoritarian; this view is exacerbated by the unequal postures of patient and analyst but is not necessarily grounded in the reality of the analyst's behavior. Similarly, patients with doting parents experience their analysts as raptly listening to their every word, as indeed analysts do spend a great deal of time listening. In addition to parental transferences like these from various developmental stages and involving both parents (or whatever group of adults are the caregivers), there are often physicianly and teacherly transferences. In sum, for every analytic case, there are many different transferential experiences that arise.[17]

The presence of these many transferences provides the first reason for my claim that classic psychoanalytic technique can best approximate extinction. What am I suggesting here? How can this work? I am proposing that it is the formation and the experience of these multiple transferences that actually (and naturally) constitute the multiple contexts necessary for any possibility of approaching extinction. And the second reason for my claim is related. Classic analytic technique not only aims to facilitate the development and experience of these many transference contexts but (and just as importantly) focuses on analyzing them—that is, resolving them toward better outcomes. Analyzing and resolving transferences mean in effect offering multiple contexts of "safe-here"/"safe-now trials" (CS-no US).

To repeat the point to be clear, it is this combined action of transference development and transference resolution, carried out intensively and extensively over many transference types that is, on my account, the essential equivalent of multiple extinction learning trials taking place in a myriad of contexts at different levels. Furthermore, I claim that it is the very success in achieving extinction (at least closely approximating it) that secures much psychoanalytic success. In short, when looking for mechanisms to explain how and why classical psychoanalysis works, the biological processes of extinction learning must be considered to be of central importance.

The next two sections elaborate on these claims. First, I will discuss the use of the couch, asserting that its use promotes the development of many transferences, never just one. Moreover, use of the couch, I will hold, allows the quality of imagination necessary to experience each of these transference contexts intensely. Then, returning to Mr. H's case, I will demonstrate how these intensive and extensive transference experiences provide the grounds for best extinguishing the psychopathological fear (and other aversive) conditioning symptoms over the many different contexts necessary for adequate extinction.

THE PSYCHOANALYTIC COUCH

Transferences are ubiquitous. However, when we see someone in just one role, as we do our dentist or mail carrier, the transference is usually of a single type and does not undergo much alteration. Our spouses, parents, children, and siblings, on the other hand, are experienced in a great many ways, over decades of time shared together. There are many different sorts of father transferences, mother transferences, and so on. When we address the issue of transferences in psychoanalysis, we must ask what is it about them that proves therapeutically effective? To answer this question, we have to first consider the aims of psychoanalysis in general.

Jacobson (1995, p. 309) maintains that an analysis is an ". . . open-ended re-living; exploration; and integration of unconscious issues, unconscious processes, and unconscious modes of functioning, with the goal of understanding them in the service of the resumption of development and the freedom to change." Particularly the phrase "open-ended re-living" suggests that a successful analysis requires a variety of different transferences. Jacobson asserted this without any thought to extinction efficacy.

But how can the development of multiple transferences be facilitated in an analysis? Even psychoanalysts who question the use of the couch for every patient recognize that, for most patients capable of undergoing a psychoanalysis, "... the use of the couch makes a good exploration better (Lichtenberg, 1995, p. 293)." Why? Because the couch allows, and can "... promote the development of transference[s] of a regressive nature" (Gedo, 1995, p. 296). Indeed that much is uncontested both by psychoanalysts like Lichtenberg and Gedo, who stress that the couch is certainly not for every patient, and those analysts who are more unreservedly pro-couch, including Grotstein (1995) and Wolf (1995). The latter adds that, with patients lying on a psychoanalyst's couch, "[s]pecific archaic trauma may be recalled that would not have been accessible without the regressive propensities of couch use" (Wolf, 1995, p. 322). The idea of an old trauma brings us closer to the topic at hand—aversive conditioning arguably contributing to the psychopathology seen in every analytic patient. Likewise, a comment of Grotstein's (1995, p. 397) is also helpful for our purposes. He says: ". . . lying down facilitates a shift from the real [here and now] to the imaginative. . ."

And so, with this background now in place, I offer the following three interrelated claims:

1. To achieve the many contexts needed for adequate extinction of aversive conditionings, multiple transferences are needed.
2. Moreover, these transferences must be intensely felt, so that a re-experiencing of the CS-US association can take place along with extinction trials (CS-no US) in many settings and at diverse levels.
3. Imaginations facilitated by use of the couch are not only instrumental but also essential in allowing the variegated transferences to first develop, and then to be deeply felt. With their patients lying on a couch, analysts are not constrained to the single role of helping professional, nor are patients as restrained by social convention as they would be sitting up and facing the psychoanalyst.

Taking up the third claim first, let me offer as evidence for the efficacy of imagination two studies, each far afield from the realm of psychoanalysis. The first is the research by Mystkowski et al. (2006). Here, the people with spider phobia who were asked simply to imagine the treatment context (the extinction trial) just prior to the subsequent test of their phobic reactions experienced significantly less fear renewal on self-report measures. The second is a study whose title, "Thought for Food: Imagined Consumption Reduces Actual Consumption," reveals much about its focus. Researchers Morewedge, Huh, and Vosgerau (2010, p. 1530) demonstrated that subjects who repeatedly imagined eating a particular food (thirty times) "subsequently consumed less of the . . . [actual] food [they had imagined] than did people who repeatedly imagined eating that food fewer times , [or than subjects who] imagined eating a different food [thirty times] . . . , or [than subjects who] did not imagine eating a food [but performed another repetitive action]." Whereas Morewedge and colleagues hypothesized (p. 1531) that having subjects imagine just three ingestions might sensitize and stimulate the appetite,[18] they found that "mentally simulating an experience that is more analogous to repeated exposure (. . .repeatedly imagining the consumption of units of a food) . . . engender[ed] habituation to the stimulus." These findings, that "mere" mental imaginations of a situation are sufficient to cause stimulus-specific extinctions (p. 1533), are extremely important in support of the idea that transferential re-experiences can constitute the many diverse extinction contexts necessary for satisfactory aversive conditioning extinction.

Next, to address the first two claims, I advance the idea that multiple transferences constitute intensely felt multiple extinction contexts.

MULTIPLE TRANSFERENCES SERVING AS INTENSE MULTIPLE EXTINCTION CONTEXTS

Freud (1914, p. 154) advocated allowing all of the patient's (unconscious) conflicts, including the fear and anxiety causing and caused by such conflicts, to be vividly present in the analytic treatment in the form of various transferences. He explained:

> . . .we regularly succeed in giving all of the symptoms of the illness . . . new transference meaning[s] and in replacing his [the patient's] ordinary neurosis by a "transference-neurosis" of which he can be cured by the therapeutic work. The transference thus creates an intermediate region between illness and real life. . .

Freud continued (p. 154): "The new condition has taken over all the features of the illness; but it represents an artificial illness [in that it is] accessible to our intervention. It is [however] a piece of real experience. . ."

The transference neurosis version of the illness can be seen, on my view, as that caused by the reappearance of the conditioned fear. Further, and of therapeutic significance, the interventions to which Freud alludes can be understood as the different transference re-experiences of extinction contexts—various contexts, in all of which the CS is no longer linked to the US.[19] Let us see how this looks for Mr. H, the patient whose psychopathology was described at length earlier in this chapter.

Recall that for Mr. H, the conditioned stimulus (CS), defined in the most narrow terms, was the exuberant unconstrained approach of beloved others (in this case, his mother and the dog). A broader description of the CS—one that might overlap with the original emotional context of the aversive conditioning event—includes Mr. H's feeling "on top of the world" following a significant accomplishment, and also a sense of himself as more successful and favored compared with his father. The unconditioned stimulus (US) was the excited dog knocking Mr. H over and biting him so that a trip to the emergency room was required; this was accompanied by blood and stitches. The conditioned response/unconditioned response (UR/CR) consisting of fear, anxiety, and pain began with the lunging dog and continued throughout the episode. To avoid the fear, anxiety, and pain associated with the unconditioned stimulus (US), Mr. H avoided the conditioned stimulus (CS)—that is, feeling good and more successful than rivals—throughout his life, in several manifestations and at many developmental stages, as was described at length earlier.

Not surprisingly, then, in Mr. H's psychoanalysis there were many transference instantiations in which some achievement or particular success was on the horizon ("threatening"), with other people about to react with (perceived) overexuberance. These situations occurred in both major and mundane ways. Taking the quotidian type first, Mr. H's own useful psychoanalytic insights, especially those overtly acknowledged by me, his female analyst, caused him a great deal of anxiety at first and occasionally thereafter. This sort of interchange, of course, occurred throughout the analysis, and Mr. H's reactions were different at different times, depending upon the nature of his transference state.

Here is one typical example. During one session, Mr. H was particularly insightful. He not only knew this, he also correctly gauged my pleasure at his work. He arrived for his next session feeling extremely anxious. At first we were perplexed, until he revealed that on his way to the session he had a fearful fantasy, one he knew to be irrational: namely, that my husband would be angry with him, maybe even try to hurt him. Why? Because my husband would feel diminished by my pleasure in working with Mr. H. Once we understood this, the rest of the session could function as an intense CS-no US trial with the following features: Despite Mr. H demonstrating his real success as a psychoanalytic patient, and despite his correctly sensing my encouragement of him, nothing untoward happened between Mr. H and my husband, between my husband and me, nor, most importantly, with Mr. H himself. All of us were unscathed, as were our relationships with one another.

The examples of major successes were those that Mr. H achieved either with his wife, in the sexual realm, or at work, as both areas continued to cause anxiety for Mr. H. In order for the analysis to represent (and actually constitute) a set of useful extinction contexts, it was necessary for us (Mr. H and me together) to figure out the nature of each specific success along with its accompanying anxiety and fear—every time, and within whatever transference pattern was occurrent. For instance, a situation arose that was quite parallel to the original aversive conditioning situation.

Mr. H got a promotion and raise at work, rising ahead of a more senior (male) colleague. He was delighted. His wife was proud, and also amorous. So here we have the set-up. Owing to a success in which he felt he had bested a father-figure rival, Mr. H started to feel "on top of the world." And then, he was met by his wife, who in the mother transference was an exuberant, ardent woman! This particular incident took place several years into the analysis, after we had done some considerable prior work on the contingent rather than causal nature of the association between Mr. H's high school successes and the financial problems his father had sustained.[20] Thus, that particular part of the CS-US association had already profited by a number of transference extinction trials. Still, at the time of his promotion, Mr. H felt he was not ready for his wife to approach him sexually. And yet as he explained to me, he felt that if he did not have intercourse with her immediately, when she was so excited about his accomplishments, then she would surely have to "bite his head off." He endured sexual intercourse anxiously, simultaneously becoming aware of the meaning of the comment about biting that he had unconsciously constructed. In his next session he summarized his predicament: "What a choice, she'll bite my head off; or her vagina will damage my penis." This ushered in a new period of the analytic work. Mr. H began to "design" his own extinction trials, increasingly allowing himself to tolerate and then gradually even enjoy sex initiated by his wife.[21]

In a similar fashion, various transference experiences provided different contexts for extinction (CS-no US) of different aspects of the original aversive conditioning situation. The aspect involving his mother's preference of Mr. H over his father/her husband is easy to demonstrate. Often Mr. H would imagine that I preferred him to other men—my other patients, my husband and other male relatives, my friends and colleagues. Allowing himself this fantasy, but also then realizing that I could value him *and* other men—something he concluded by watching me interact with other men in tiny episodes over many years[22]—proved to be yet another extinction context. During work on this matter, Mr. H also came to believe that his mother did love and respect his father, notwithstanding the periods of financial difficulty his father had sustained.

The generalizations of the original aversive conditioning outward to other associatively related conditioned stimuli (CSs) were of interest, too, whenever they could be experienced and appreciated in a transference context. Never as problematic as his main symptom, Mr. H, just prior to beginning his psychoanalysis, did report mild fears of animal traps, jagged can openings, and elevators. One example of a trial of aversive conditioned stimulus paired to unconditioned stimulus (CS-US) conditioning that occurred within the analysis (with its predominance of CS-no US trials) involved his having cut himself on just such a jagged can one afternoon at work. He bled quite a bit and did require stitches at a local emergency room. Mr. H admitted that he felt very anxious to the point of dizziness during much of the experience. And yet, as he told me at our next session, "I lived through it."

Similarly, although pertaining this time to the generalizing of the unconditioned stimulus (US), there was the matter of Mr. H's changing reactions over the years to the occasional dog barking to which we would be subject. My dog, although usually quiet, would once in a while surprise us with loud barks. In the beginning, Mr. H jumped every time this happened. I wondered with him, "Did he worry she was close at hand?" Only later did I realize my own association to his bloody hand following the dog-bite trauma. In any case, over the years my dog, helpful as always, allowed the analysis to provide yet another set of extinction contexts. Indeed, after some years of experiencing these rare, but surprising, barking jags, Mr. H's reactions extinguished. This can be understood as follows: No matter how excellently the analysis was progressing and no matter how good Mr. H felt, my dog never burst into the consulting room, and never bit him. Indeed, she barked, but this helped to establish several instances of conditioned stimulus with no unconditioned stimulus associated—that is, "safe-here"/ safe-now" trials (CS-no US).

CONCLUSION

The case of Mr. H is a typical psychoanalytic case. Both his psychopathology and the classical psychoanalytic work with him—four sessions per week with patient and analyst physically present, with the patient reclining on the couch; these technical matters in the service of promoting free association and extensive/intensive imaginative experiences of many transferences at many levels—have been presented in some detail here. This was done to demonstrate:

1. the ". . . countless ways in which the conflictual [aversive] situations are embedded . . . " in his psychopathology,[23]
2. the view that the many transferences constitute the multiple extinction contexts at the diverse levels needed to best approximate extinction of aversively conditioned psychopathology.

Indeed, to the extent that the etiology of much psychopathology is related to aversive/fear conditioning, and since such aversive conditioning is now understood to be easily generalized while never fully eradicated, psychoanalysis, in providing the myriad of extinction contexts necessary, does seem potentially more effective in preventing aversive conditioning reappearances (particularly renewal) than any other extant treatment. That said, I am not contending that because psychoanalysis can effect these extinction contexts, psychoanalysis should be the treatment of choice for phobias, post-traumatic stress disorder, panic attack, and other anxiety disorders. That sort of recommendation would clearly not be practical, especially in the current climate. I am, however, making this claim: It is through the rather unique[24] use of multifaceted transferences, now shown to serve as multiple extinction contexts, that the success of classical psychoanalysis can be understood. Appreciated in this way, psychoanalysis reveals itself to be as foundationally biological as it is psychological.[25]

REFERENCES

Bouton, M. (1988). Context of ambiguity in the extinction of emotional learning: Implications for exposure therapy. *Behaviour Research and Therapy, 26*, 137–149.

Bouton, M. (1993). Context, time, and memory in the interference paradigms of Pavlovian learning. *Psychological Bulletin, 114*, 80–99.

Bouton, M. (2004). Context and behavioral processes in extinction. *Learning and Memory, 11*, 485–494.

Bouton, M., & Swartzentruber, D. (1991). Sources of relapse after extinction in Pavlovian and instrumental learning. *Clinical Psychology Review, 11*, 123–141.

Bouton, M., Westbrook, F., Corcoran, K., & Maren, S. (2006). Contextual and temporal modulation of extinction: Behavioral and biological mechanisms. *Biological Psychiatry, 60*, 352-360.

Bouton, M., Woods, A., & Pinero, O. (2004). Occasional reinforced trials during extinction can slow the rate of rapid reacquisition. *Learning and Motivation, 35*, 371–390.

Brakel, L.A.W. (2009). *Philosophy, psychoanalysis, and the a-rational mind*. Oxford: Oxford University Press.

Brakel, L.A.W. (2010). *Unconscious knowing and other essays in psycho-philosophical analysis*. Oxford: Oxford University Press.

Chang, C., Knapska, E., Orsini, C., Rabinak, C., Zimmerman, J., & Maren, S. (2009). Fear extinction in rodents. *Current Protocols in Neuroscience, 47*, chap. 8.23, 1–19.

Fernando, C., Liekens, A., Bingle, L., Beck, C., Lenser, T., Steckel, D., & Rowe, J. (2009). Molecular circuits for associative learning in single-celled organisms. *Journal of the Royal Society Interface, 6*, 463–469.

Finn, M., Shevrin, H., Brakel, L.A.W., & Snodgrass, M. (2012). *Phobic fear impacts represented object size: A quantitative study of drawings made by patients with specific phobias of their phobic object.* Manuscript submitted for publication.

Freud, S. (1914/1958). Remembering, repeating and working-through. In J. Strachey (Ed. & Trans.), *The standard edition of the complete psychological works of Sigmund Freud* (Vol. 12, pp. 145–156). London: Hogarth Press.

Gedo, J. (1995). Channels of communication. *Psychological Inquiry, 15*, 294–303.

Grotstein, J. (1995). A reassessment of the couch in psychoanalysis. *Psychological Inquiry, 15*, 396–405.

Hermans, D., Craske, M., Mineka, S., & Lovibond, P. (2006). Extinction in human fear conditioning. *Biological Psychiatry, 60*, 361–368.

Herrnstein, R., & Loveland, D. (1964). Complex visual concept in the pigeon. *Science, 146*, 549–551.

Jacobson, J. (1995). The couch: Facilitator or sine qua non? *Psychological Inquiry, 15*, 304–313.

Ji, J., & Maren, S. (2007). Hippocampal involvement in contextual modulation of fear extinction. *Hippocampus, 17*, 749–758.

Lichtenberg, J. (1995). On, behind, and without the couch. *Psychological Inquiry, 15*, 280–293.

Martin-Soelch, C., Linthicum, J., & Ernst, M. (2007). Appetitive conditioning: Neural bases and implications for psychopathology. *Neuroscience and Biobehavioral Reviews, 31*, 426–440.

Mineka, S., Mystkowski, J., Hladek, D., & Rodriguez, B. (1999). The effects of changing contexts on return of fear following exposure therapy. *Journal of Consulting and Clinical Psychology, 67*, 599–604.

Moore, B., & Fine, B. (Eds.). (1990). *Psychoanalytic terms and concepts*. New Haven, CT: American Psychoanalytic Association and Yale University Press.

Morewedge, C., Huh, Y., & Vosgerau, J. (2010). Thought for food: Imagined consumption reduces actual consumption. *Science, 330*, 1530–1533.

Mystkowski, J., Craske, M., & Echiverri, A. (2002). Treatment context and return of fear is spider phobia. *Behavior Therapy, 33*, 399–416.

Mystkowski, J., Craske, M., Echiverri, A., & Labus, J. (2006). Mental reinstatement of context and return of fear in spider fearful participants. *Behavior Therapy, 37*, 9–60.

Mystkowski, J., & Mineka, S. (2007). Behavior therapy for fears and phobias: Context specificity of fear extinction. In T. Baker, R. Bootzin, & T. Treat (Eds.), *Psychological clinical science: Papers in honor of Richard M. McFall* (pp. 197–222). New York: Psychology Press.

Pavlov, I. (1927). *Conditioned reflexes*. Oxford: Oxford University Press.

Porter, D., & Neuringer, A. (1984). Music discrimination by pigeons. *Journal of Experimental Psychology: Animal Behavior Processes, 10*, 138–148.

Quirk, G. (2002). Memory for extinction of conditioned fear is long-lasting and persists following spontaneous recovery. *Learning and Memory, 9*, 402–407.

Quirk, G., & Mueller, D. (2008). Neural mechanisms of extinction learning and retrieval. *Neuropsychopharmacology Reviews, 33*, 56–72.

Rangel, A., Camerer, C., & Montague, P. (2008). A framework for studying the neurobiology of value-based decision making. *Nature Reviews/Neuroscience, 9*, 545–556.

Skinner, B. F. (1938). *The behavior of organisms: An experimental analysis*. New York: Appleton-Century-Crofts.

Snodgrass, M., Shevrin, H., Brakel, L.A.W., & Kushwaha, R. (2013). *Unconsciously formed memories are smarter than you think: Subliminal theta synchronization moderates extinction*. Manuscript in preparation.

Vansteenwegen, D., Hermans, D., Vervliet, B., Francken, G., Beckers, T., Baeyens, F., & Eelen, P. (2005). Return of fear in human differential conditioning paradigm caused by a return to the original acquisition context. *Behaviour Research and Therapy, 43*, 323–336.

Vervliet, B., Vansteenwegen, D., Baeyens, F., Hermans, D., & Eelen, P. (2005). Return of fear in human differential conditioning paradigm caused by a stimulus change after extinction. *Behaviour Research and Therapy, 43*, 357–371.

Walters, E., Carew, T., & Kandel, E. (1979). Classical conditioning in aplysia. *Proceedings of the National Academy of Science, 76*, 6675–6679.

Wolf, E. (1995). Brief notes on using the couch. *Psychological Inquiry, 15*, 314–323.

Part III

Psychological Biology

3 The Ontology of Psychology

INTRODUCTION: WHAT IS THE PROBLEM?

As a long-time practitioner of both psychoanalysis and psychiatry, I recently had the unhappy realization that each of these fields has changed—and, in my opinion, not for the better. Over the thirty years of my career, psychoanalysis has become more marginalized, and psychiatry has become medicalized. This has led to an uncomfortable puzzle. I found serious cause to wonder: Just what is it that constitutes psychology? Of what does it consist? And what level is the psychological level? Is there something in the study of the mind over and above, or even just different from, a more complete understanding of the brain? Or pursuing this question in an opposite direction, is there anything *psychologically* distinct from manifest behavior?[1] In other words, what is the ontology of the mental? What is the ontology of psychology?

SOME EXAMPLES OF PSYCHOLOGICAL LEVEL ENTITIES

As a preliminary step, it might be helpful to list possible candidates that appear to have a clear and distinct psychological status. Qualia—that is, the qualities of consciousness; for example, what pain *feels* like and the *experience* of red—seem like prime examples of entities that are essentially psychological. In fact, all sensations felt and perceptions experienced, even consciousness itself—both in a primary way and in a secondary reflective way, in which an agent's awareness includes consciousness *of* a feeling, percept, or sensation—all of these seem to require a psychological-level definition.

Another class of psychological entities includes all those with representational contents.[2] So, for example, take the simple perception "I see a black horse." The percept has "black horse" as its content.[3] Knowledge also has representational contents (I know that what I am seeing is a black horse); as do the cognitive attitudes—for instance, belief, supposition, and hypothesis—and the conative attitudes—for example, desire, want, and wish. The cognitive and conative attitudes are often aligned toward effective action. Thus I *want* to take a photo of a black horse, and since I *believe* I see one in the distance, I will go a little closer, make sure it is not a black cow, and then take the photo.

More complicated attitudes like intentions and motivations seem intrinsically psychological, too. Thus, if I desire to see movie M today, and I believe M is playing nearby, I can readily form the intention of going to the movies. If I go, I have acted on this intention. Of more moment, suppose A has the strong motivation to continue to smoke, despite knowing the risk. Each time A lights up and smokes, A has acted on an intention. Or take an even more dire case. If B acts knowingly to commit suicide, then likely B has had motives, has formed an intention, and has acted upon this intention. Not only do motives and intentions have representational contents, they seem to possess causal powers, and thereby strengthen the case for psychological causation.[4]

Perhaps even more structurally complex than motivations and intentions[5] are behaviors that seem best predicated on the psychological level rather than (1) from a strictly biological domain or (2) due solely to sociological processes such as learning. For instance, magicians note that their tricks are not discovered because people almost invariably look at the magicians' eyes and not their hands. Were the audience to follow the magicians' hands, the tricks would be revealed and the magic spoiled. A predominantly biological explanation, describing perceptual proclivities and visual limits owing to biological determinants such as sensitivity to differential motions and edge detectors, does not seem to figure here at all. Related to this, several studies (for example, that of Brauer, Kaminski, Riedel, Call, and Tomasello, 2006) have found that dogs (like children) follow human communicative cues better than apes in tasks involving finding hidden food, whereas apes outperform the dogs when physical causal cues are offered. A sociological explanation would suggest that dogs have acquired this as a learned behavior after many overt trials. Instead, according to Brauer et al. (2006, p. 39), the dogs' responses are psychological, since even ". . . very young puppies with almost no experience with humans are skillful . . . suggest[ing] that dogs' ability to read human communicative cues is independent of their individual history . . ." Apes, the researchers hold, also acted on a largely psychological basis. The clear behavioral divergences between dogs and apes on the experimental tasks demonstrate the wide differences in the psychologies of the two species. The apes ". . . understood the causality . . . [but] were not attracted to the human actions, as were the dogs" (Brauer et al. p. 44).

GIVEN THESE PSYCHOLOGICAL ENTITIES, WHAT IS THEIR ONTOLOGY? DUALISM VERSUS PHYSICALISM

Can psychological entities—such as consciousness itself; qualia of all sorts, including pain and the experience of color; actions and behaviors that seem not well described either in terms of brain biology or sociocultural factors—be ontologically understood? Are they ontologically explainable? Any hope of addressing this issue cannot get around an age-old question—the famous mind/body problem. And so we shall confront this problem head on now.

There have been two classic ways to characterize the mind/the psychological/the mental ontologically: one is physicalism (materialism),[6] and the other is dualism. The basic claim of all physicalists is that there is nothing other than the physical/material world with its substances, properties, events, and laws. Thus, in any physicalist catalog of "what there is," all mental phenomena will be found fitting (in some fashion) within the category of physical phenomena. There are two prominent branches of physicalists: reductive physicalists, for whom mental phenomena can be reduced to physical phenomena, and nonreductive physicalists, who allow that mental phenomena cannot be so reduced. Nonreductive physicalists maintain that this is so despite their view that ontologically mental phenomena can be nothing other than strictly material. Since most of this chapter will be devoted to the physicalists, including various types of both reductive and nonreductive materialists, I shall first and more quickly explore important aspects of prevailing dualist views.

Dualists, who hold that there is a radical difference between the mental and the physical, also have two major branches. The substance dualists argue that the mind and body are composed of ontologically different materials. While the property dualists aver that ". . . mental states are irreducible attributes of brain states . . . and that mental phenomena are non-physical properties of physical substances" (Calef, 2005, p. 1). Property dualism does not entail that mental phenomena are nonphysical properties of nonphysical substances. Hence, property dualists have no need to posit the existence of nonphysical substances (see Calef, 2005, p. 2). Nonetheless, from a modern scientific standpoint, the burden of characterizing the nonmaterial nature that dualists ascribe to the nonphysical properties of the mental remains a daunting problem.[7] On the other hand, perhaps the enduring strength of the property dualist view owes much of its potency to the difficulties materialists inevitably must face in providing a satisfactory account of the important phenomenal aspects of the mental realm—in particular, qualia and the experience of consciousness.

RULING OUT DUALISM: ZOMBIES AND OTHERS

The Zombie/Conceivability Argument

Since my own view (to be developed in the course of this chapter) is an antidualist one, let me turn first to a consideration of dualist arguments, exploring their strengths and weaknesses. To begin, I will focus on what is perhaps the most convincing of these arguments—the Zombie Case, starting with its basic form and then introducing some related versions.

Chalmers (2010, p. 106) paraphrases his earlier work (and that of others) and sets up the Zombie Case/Conceivability Argument as follows: ". . . It is conceivable that there be a system that is physically identical to a conscious being but lacks . . . that being's conscious states. Such a system might be a *zombie*: a system that is physically identical to a conscious being but that lacks consciousness entirely." He continues (p. 107) that such a being/system

> . . . will look identical to a normal conscious being from the third-person perspective. In particular . . . brain processes will be molecule-for-molecule identical with the original,[8] and their behavior will be indistinguishable. But things will be different from the first-person point of view. What it is like to be . . . a . . . zombie will differ from what it is like to be the original being. [For] there is nothing it is like to be a zombie.

The next step in the Zombie Case, according to Chalmers (p. 107), is to acknowledge that since such zombie systems/beings are coherently imaginable with "no contradiction," it can be inferred that they are a *metaphysical possibility*: "From here, it is inferred that consciousness must be nonphysical. If there is a metaphysically possible universe that is physically identical to ours but that lacks consciousness, then consciousness must be a further, nonphysical component of our universe." Again, quoting Chalmers (p. 107) and putting it in the clearest possible notation:

1. It is conceivable that there are zombies.
2. If it is conceivable that there are zombies, it is metaphysically possible that there are zombies.
3. If it is metaphysically possible that there are zombies, then consciousness is nonphysical.

---

4. Consciousness is nonphysical.

Now, before addressing this argument critically, I will take a detour to set out several other dualist arguments of similar type, pointing out serious flaws in each of these versions, all of which the Zombie Case avoids. Then I will return to raise objections to the Zombie Case itself.

DUALIST ARGUMENTS SIMILAR IN KIND TO ZOMBIE CASE

The Knowledge Argument

Here is Frank Jackson's (1982, p. 130) famous argument featuring Mary, the color scientist:

> Mary is a brilliant scientist who is . . . forced to investigate the world from a black and white room *via* a black and white television monitor. She specializes in the neurophysiology of [color] vision and acquires . . . all the physical information there is to obtain about what goes on when we see ripe tomatoes, or the sky, and use terms like "red," "blue," and so on.

Jackson (p. 130) then asks what will happen when Mary is released from her room and sees colors for the first time in her life. "Will she *learn* anything or not?" He concludes (p. 130):

> It seems just obvious that she will learn something about the world and our visual experience of it. But then it is inescapable that her previous knowledge was incomplete. But she had all the physical information. *Ergo* there is more to have than that, and Physicalism is false.

Despite the elegance of this argument, I believe it to have a fatal flaw. But to make my case, I will have to change Jackson's use of the word *information* to *knowledge* in the two instances in which he uses it above. If this is sanctioned (and it seems to be in keeping with the spirit of things; this is, after all, a version of the Knowledge Argument), then what we have is the following: A stipulation that Mary has complete knowledge (which, of course, includes complete physical knowledge) of color vision, but then the *conclusion* that Mary does not *know* what it is like to see and experience red. But this, in turn, *assumes* that what it is like to experience, see, and know red is not a part of physical knowledge.

So is there a way out for Jackson? One could instead consider experiencing red-as-red as an example of *know-how* physical knowledge. Taking this to be the case, there are three possibilities. But as it turns out, none of the three are any better for "Mary, the color scientist" as a potent argument for dualism. These three possibilities are: (1) Mary didn't have all the physical knowledge after all; (2) know-how knowledge is excluded from the domain of knowledge; or (3) the argument begs the question, assuming what it is trying to prove—namely, that know-how knowledge, that is, knowing red experientially, is a nonphysical sort of knowledge.

The Sensation Argument

Hill (1991, p. 86), no dualist himself, provides another version of the Knowledge Argument in order to demonstrate a similar sort of question begging. This argument is called the Sensation Argument. Hill sets it out thus:

> **First Premise.** It is possible to be directly aware of one's sensations.
> **Second Premise.** It isn't possible to be directly aware of physical occurrences.

Third Premise. If x has a property that y fails to have, then x is not identical with y.

Conclusion. Sensations are not identical with physical occurrences.

From here, Hill (1991, p. 86) argues in much the same fashion that I have above, asserting: "The second premise begs the question." This is so, he continues (p. 87), because: "It is true in most cases that awareness of physical occurrences has to be mediated by internal representations that are distinct from the occurrences themselves. But what if sensations are identical with a subset of the set of physical occurrences? . . . then there is a set of physical occurrences that are . . . exceptions to the second premise." Hill (p. 87) sums up his critique, clearly indicating the question begging circularity, in observing: ". . . it appears that it is necessary to show that materialism is false before one can be in a position to claim that the second premise is true."

The Argument Concerning "What Is It Like to Be a Bat?"

Interestingly, Hill (1991, p. 87) also illustrates a way in which Thomas Nagel's main argument in his celebrated 1974 article "What Is It Like to Be a Bat?" can be seen as a version of the Knowledge Argument. While Hill (p. 87) does not aver that Nagel intended to support dualism (in fact he suggests that Nagel had no such intent), Hill maintains that Nagel's argument instead is one that sets out to question ". . . the validity (and even the intelligibility) of token materialism."[9] Hill's version of Nagel's argument can be paraphrased as follows (p. 87):

First Premise. It is impossible to know what it is like to have the sensations that another creature has unless one is capable of taking (and having) the point of view of that creature.

Second Premise. It is possible to have all the physical knowledge about a creature without having or taking the point of view of that creature.

Conclusion. Since having complete physical knowledge of another creature does not entail having or taking that creature's point of view, it does not entail knowing what it is like to have that creature's sensations. Hence, sensations do not admit of a physicalist reduction.

Although aspects of this argument are very compelling—most people would agree that they cannot know what it is like to be a bat—the trouble here is again the second premise. As with the Mary case above, this version of the Bat Argument presumes that having/taking a creature's point of view and having its sensations are not part of the complete physical knowledge of that creature. Thus, while Hill (probably) and I (surely) can agree that we may not be able to assume a bat's viewpoint nor have its sensations, this can reflect our human incapacity to obtain what would constitute *the complete physical knowledge* of a bat.

Evaporating Indexical Argument

Problems very similar to the ones we've been discussing concerning the Knowledge Arguments are seen with a different sort of dualist argument—an argument I shall term Evaporating Indexicals.[10] Chalmers (2010), contending that complete physical knowledge excludes indexical knowledge, first asserts (p. 162): "There is good reason to believe that our core phenomenal concepts are not indexical." Thus, for Chalmers (p. 162), someone thinking ". . . *this phenomenal property is R[ed]*, involving an indexical concept [i.e., *this*] and a phenomenal concept of phenomenal redness, is [analogous to someone thinking] . . . *this shape is circle*, involving an indexical [i.e., *this*] and a geometric concept of circularity."[11] In both cases, Chalmers (p. 162) claims that ". . . the phenomenal [or geometric] concept is distinct from the indexical concept." Moreover, he continues with the following case designed to show that indexicals contribute nothing to physical knowledge (p. 163):

> Say that I am physically omniscient but do not know whether I am in the United States or Australia (we can imagine . . . appropriate qualitative twins in both places). Then I am ignorant of the truth of "I am in Australia" and discovering that I am in Australia will constitute new knowledge. However, if other people are watching from the third-person point of view and are also physically omniscient, they will have no corresponding ignorance . . . There is no potential knowledge that they lack . . . So my ignorance is essentially indexical and evaporates from the objective viewpoint. The same goes for indexical ignorance concerning what time it is. When I am ignorant of the truth of "It is now 3 am," a physically omniscient historian in later years will have no corresponding ignorance about whether it was then 3 am.

The basic trouble with this argument is similar to the begged questions and the presumed truth of premises made in many of the Knowledge Argument cases described above. But here the assumption that indexical knowledge does not contribute to one's physical knowledge seems, if anything, a more extreme and wrongheaded claim. For how is it that I do not have knowledge of where I am located—both in time and in space—and still claim to be physically omniscient? What sort of knowledge is knowledge of my own *whens* and *whereabouts* if it is not physical knowledge?

Now, after this brief exploration of arguments related to the Zombie Argument—including several Knowledge Arguments and the Evaporating Indexicals, it is time to have a more critical look at the original Zombie Case.

Revisiting the Zombie/Conceivability Argument

Although the Zombie/Conceivability Argument for dualism avoids the sort of drawbacks discussed above with respect to the Knowledge Arguments (and related cases) and is, in this sense, a stronger and perhaps more appealing argument, it is not without problems of its own. To address these, let me start with the question: What is the relationship of conceivability to possibility anyway?

Physicalists of all stripes[12] would be happy if they could only feel justified in summarily dismissing the Zombie/Conceivability Case with an argument as simple and basic as the generic one Levine (1993, p. 122) provides: "One's ideas can be as clear and distinct as you like, and nevertheless not correspond to what is in fact possible. The world is structured in a certain way, and there is no guarantee that our ideas will correspond appropriately." In other words, there is no case to be made from the fact that zombies are conceivable.

But, of course, physicalists know they cannot be easily rid of the Zombie Problem in this way. And in a later work, Levine (1998, pp. 452–454), for his part, makes it harder for them, drawing an important distinction between metaphysical and conceptual/epistemic possibility—a distinction that he recognizes could provide some support for the Zombie/Conceivability Argument. Levine (1998) proceeds as follows. First, assume that one accepts the Kripke (1972, esp. pp. 116–143) rigid designator account for natural kinds and proper names—for example, water is H_2O in every possible world. Next Levine (1998, p. 452) suggests that we consider the difference between conceiving of water as XYZ and conceiving of the weather here and now ". . . as both raining and not raining. The former is epistemologically possible, or still conceivable in some narrow sense, while the latter is neither." Both are metaphysically impossible. Introducing "married bachelors" to provide another example of this difference, Levine (1998, p. 453) affirms that

> . . . situations involving married bachelors and situations involving water made out of XYZ are [both] metaphysically impossible . . . However, we can capture the difference with . . . epistemic possibility this way. The statement, "There are married bachelors" is also conceptually [/epistemologically] impossible, but the statement, "There is water made out of XYZ" is not.

Now, with this distinction at hand, it seems plausible that the possibility argued for in the Zombie/Conceivability Case need not be of the metaphysical ort, but could be of the epistemological/conceptual type. Put another way, perhaps the Zombie Case could even withstand empirical findings ruling out metaphysical possibility—demonstrating, for instance, that molecule-for-molecule identity with human brains would always result in consciousness—*if* the sort of conceivability required were conceptual/epistemological, not metaphysical.

But even if conceptual/epistemological possibility were the only type of possibility at issue,[13] there would be problems ahead for the Zombie

Argument, notwithstanding this seemingly less demanding requirement. Several authors (no matter what their ultimate position on the mind/body problem) suggest that the Zombie/Conceivability Case, turning as it does on the conceptual conceivability of zombies, is flawed because *our capacity* to imagine consciousless human physical duplicates is paradoxically a function of the *makeup* of *our own human concepts*. It is not in any way an accurate reflection of what *is* really the case. In other words, we may be drawn to dualism, finding the conceiving of zombies seductive, owing to the nature of our own psychology.

Jackson (2003, p. 9 and p. 30, footnote 9) pursues this line, stating that only ". . . an illusion fuels the epistemic intuition" that we can conceive of zombies. Nagel (1998), too, is clear about the human limitations inherent in assessing conceptual possibility generally, and with respect to zombies in particular (p. 346): "The following seem[s] *prima facie* conceivable . . . [but is] pretty certainly impossible in a very strong sense, namely: A living, behaving, physiologically and functionally perfect human organism that is nevertheless completely lacking in consciousness, i.e. a zombie." He continues with his diagnosis (p. 346):

> I believe that the apparent conceivability of these things reveals something about our present concepts but not about what is really possible . . . [Zombies] are not true logical possibilities, and if [that is] so, our concepts are missing something. Our current concepts don't lead to contradiction—it's not as bad as that—but they fail to reveal a logical impossibility.

Along similar lines, Hill (1997, pp. 75–76) argues:

1. There are no substantive a priori ties between sensory concepts [qualia and consciousness] and neuroscientific concepts. . .
2. If there are not substantive a priori ties between two concepts, then it is possible to conjoin either of the concepts with the negation of the other without producing an inconsistency. . .
3. If it is within a subject's power to conceive coherently of its being that p, then, unless the subject has a good a posteriori reason to think that the proposition p could turn out to be inconsistent with a set of propositions that have been shown independently to be necessary, the subject will come to believe that it is possible . . . for it be the case that p.
4. [since] . . . materialism is not part of our commonsense metaphysics, we do not *normally* regard ourselves as having a good a posteriori reason to think that propositions about . . . the existence of zombies are incompatible with necessary truths that have been independently established.

He next adds the noncontroversial claim "that human beings can fail to be in possession of the standard scientific reasons for affirming the necessary coextensiveness of . . . [certain] concepts . . ." (p. 77). This, along with the four-step argument listed just above, allows Hill (p. 77) to conclude, "that the mechanisms that are responsible for conceivability-based intuitions about . . . zombiehood belong to a certain category of [psychological (p. 76)] mechanisms, H, and . . . that a number of the mechanisms that belong to H are highly unreliable."[14]

A variation on the problem for the Zombie Case with which we've been dealing—namely, that what is conceivable by humans with our human cognitive capacity is not a good indicator of what there *is* and what *is possible* (conceptually, epistemologically, and metaphysically)—is the situation described (but not embraced) by Leuenberger (2008). He presents the interesting possibility (p. 149) "that our judgments [even] about what we can conceive are not to be trusted. We may [only] seem to be able to conceive zombies, but [actually] fail to do so." This sort of self-deception regarding conceivability is not unrelated to a position Leuenberger (2008) does endorse—a view he calls "*ceteris absentibus* physicalism." He begins to explain this type of physicalism as follows (p. 149):

> There is a possible world that is a physical duplicate of ours where nobody is conscious. But our conceiving does not show that there is a possible world that is a physical duplicate of ours where nobody is conscious, and where there is no blocking fact. The blocking fact prevents consciousness from arising; without it, the physical properties would be sufficient to give rise to consciousness.

He continues (p. 149): "Thus the conceivability of zombies is compatible with *certeris absentibus* physicalism"—a physicalism that requires two additional claims, which Leuenberger next makes. The first of these is: ". . . that it cannot be positively conceived that there are not blockers" (p. 149). Thus, on Leuenberger's account, if you are conceiving of zombies—physical replicas of humans but without consciousness—you cannot conceive that there are no blockers to that consciousness. Putting this more positively, if you are conceiving of zombies, then you are conceiving of consciousness blockers, regardless of whether you know you are. With this first additional claim, the link to the self-deception alluded to above can be spelled out. If you are able to conceive of zombies, unless you also allow blockers, you are deceiving yourself about what you seem to be able to conceive. The second claim is that "physicalism is compatible with the possibility of blockers for actual positive facts" (p. 149).

Not everyone concurs with the conclusion that that *ceteris absentibus* physicalism provides a potent attack on dualism. Chalmers (2010), for example, offers two objections. First, he asserts that "I could respond by denying that *ceteris absentibus* is strong enough to count as physicalism . . ." (p. 164). But he then adds that, even if he allows that it is a form of physicalism, there can be an argument mounted. Thus, Chalmers states his second objection: "I think it is clear that when we conceive of the zombie world, we do not conceive of a world with blockers. We conceive of a world with physics and *nothing else*: no blockers, no consciousness" (p. 164). Leuenberger has a response to this objection. He asserts that "blockers are too unfamiliar for their absence to be positively conceivable." (The quote is from Chalmers, 2010, p. 164 paraphrasing Leuenberger, 2008). Note that Leuenberger's view here again suggests that those who conceive of zombies also conceive of blockers, *whether or not they are aware of conceiving of blockers.*

For those not convinced by Leunberger's argument, there is an even more elegant defense for the *ceteris absentibus* physicalist position—one that addresses Chalmers's second objection without Leuenberger's response and without positing unconsciously conceiving of blockers. Thus, when Chalmers declares (p. 164) that "when we conceive of the zombie world . . . we conceive of a world with physics and *nothing else*; no blockers. . . ," he could not have made it plainer that he is ruling out blockers as part of the physical world. But why does he do this? Not unlike the dualist question-begging circular presupposition that consciousness is nonphysical, this assumption is even more puzzling because it would seem most natural to presume that blockers would be physical! After all, what else would they be?[15] So, with physical blockers in place, a physicalist could allow one to conceive of zombies as those with brains physically identical to humans and yet lacking consciousness, stipulating, however, that for every zombie there would be a physical blocker interfering with what would otherwise be the proper-function emergence of consciousness from his/her brain.[16,17]

ACCEPTING PHYSICALISM

Having addressed and argued against what some consider the best claims for dualism in the Zombie/Conceivability Case (and related arguments), I will now move on to discuss at length various physicalist/materialist/ monist views. Although all the physicalist positions can more readily accommodate current scientific understandings,[18] they are not without problems of their own. In the remaining sections of this chapter, I will outline both the strengths and weaknesses of several physicalist accounts, endorsing an original view at the chapter's conclusion. But to begin, I will present an important defining feature of physicalism.

PSYCHOPHYSICAL SUPERVENIENCE IN PHYSICALISM

Minimally, let us start with defining physicalist (or materialist) views as those which endorse ontological material monism—briefly, that everything is physical; nothing exists that is not physical. Given this as a starting point, we can also state that all forms of reductive physicalism and nonreductive physicalism[19] accept that the mental *supervenes* upon the physical. Here is how Kim (1993), perhaps its foremost proponent, explains this supervenience relationship (p. 76): "If strong psychophysical supervenience holds,[20] what happens in the realm of the mind is determined in every detail by what happens in the physical realm." Kim (p. 76) continues:

> This determination is an objective matter; it does not depend on whether anyone knows anything about it, or what expressions are used to talk about mind and body . . . epistemological considerations do not intrude here. That is perhaps why global supervenience is often used to state the doctrine of materialism.[21]

Then, making abundantly clear the limits of a supervenience relation, Kim (1993) stresses again that

> . . .the thesis that a given domain supervenes on another is a metaphysical thesis about an objectively existent dependency relation between the two domains; it says nothing about whether or how the details of the dependency will become known so as to enable us to formulate explanations, reductions, or definitions. (p. 76)

NONREDUCTIVE PHYSICALISM

For the nonreductive physicalist, certain objects and events have mental properties (e.g., the property of being a wish or being a pain). These properties exist, they are real, and they have autonomous causal powers. Even though most nonreductive physicalists agree with their reductive physicalist counterparts that mental properties are dependent and supervene upon the physical—which at minimum means there cannot be events/objects having *only* mental properties (Kim, 1993, p. 340)—*all* non-reductive physicalists hold that mental properties are not reducible to the physical. So what is the relationship between the mental properties and the physical realm? Nonreductive physicalists usually accept *strong supervenience* to the effect that the physical facts (and physical relations) determine all of the facts, including mental properties. And they also endorse *physical realization*, in which every mental event/state must be instantiated physically.[22]

With so much in common with reductive physicalists, and yet so much that is different, to more fully appreciate nonreductive materialism generally, let us next investigate in detail several different kinds of nonreductive physicalist positions.

Several Nonreductive Physicalist Accounts

Nonreductive physicalists come in many forms.[23] There are, for instance, those philosophers embracing emergentism (and there are emergentist subtypes too). Here the general notion is that higher-order properties such as mental properties emerge from relations among the more basic physical properties and objects and that the new higher-order emergents have autonomous ontological standing and causal efficacy. (Emergentism will be taken up in a separate section below.)

Then there are also several kinds of nonemergentist nonreductive physicalists. One such is Louise Anthony (1999, p. 37), who holds "... that mental properties are only irreducible in the ontological sense." She continues (pp. 37–38), "... there must be micro-physical explanations of all non-basic properties and laws, including intentional ones ... but at the same time we hold out for the ontological distinctness of at least some non-basic [mental] properties."

Other philosophers, who are (at least sometimes) classified as nonreductive materialists, draw the line between themselves and the reductionists at different points. Donald Davidson (1970/1980, esp. p. 214), in advocating anomalous monism, is a material monist, affirming that all events have physical properties, but allowing that some events have mental properties, too. For Davidson each such mental event is tokened by the physical world—that is, physically realized in a spatiotemporal particular—but that these mental events—unlike physical ones, which are under physical laws—obey no psychological laws and have no predictable causes. There are not even casual laws connecting psychological events to physical events. Indeed, there are instead *reasons* operative in the realm of mental events, a realm which prominently includes first-person intentionality. But, since these are not causes, Kim (1994, pp. 269–270) can proclaim:

> The fact is that under Davidson's anomalous monism, mentality does no causal work. Remember that under anomalous monism events are causes or effects only as they instantiate physical laws, and this means that an event's mental properties make no causal difference ... not even in relation to other mental properties.

So, Davidson's nonreductive materialism cannot claim causal efficacy for autonomous mental events. Further, Davidson himself does not endorse the explanatory supervenience Anthony (1999) allows. Davidson (1970/1980, p. 214) states: "Anomalous monism ... rejects the thesis ... that mental phenomena can be given purely physical explanations."

For Galen Strawson (1994, 2009), too, materialism is endorsed, but not reduction. Mental experiential properties are instrinsically physical, hence already physically realized; they are ontologically real and have real causal powers. In the more recent work, Strawson (2009, p. 273) demonstrates the nonreductive token identity view he's developed: "I take it as a materialist that the existence of *e* [an experience] consists in, is literally identical with, the existence of a complex group of neurons in a certain complex state of interaction, a certain sort of *synergy* . . . (this claim is not reductive. . .)."[24] His earlier work shows some of the steps he has taken. Strawson writes (1994, p. 60):

> If one is a materialist and a realist about experiential properties then one holds that experiential properties like the property of having color experience just are physical properties . . . Either experiential properties, being natural physical properties, are reducible to other natural physical properties . . . or they are not.

He continues (1994, pp. 61–62): "to be a nonreductive materialist monist, then . . . is simply to hold that experiential properties are—that experientiality is—among the fundamental [i.e., nonreducible] properties that must be adverted to in a completed or optimal physics." And here is how Strawson sums up his view (1994, p. 74):

1. All reality is physical (the basic materialist premise).
2. There are experiential and nonexperiential phenomena (unavoidable realism about the experiential, *plus* the assumption [!][25] that there is more to physical reality than experiential reality.
3. Among physical phenomena, experiential physical phenomena do not depend on nonexperiential phenomena.

Another philosopher who fits into the category of nonreductive physicalist is John Searle. This is the case, despite the fact that he does not identify himself as dualist or materialist (1992, p. 28): "I reject both property and substance dualism; but . . . I reject materialism and monism as well. The deep mistake is to suppose that one must choose between these views."[26]

And yet Searle (1992) does seem to offer a rather classic nonreductive materialist account, and one that is quite compelling. For example, he states forcefully (p. 28):

> I want to insist . . . that one can accept the obvious facts of physics—for example, that the world is made up entirely of physical particles in fields of force—without at the same time denying the obvious facts about our own experiences—for example . . . that our conscious states have quite specific *irreducible* phenomenological properties.

He makes the point about no reduction even more colorfully several pages later (p. 51): "You cannot reduce intentional content (or pains or 'qualia') to something else, because if you could they would be something else, and they are not something else." Moreover, although he dismisses reduction and with it ontological supervenience (much as does Anthony), Searle (1992) too does countenance that mental states are causally supervenient and dependent on neurophysiological states (pp. 124–125):

> . . . mental states are totally dependent on corresponding neurophysiological states in the sense that a difference in mental states would necessarily involve a corresponding difference in neurophysiological states . . . On this characterization of the supervenience relation, the supervenience of the mental on the physical is marked by the fact that physical states are causally sufficient, though not causally necessary,[27] for the corresponding mental states.

Finally, to fill out his nonreductive physicalist credentials, Searle (1992) holds that mental properties are real and causally active. He states (pp. 125–126):

> It seems . . . obvious from everything we know about the brain that macro mental phenomena are all caused by lower-level micro phenomena . . . such bottom up causation . . . is quite common in the physical world. Furthermore, the fact that the mental features are supervenient on neuronal features in no way diminishes their causal efficacy.

Advantages of Nonreductive Physicalism, and Yet. . .

There is no question that nonreductive materialism is intuitively appealing. Which of us can deny the reality our own consciousness, the qualia we experience, our intentional acts, the beliefs and desires we have, and the contents thereof? And yet which of us can countenance something over and above the physical world, its laws, and its entities, objects, properties, events, and relations therein? First-person nonreductive physical ontology of the mental—especially as elaborated by philosophers as talented and diverse as Anthony, Davidson, Strawson, and Searle—seems to promise all of the advantages of dualism without any of the unhappy, weird consequences that even minimal property dualism demands.[28]

And yet, there are problems—or at least one major problem—with all the solutions the nonreductive materialists have offered. The problem, equal in intuitive strength to the advantage, concerns a gap. *In every nonreductive physicalist view there is some sort of gap between the physical and mental* (or, in Strawson's terms, between the nonexperiential-physical and experiential-physical).[29] The gap can be ontological, explanatory, epistemological, causal, or some combination, depending on the particular nonreductive physicalist account considered. But in each case there is a chasm. Let me try to express the problem in a general way as follows: Given that all reality is physical, concerning mental properties—for example, qualia, consciousness, intentionality, mental content—how can these mental properties:

1. be as they are (i.e., mental) and at the same time be (or be related to) fundamental physical facts?
2. arise from fundamental physical properties and laws?
3. be explained in terms of these physical realities?
4. be caused by physical properties and physical relations?[30]

There is another group of philosophers, a number of whom consider themselves nonreductive materialists, who believe they have certain solutions to at least some of these gap problems. These are the emergentists, referred to in the very beginning of this section on nonreductive physicalism. And so it is to emergentism that we now turn.

Emergentism

Roger Sperry's (1969) assertions about the mind/body relationship are drawn from his neuropsychological work with patients who have had a surgical separation between the two cerebral hemispheres called commisurectomies. He provides a succinct introduction to emergentism and the claims made by emergentists, stating (p. 532):

> The long-standing assumption in the neurosciences that the subjective phenomena of conscious experiences do not exert any causal influence on the sequence of events in the physical brain is directly challenged in this current view of the nature of the mind-brain relationship . . . [Here] consciousness, interpreted to be a direct emergent property of cerebral activity, is conceived to be an integral component of the brain process that functions as an essential constituent of the action and exerts a directive . . . control over the flow pattern of cerebral excitation.

Sperry's account, according to both O'Connor (1994, p. 97) and Ganeri (2011, p. 672), contains the core features of any satisfactory theory of property emergence—supervenience, nonstructurality, and novel causal influence (in this case of the mental). The unfamiliar term, *nonstructurality*, is described by O'Connor (1994, p. 97) as involving "three components: the property's being a) potentially had only by objects of some complexity, b) not had by any of the object's parts, c) distinct from any structural property of the object." Subjective experiences, including consciousness, emergent from brain processes certainly fit this description.

As with nonreductive physicalism in general, property emergentism of the mental has great intuitive appeal. Ready analogies can be made with other complex systems—take cities as a commonplace and rather simple example. Cities, for physicalists, indeed can consist of nothing over and above all of their myriad physical components, as diverse as these may be: for example, cars, people, buildings, streets, signs, trees, trash, traffic lights, and sewers. Yet cities develop their own rules and laws, laws which then have causal influence on at least some of the physical constituents of the city—for example, traffic laws, rental agreements, and fire regulations.

But there is a serious problem with emergentist views—a tension between supervenience and novel causal power that threatens a possible contradiction. The problem is recognized by friend and foe of psychophysical emergentism alike. Friend O'Connor (1994) states (p. 98):

> If an emergent property is a necessary consequence of certain base-level properties (as is implied by the supervenience condition), then its instantiation is one of the potentialities of that set of properties. But then are not the further potentialities of this emergent property also a subset of the total set of potentialities of the base properties, in virtue of the connection between the base properties and it? . . . One is led to wonder why we might ever . . .postulate an emergent property at all, since it provides no explanatory gain. . .

He sums up the problem (p. 98): "This objection implies, in effect, that the features of supervenience and novel causal influence are incompatible."

Foe of emergentism Kim (1999a) similarly argues (p. 32): "If an emergent, *M*, emerges from basal condition *P*, why can't *P* displace *M* as a cause of any putative effect of *M*? Why can't *P* do all of the work in explaining why any alleged effect of *M* occurred?" Thus, if the emergence relation is causal, and *P* has caused *M*, and *M* looks to have caused further physical effect *P**, Kim holds (p. 32), ". . . the emergent property *M* [is] otiose and dispensable as a cause of *P**." In other words, if that which is emergent has no real or novel causal powers, how can emergent properties be viewed as anything other than merely epiphenomenal?

A fuller appreciation of the problem of mental causation, and the closely related problem of downward causation—downward insofar as the mental which supervenes upon the physical is characterized as having new causal effects on physical properties downstream—must await the next section of this chapter, where they will be the main topics. Meanwhile, for this section, I will continue with emergentism as the central focus—notwithstanding the fact that attempts to deal with mental causation and downward causation are often intertwined in such considerations. Let me also note that when one discusses emergence, there are a few different sorts of emergentism in play crosscutting with one another. These are weak and strong emergentism and ontological and epistemological emergentism, distinctions among which I now turn.

Weak emergence, according to Bedau (1997)) requires only that emergent properties can be derived from micro-level information but only in a certain complex way. Ganeri (2011), commenting on Bedau's view, suggests

(p. 683) "That the complexity requirement is what distinguishes weak emergent causal powers from the resultant [regular nonemergent] properties of the system: one cannot *deduce* weakly emergent phenomena [directly] from one's knowledge of the basal conditions. . . " But even with the complexity of dynamical systems, since weakly emergent mental properties would be derivable in principle (and therefore in some sense deducible indirectly), the worry Ganeri (p. 683) notes is that such weakly emergent mental properties would be epiphenomenal—not autonomously causally effective after all. Strong emergence, on the other hand, at least as characterized by Chalmers (2006, pp. 252–253), yields properties that must be considered emergent in that they are marked by their "non-deducibility even in principle."

Carl Gillett (2006) has a somewhat different view of strong emergence for mental properties. Gillett's account is summarized clearly and succinctly by O'Connor and Churchill (2008, p. 274) as follows: Mental properties are emergent. Like all macro-level properties, they are realized microphysically. However, in the special case of emergent properties, the same microphysical properties contribute different fundamental causal powers to the microphysical individuals as they realize different macro-level properties.

An account of strong emergence that resembles Gillett's is advanced by Shoemaker (2007, p. 73): "The component entities have powers that, collectively determine the instantiation of the emergent property when they are combined in an emergence-engendering way. But these being cases of emergence, these cannot be powers that manifest themselves when the components are not combined in emergence-engendering ways."

Related to emergence as described by Shoemaker and Gillett above, but like Bedau's position in that complex systems are centrally featured, are the views advanced by Rueger (2000), Ganeri (2011), and O'Connor and Churchill (2008). All of these theorists are unsatisfied with weak emergence, stressing instead the importance of unpredictability and new causal powers for emergent properties. Rueger (2000, p. 467), for instance, argues for *diachronic* or *evolutionary property emergence*, describing dynamic systems (pp. 480–481) with "stable instability" over a time period that allows ". . . *diachronic* property emergence: a slight [quantitative only] change in the base properties [from] A→A* can lead to supervening properties B* which are [emergent and] qualitatively different from the properties B that supervened on the unmodified base A."

Ganeri's (2011) view of emergence also features diachronicity, but he first introduces *transformation* (pp. 684–688). He explains (p. 688): "The proposal motivating the transformational theory is that, when micro-entities come together in appropriately complex systems of organization, the micro-properties they instantiate are transformed so as to give rise to novel causal powers in the macro-entity they constitute." He continues (p. 688): "What powers an element has is conditional on what combination it is in . . . The emergence of conscious states is not merely a fact about our inability to predict the behaviour of very complex systems . . . It is a fact about the power of micro-entities [only] when they belong to macrophysical structures." Completing his account, Ganeri asserts (p. 691):

> The new idea is that the physical base P* of the newly produced mental event M* has M as an assistive cause . . . combin[ing] the idea of assistive causation with the earlier idea of transformation. The point of the proposal, then, is that . . . the earlier emergent mental event contributes to the transformation of the physical base of the later emergent mental events.

In other words, there is, on Ganeri's view, downward causation (mental to physical), but (p. 691) ". . . the only downward causation is diachronic, while the synchronic relation (the 'material causation' relation) is constitutive."

Finally O'Connor and Wong (2005) state (along the same lines but more vaguely) that it is vital (p. 664) ". . . to recognize that the relationship of micro-level structures and macro-level emergent properties is dynamic and causal, not static and formal . . . and that . . . [a]n emergent property of type E will appear only in physical systems achieving some specific threshold of organized complexity." O'Connor (2008, p. 277) then adds that such emergent properties ". . . persist if and only if the system maintains the requisite complexity."

One can observe that in all these accounts of both weak and strong emergence, there is an undercurrent of a confound between epistemic and ontologic emergence. This both reflects and is based upon the unresolved problem: Can a mental property supervene on physical properties and still be novel, unpredicted (in principle), and have autonomous causal powers? Novel and unpredicted (in principle) suggest that for a macroproperty like M to be considered emergent, its supervenience upon microproperty P (or various Ps) cannot admit of a physical explanation. O'Connor (1994, p. 98), commenting on both sides of this dilemma, talks of "quirky" emergent properties which ". . . would have (we may suppose) various effects in a lawlike way (as ordinary non-emergent properties do), . . . [about which then] there seems to be no bar in principle to our physicists' revising their formulation of the fundamental laws to take account of this quirky phenomenon." The upshot of this, O'Connor (p. 98) recognizes, would be that ". . . even the quirky phenomenon could be described in terms of functions from the base-level properties alone." And yet, just after stating this, O'Connor adds (p. 98): "But this does not motivate the repudiation of the presence of emergent properties. For the laws adequate to describe the quirky phenomenon will themselves have a very odd complexity. . . "

Searle (1992) faces the same dilemma with much less consternation (p. 112):

> . . .consciousness is a causally emergent property of systems. It is an emergent feature of certain systems in the same way that solidity and liquidity are emergent features of systems of molecules. The existence of consciousness can be explained by the causal interactions between elements of the brain at the micro level, but consciousness cannot itself be deduced or calculated from the sheer physical structure of the neurons without some additional account of the causal relations between them.

But Searle has no qualms that this additional account can in principle be provided. Continuing, he contends (p. 112):

> This conception of causal emergence, call it "emergent1", has to be distinguished from a much more adventurous conception, call it "emergent2". A feature F is emergent2 iff [if and only if] F is emergent1 and has causal powers that cannot be explained by the causal intereactions a, b, c . . . If consciousness were emergent2, then consciousness could cause things that could not be explained by the causal behavior of the neurons. The naïve idea here is that consciousness gets squirted out by the behavior of the neurons . . . but . . . then has a life of its own.

Finally, Searle states (p. 112): "It should be obvious that on my view consciousness is emergent1, but not emergent2, and it seems unlikely that we will be able to find any features that are emergent2, because the existence of any such features would seem to violate even the weakest principle of the transitivity of causation."

But the key point here is seen in Searle's comment ". . . unlikely that *we will be able to find any* features that are emergent2 . . ." Isn't this just a version of Chalmers's claim—that strongly emergent properties are not deducible in principle—made stronger and turned around. In other words, *our* physical science laws will *not allow us to be able to* deduce or (an even stronger claim) explain these phenomena—an epistemological limitation. This epistemologic turn is not something Searle makes manifest. O'Connor, too, as quoted above (1994) only deals with the epistemological problem implicitly, saying that either we will have quirky emergent properties that we can't explain, or quirky disjunctive physical explanations. But the problem *is* recognized and commented upon by Rueger (2000, p. 471): ". . . the doctrine of emergence, if explicated in terms of a failure of explainability, seems to turn from a metaphysical position into an essentially epistemic doctrine." And the problem is also directly addressed by Kim (2010, p. 93): ". . . deducibility, or the absence thereof, is the key to the standard conception of metaphysical emergence . . . [but] do we now have a properly characterized ontological concept of emergence, a conception that makes emergence something objective in the world, not a phenomenon that has to do with our own cognitive resources and powers?" He continues with the question (p. 93): "Is deducibility, or nondeducibility, itself a wholly nonepistemic concept?" Certainly his answer is a resounding no, but

Kim's diagnosis of the problem is telling (p. 104): ". . . epistemic emergence, unlike metaphysical emergence, seems . . . rather unremarkable . . . But it may well be that in our search for a coherent concept of metaphysical emergence, we are looking for something that does not exist."[31]

***

So, with emergentism, too (at least emergentism as a branch of nonreductive physicalism),[32] we are left with problems that are just as thorny as the gap problems for other nonreductive physicalists: If there is ontologic emergence and emergent properties, can they can be explained or deduced in principle from physical laws (even laws of great complexity)? If yes, how are these properly considered emergent; if no, how can we ever understand them as part of physicalist physical-only world?

Further Problems for Nonreductive Physicalism: Mental Causation and the Exclusion Argument

Perhaps the most important problem facing nonreductive physicalism is raised by the Exclusion Argument. The argument, in skeleton form, holds that, given causal closure of the physical domain (i.e., physical events must have physical causes), any and every physical event/property/relation must have a physical cause as its cause. This means that there can be no downward causation—there are no mental events/properties/relations that can independently cause physical ones. And this is important because only independent causes are real causes. Thus, mental properties that seem to be genuine causes are now shown to be merely pseudo causes, parasitic upon physical causes, and thereby rendered epiphenomenal. I'll proceed to fill out the basic argument as proposed by Kim in two essays from his 1993 collection.[33]

Addressing the nonreductive physicalists who are mental realists, Kim (1993) begins the argument with a definition (p. 279): "[T]o be a mental realist, your mental properties must be *causal properties*—properties in virtue of which an event enters into causal relations it would otherwise not have entered into." He continues by assuming exactly the issue that he will challenge (p. 279): "[Assume] psychophysical causation takes place—that is, some mental events cause physical events. For example a sudden sharp pain felt in my hand causes a jerky withdrawal of the hand." Kim then clarifies (p. 279): ". . . when I say that mental events cause physical events, something stronger is intended, namely that an event, *in virtue of its mental property*, causes another event to have a certain physical property." He gives examples most would find unobjectionable—for instance, our beliefs and desires causing us to move toward something we want. Finally, Kim (p. 280) offers an additional assumption that "any physicalist would grant, namely 'the causal closure of the physical domain'. Roughly it says this: *any physical event that has a cause at time t has a physical cause at time t.*"

With these steps in place, Kim (1993, p. 280) continues by looking at the consequences that would arise were a mental event (M), in virtue of its mental properties, to cause a physical event (P). Immediately it is clear that P must have a physical cause, too, in accord with causal closure of the physical domain. But then what could be the relationship between the mental and physical causes? Kim (p. 280) nominates two candidates: (1) co-causes combine for a sufficient cause and (2) two independent causes. Quickly Kim rules out the co-cause relation because it is a violation of the causal closure of the physical (p. 280): "[I]t regards the mental event as a necessary constituent of a full cause of a physical event; thus, on this view, a full causal story of how this physical event occurs must . . . go outside the physical domain." Next, and almost as quickly, he claims that having two independent causes is tantamount to overdetermination, which also violates the same causal closure principle in two ways. First, he reasons (p. 281):

> . . . if the pain sensation causes my hand to withdraw, the causal chain from the pain to the limb motion must somehow make use of the causal chain from an appropriate central neural event to the muscle contraction; it makes no sense to think there might be an independent, perhaps telekinetic, causal path from the pain to the limb movement.

In other words (p. 247), ". . . it would be more credible to think that if the belief-desire pair is to cause the movement of my arm it must 'work through' the physical causal chain starting from . . . some neural event in the brain, culminating in a muscular contraction." Second, if both the physical and mental causes were independently sufficient to cause P, the mental cause M would be able to cause P, even if the physical cause of P had not occurred. But then P would be without a physical cause, again violating the causal closure of the physical domain. Concluding that neither the relationship of co-cause nor that of two independent causes will work for mental and physical causes, Kim asks and answers the final damning question (p. 281): "Given that any physical event has a physical cause, how is a mental cause *also* possible?" It is not, he concludes, because ". . . 'the problem of causal explanatory exclusion' . . . [in which] a cause . . . of an event, when it is regarded as a full, sufficient cause . . . appears to *exclude* other *independent* purported causes . . . of it."[34]

The upshot of this for Kim is that mental causes are mere pseudo-causes, epiphenomenal causes, dependent upon physical causes. As discussed by Salmon (1984/1999, p. 449)[35] a pseudo-causal or epiphenomenal process exhibits regularity as does a genuine causal process; however, the regularities of a pseudo-cause is "parasitic upon causal regularities exterior to the process itself." (A demonstration of the difference can be seen in an example Salmon (p. 448) offers about a car traveling on a sunny road at 100 kilometers per hour. "As the car moves . . . its shadow moves at the [same] speed. The moving car . . . constitutes a causal process; the shadow is a pseudo-process.") The implication of mental causes being mere pseudo or epiphenomenal causes is that there can be no downward causation, which can also be understood in relation to a principle Kim (1993, p. 355) terms the Causal Inheritance Principle, as follows. From the Exclusion Argument, Kim (1993, p. 354) states: "Given that P is a sufficient cause of P*, how could M also be a cause, a sufficient one at that, of P*? What causal work is left over for M, or any other mental property, to do?" And the answer, of course, for Kim (1993, p. 355), is that M can do no real causal work as ". . . the causal work [including downward causation] we impute to higher-level processes [like mental processes] are derivative from and grounded in the fundamental nomic processes at the physical level." Kim claims (1993, p. 355) that this can be stated in a balder way with what he calls the Causal Inheritance Principle. This principle holds that higher-level mental states that supervene on physical ones have no independent causal powers. Instead, "these higher [mental] states . . . inherit their causal powers from the underlying [physical] states that realize them." And so there is no downward causation. Even sparser is Kim's (2005, p. 44) assertion that ". . . *the assumptions of causal exclusion and lower-level causal closure disallow downward causation*" (Kim's italics).[36]

***

Nonreductive physicalism has taken some hits. The gap problem is always on hand in any and every view. That is, there is always some uncomfortable space between the mental and the physical—on an ontological, explanatory, epistemological, causal basis, or some combination thereof. There are also serious problems with emergentist solutions. And now, in combination with the principle of causal closure of the physical domain—a principle unobjectionable to physicalists—the Exclusion Argument renders (or at least threatens to render) mental causes merely epiphenomenal, with no independent causal role in either lateral ($M \rightarrow M^*$) or downward ($M \rightarrow P$) causation. This is the state of affairs so far. But in the next subsection we will have a look at some possible solutions for nonreductive physicalists.

Possible Solutions for Nonreductive Physicalism

Revisiting Emergence1

Returning to Searle's (1992, p. 112) notion of emergent1 versus emergent2 (described above), perhaps there *is* a way that nonreductive physicalism can allow mental and therefore downward causation. How? If the mental causative properties could be seen as ontologically emergent from physical properties in a strictly emergent1 "nonadventurous" manner. True, they would not be predictable by our current knowledge of physical laws. But mental causative properties could be understandable by applying these laws after the fact, postdictively. Or, as Searle (p. 112) seems to suggest is already the case, our knowledge of the physical world allows us to understand *that* the mental (including consciousness) emerges from the "causal behavior of neurons"—much as liquidity emerges from the causal behavior of water molecules—even though it is clear that we cannot yet understand *how* the mental emerges from the physical microconstituents. For Searle, this lack of knowledge in no way detracts from his position. Searle is dealing with ontologic emergence, not epistemic. And, since for Searle (p. 28) the facts of physics—"that the world is made up entirely of physical particles in fields of force"—are the only facts, the emergence of mental properties from physical ones is as physical a process as liquidity emerging from many molecules of H_2O.

Kim, however, does not accept Searle's analogy and offers the following objection. For liquidity and H_2O molecules, Kim is an unswerving proponent of ontologic emergence. He states (1998, p. 85):

> H_2O molecules have causal powers that no oxygen or hydrogen atoms have. A neural assembly consisting of many thousands of neurons will have properties whose causal powers go beyond the causal powers of the properties of its constituent neurons, or subassemblies, and human beings have causal powers that none of our organs have. Clearly then *macro-properties can, and in general do, have their own causal powers, powers that go beyond the causal powers of their micro-constituents.* (Kim's italics)

But with respect to mental properties and their neural constituents, for Kim there are no emergent causal powers and the Exclusion Argument holds sway. Discussing a belief/desire to raise one's arm to get a drink of water, Kim (2010, pp. 261–262) says:

> . . . mental events and states have the causal efficacy they have because their neural/physical realizers have causal efficacy. In fact, a mental state, occurring on a given occasion, in virtue of being realized by a certain neural/physical state, has exactly the causal powers of that physical state . . . [T]he next natural step . . . we are compelled to take—is to reductively identify this particular mental state with its neural/physical realizer . . . To say . . . that the belief is a distinct state from its neural realizer and go on to take each as a sufficient cause of the arm rising, is to walk smack into the problem of overdeterminism. And to say that the mental state has causal efficacy "via" the causal efficacy of its neural realizer carries an apparent epiphenomenal implication: Given that the neural realizer is a full cause of the arm rising, what causal work is there for the mental state to contribute? . . . what could "via" mean here?

So what is going on in these two contrasting passages? Why does Kim accept the novel causal powers of the liquid state of water, in which the liquidity supervenes and emerges in an emergent1 fashion from the collection of H_2O molecules and their relations, but does not allow novel causal powers for a mental state—say, a belief or a desire? Could one not characterize this mental state (or any particular mental state) in an analogous way as supervening upon and emergent (in an emergent1way) from a specific array of interacting neurons? Or, getting at this from the other side, why does Kim grant liquidity novel causal powers, when he could say this instance of liquidity owes its total causal efficacy to this particular (enormous) number of interrelating H_2O molecules, and so on for each instance of liquidity? I will try to answer this question, and a similar one that arises, in the next subsection.[37] But before I attempt this diagnostic feat, it may be instructive, and maybe even fun, to look at other examples of potential emergent1 phenomena, comparing and contrasting these both with mental properties and with liquidity.

There is the case of a fist. Is this an emergent property with distinct causal powers? Or are the more fundamental elements constituting the fist, and their interactions—fingers, hand, knuckles—sufficient? This just seems like a case of arrangement and is simpler than the examples to follow. But despite its simplicity, would Kim grant fists novel causal powers, or would fists be epiphenomenal with the true and sufficient causal work done by the constituents of fists?

Cities are very complex aggregates of ever-shifting components—including people, with some moving away and some immigrating into the city, others being born, and still others dying. Cities have streets, electrical and communication wires, vehicles, traffic lights and signs—all of which get repaired, replaced, and updated. They have stores with ever-changing merchandise; food, some that gets eaten and biologically processed, some that spoils and gets thrown out, some that is replenished with more food. Stores also sell clothes, toys, and technical items. Cities include grassy areas, trees, and shrubs. Cities need fire and police departments, other city agencies, and airports, hospitals, libraries, court houses, jails, schools, and city halls. In cities one finds dogs, cats, rats, birds, insects, bacteria, fungi, squirrels; raw materials of various sorts; and hazardous wastes. How does the Searle/Kim debate figure here? Are city ordinances, city histories, city-sponsored teams, parades, and elections instances of emergent1, emerging from the huge number of complexly interacting elements comprising the city at a particular time? Or are the city's causal powers really epiphenomenal to the causal powers of its constituent parts, granting that they must operate in a very complex interactive fashion, almost impossible (but maybe not in principle) to track? This seems too close to call, because both views are quite plausible.

Relatedly there are the biological cases: cells and the parts of cells (e.g., organelles such as mitochondria, ribozymes, nuclei with DNA and nuclear membranes, RNA, vacuoles); multicellular organisms and the particular cells aggregated to form the organs of these more complicated forms; and the eusocial insects (bees, wasps, ants, and some species of termites and aphids) whose individual members have specialized functions facilitating their colonies' success. Interestingly, all of the parts constituting the more complex entities give up some of their freestanding capacities when they form the more complicated cell, organism, or colony. Again, in all these cases, the new, more complex entities seem to have novel causal powers because they are ontologically emergent1 from their constituent parts; but *is* it also true that the causal work could be done by the more fundamental contributing parts, their new, specialized, within-a-compound functions taken rather easily into account?

Only somewhat different are the chemical cases. Not only do we have liquidity as an uncontested emergent1 property from the interaction of many H_2O molecules, we have the equally unproblematic emergent1 phenomenon of water (H_2O) arising from hydrogen (H) and oxygen (O). In this case, each of the elements, hydrogen and oxygen, when not bonded to each another, has a set of properties quite different from that when these elements bond to form the compound water, with water molecules clearly having novel causal powers. As we've seen, these molecular and group phenomena are endorsed by Kim as truly emergent properties and not epiphenomena. This seems right. And yet, could one not plausibly make the claim that the lower-level physical elements, with the lawful changes occurring in their interacting and combining, are still doing all the real causal work and are sufficient under causal closure of the physical? It would even seem quite possible to track—human knowledge of chemistry being sufficiently extensive that we could understand how the causes operate—and moreover to predict physical changes, all well within the natural physical world. So, again, it is hard to decide between the Searle and Kim views.

As will be clear immediately below, these examples and the questions that arise from them constitute a sort of rehearsal for the topic of the next section, on the Generalization Argument. This is an argument used by nonreductive physicalists to counter Kim's Exclusion Argument, which is why I have placed it in the section of this chapter reviewing possible solutions for nonreductive physicalism.

The Generalization Argument: An Argument Mounted Against the Causal Exclusion Argument

Ned Block (2003) presents a serious challenge to the Causal Exclusion Argument in his evocatively titled article, "Do Causal Powers Drain Away?" Block states (p. 133):

> The issue is whether it is a consequence of the Causal Exclusion Argument that all macro level causation (that is, causation above the level of fundamental physics) is an illusion, with all of the apparent causal powers of mental and other macro properties draining into the bottom level of physics.[38]

Robert Van Gulick (1992, p. 325) similarly contends ". . . reserving causal status for strictly physical properties . . . would make not only intentional [and other mental] properties epiphenomenal, it would also make the properties of chemistry, biology, neurophysiology and every theory outside of microphysics epiphenomenal." The conclusion of this challenge is to reject the Exclusion Argument, allowing mental properties to have real causal powers.

Kim (1998, p. 85) has a counterargument, claiming that the Generalization Argument is not a consequence of the Exclusion Argument. As quoted above, Kim states (p. 85) that ". . . *macro-properties can, and in general do, have their own causal powers, powers that go beyond the causal powers of their micro-constituents*." He reiterates (1998, p. 118) that ". . . we must grant novel causal powers to micro-based properties at higher levels—novel in the sense that these causal powers are not had by any lower-level properties that constitute them."

To understand what Kim is getting at here, it is essential that we understand what he means by "micro-based properties at higher levels"—that is, "macroproperties." He explains (1998, p. 84): "A micro-based property . . . is constituted by micro-constituents—that is, by the micro-parts of the object that has it and the properties and the relations characterizing these parts. But we should be clear that such properties are macroproperties, not microproperties." So by this definition, for Kim all of the following are macroproperties—micro based and constituted by their microconstituents—but also higher level and having real and novel causal powers: water molecules, constituted by hydrogen and oxygen atoms bonding (p. 85); liquid water, consisting of many molecules of water interacting (p. 85); brain circuits, made up of "many thousands of neurons" in neural assemblies (p. 85); as well as baseballs (p. 81), and tables and chairs (p. 86), familiar items, variously constituted by variegated microconstituents. Thus, according to Gillett and Rives (2001, p. 92), Kim's Exclusion Argument has escaped the damaging blow of the Generalization Argument because, for Kim, "the fact that micro-based [macro]properties have causal powers that are, in a certain sense, novel . . . prevent[s] his [causal exclusion] argument from generalizing."

But, a nonreductive physicalist might counter: Why, then, are mental properties not seen also as macroproperties, micro based, and constituted by their microconstituents? After all, there seems to be basic agreement that the mental supervenes ontologically and mereologically (part-whole composition) on the physical. Kim responds (1998, p. 86) that ". . . microphysical, or mereological supervenience does not track the micro-macro hierarchy. . ." It is obvious that, for Kim the trouble with this query and thereby with the Generalization Argument itself, is that questions such as these are (p. 866) ". . .based on the assumption [for Kim clearly false] that the mental-neural relationship is, in all relevant respects, the same relationship that characterizes, say, the chemical-microphysical, biological-physiochemical, or other interlevel cases."

But the nonreductive physicalist should certainly not be satisfied with this. Why is the mental-neural relationship different for Kim? Why can't mental properties be considered micro-based macroproperties? Here is Kim's answer in two parts. First, Kim (1999b, p. 116) states that ". . . a micro-based property is the property of being made up of certain proper parts, each with a certain specified intrinsic physical property, in a certain specific structural configuration." Second, for Kim, as clarified by Gillett and Rives (2001, p. 91), mental properties cannot be micro-based, since, according to Kim, "mental properties are plausibly multi-realized and hence, neither identical to combinations of microphysical properties nor micro-based." Indeed there is little argument that mental properties can be multiply realizable.[39] Yablo (1992), for example, affirms (p. 254) ". . . that the mental is supervenient on, but multiply realizable in, the physical . . . [is] a view [that] is in fact implicit [or, as Yablo adds in a footnote, 'All but explicit'] in the reigning orthodoxy about mind-body relations. . . " However, that they are multiply realizable does not close the book on whether mental states/events/properties can be micro-based macroproperties, as we shall see in a later section on token physicalism below.

But for now, since it turns out that Kim's objection to mental properties as micro-based macroproperties (which, it follows, would then also be an objection to mental properties as emergent1 types) rests on the idea that mental properties can be multiply realized, let me take a brief detour to introduce multiple realizability. (I will do this before continuing with other solutions for nonreductive physicalism despite the fact that multiple realization and realizability will be explored more substantively in the section below on reductive materialism.) Kim's own description of multiple realization, one that specifically concerns the multiple realizers for a mental property, will serve this introductory purpose well. Kim (2005, pp. 24–25) states:

> . . . being in pain is definable as being in a state (or instantiating a property) that is caused by certain inputs . . . and that in turn causes certain outputs . . . More generally, instantiating a mental property M . . . will turn out to be being in some state or other that is typically caused by a certain specified set of stimulus conditions and that in turn typically causes a certain specified set of outputs . . . [W]e can look for . . . [a mental property's] "realizers"—that is, states or properties that satisfy the causal specification defining that mental property . . . [F]or pain . . . [c]onventional wisdom has it that pain and other mental states have multiple divers realizers across different species and structures,[40] and perhaps even among members of the same species (or even in the same individual over time).

Observe how different this description of multiply realizable mental properties, like pain, is from Kim's description of a physical property like being a water molecule. Being a molecule of water, Kim (1999b, p. 117) reports, "is the property of being composed of two hydrogen atoms and one oxygen atom in a bonding relationship of kind R." Every water molecule everywhere and at any time, is always realized in this one and only way, exactly. But one could (and should) remind Kim, the same uniformity is certainly not true of baseballs, even less of tables and chairs; and yet he allows these in the category of micro-based macroproperties. Why?

We will leave this issue unresolved for now. We will revisit it again when multiple realization is explored at greater length in the section on reductive physicalism. But first, there is another possible solution for nonreductive physicalism—a different argument to examine directed against the Exclusion Argument.

Yablo's Determinate/Determinable Explanation: Another Important Argument Against Causal Exclusion

Yablo (1992) proposes that mental/physical properties and events can be considered an example of determinable/determinate relations (p. 256): "Necessarily, something has a mental property iff [if and only if] it has also a physical determination of that mental property." That statement, he continues (p. 256), "is an instance of the standard equation for determinables and determinates generally, namely, that something has a determinable property if it has some determinate falling thereunder."[41] Typical examples include colors and their shades. Thus, red would be the determinable and rose, scarlet, crimson, and ruby would be red's determinates.

Continuing with the determinable/determinate relation between the mental and physical, respectively, as outlined by Yablo, since mental events occur if and only if they have *some* physical determinate, we can infer (p. 271):

1. That the mental is metaphysically dependent and supervenient on the physical. Destroy all Ps and there will be no Ms. Destroy all Ms and there can still be Ps;
2. There is multiple realizability—different Ps can in principle have realized the same M.

With this stated, we now have sufficient background for the importance of Yablo's thesis. The following problems for nonreductive physicalists are removed from the problem list: causal overdetermination, causal closure and therefore causal exclusion of the mental, and mental events/states/properties as mere irrelevant epiphenomena. These problems are now obviated—not owing to some strange idiosyncratic view of the mental and the physical, but rather, as Yablo (1992) puts it, because (p. 259) "determinates and their determinable . . . are not causal rivals." Just as wholes and parts *both* fully occupy a space completely filled by one object without "the object's *parts* being crowded out [,] . . . rather than competing for causal honors, determinables and their determinates seem likelier to share in one another's success" (p. 272).

Yablo (p. 257) strengthens his case with the lovely example of Sophie the pigeon trained to peck at red and only red. She's shown a scarlet triangle and, true to her conditioning, she pecks. So which property should be excluded as causally irrelevant—the determinable *red* or its determinate *scarlet*? Suppose the determinable red, which seems so obviously causally relevant, is eliminated as a relevant cause (as would be predicted from the analogue with mental/physical). Reacting to the notion of red as causally impotent for Sophie, Yablo asks (p. 258) "... if even paradigm cases of causal relevance [like this] fail the exclusion test, what passes it?" And he answers: "Not much it turns out." In a footnote Yablo adds, "we are trying to show that the assumption needed to disempower mental properties—namely, that determinates are causally competitive with their determinables—would, if true, disempower virtually all properties."

While this is an impressive argument and indeed might be of some help to nonreductionist physicalism, there are a few problems with Yablo's account. These have to do with his original mapping. There is an imperfect congruence between red and shades of red, on the one hand, and mental events/states/properties and physical realizations/determinates/instantiations on the other. As Sophie the pigeon has learned, crimson is a version of red. In fact, a bird researcher interested in pigeons' color categories may try different shades to develop the class of shades that constitute "red" for pigeons. But various physical determinates of a mental event do not seem likewise to be properly considered versions of that mental event. Equally important, and as Yablo himself recognizes (1992, p. 256n), "There is a crucial difference: My mental properties *result* [causally] from my physical condition, but in no sense does a thing's redness result from its being scarlet."

These problems with Yablo's view raise again the vexing problems of just how to relate the physical to the mental. Although we know that the mental is metaphysically dependent on the physical, and supervenes upon it, we have questions: Does the physical cause the mental? Yes, but it is not clear how. Does the physical ontologically comprise the mental? Yes, it seems so. But is the physical just some part of the mental, with something extra required for the mental? Well, maybe, but how would this work? And furthermore, what are the other parts—nonmental—but what does that actually mean? Or, on the other hand, is the physical identical with the mental? And if so, how and why are we even making this distinction?

* * *

Having explored some important aspects of nonreductive physicalism—its advantages, some problems, and possible solutions—it is time to turn to reductive physicalism. Multiple realizability, introduced in the sections above, will be more fully explored in these sections. This concept, which has played an important and highly problematic role in *type* reductive physicalism, may prove very helpful for a new version of *token* physicalism.

REDUCTIVE PHYSICALISM

Dualists and materialists of all stripes are striving for answers to the same metaphysical questions about the nature of such psychological/mental properties (or events) as consciousness, including sensations with qualia, and cognitive and conative attitudes with intentionality and content. Since much has been said in this chapter about dualist views, and even more about the nonreductive physicalists, it is time to turn our attention to reductive physicalism/materialism—or identity theory, as it sometimes called (for a reason that will become obvious just below). Let us start by noting that there are two forms of identity theory or reductive physicalism: type and token.[42] These two forms, while having important commonalities, also have very salient differences.

Hill (1991, p. 6), a type physicalist himself, first gives a succinct account of reductive materialists generally: "Materialists [those who are identity theorists/reductive physicalists] maintain that we obtain a simpler and more straightforward picture of the universe if we assume that sensory events [mental events] are identical with physical events." Then, in describing the important difference between token and type materialism Hill (p. 11) states the following about type materialism:

> *Type materialism* is like token materialism in claiming that sensory events are identical with physical events. However, it [unlike token materialism] also claims that there is a set of physical characteristics with which qualitative[/mental] characteristics are universally and lawfully correlated, and that every qualitative[/mental] characteristic is identical with its physical correlate.

Regarding token physicalism, Hill (p. 11) states:

> *Token materialism* is the view that results from combining the proposition that every sensory event is identical with a physical event with the proposition that the characteristics by virtue of which events count as sensory . . . [their] qualitative characteristics[,]are not identical with physical characteristics of any [particular] kind. [Thus,] [t]oken materialism does not presuppose the existence of a universal correlation between sensory characteristics and physical characteristics, and it is therefore compatible with the possibility of there being two or more events of the same sensory type that are respectively identical with events that are of quite different physical types.

As such, multiple realization/realizability (MR) is no problem at all for token physicalists, and in fact, as we shall advance later in this chapter, MR could prove quite central toward making token identity materialism a very advantageous view. But before we examine token identity in any depth, there are important matters about both type identity—the more popular of the reductive physicalist views—and especially reductive materialist views in general that must be considered.

Advantages

Reductive physicalism has several advantages, not the least of which is its removing the ontological gap. If mental events/states/properties are reducible to and/or identical with physical events/states/properties, then there is no ontological gap. This obviates any need to posit anything mysterious—regular science will suffice, even if the details have not yet been worked out.[43]

On this matter, Hill (1991, p. 42) adds ". . . there is broad inductive support for the thesis that all concrete particulars—all natural objects and natural events—are composed of physical particulars in the sense of being made of objects and/or events that are ultimately physical in nature." He continues (p. 43):

> Further it seems entirely appropriate to count sensations as natural events: They are located in time and, by most accounts, in space (though dualistic doctrines often deny [that they have] . . . "definite" locations in space), and they depend nomologically for their existence on events that are paradigmatically natural (namely, brain processes). Hence it is entirely appropriate to think that sensations fall under generalizations that apply to all natural objects and events.

Related to this is another big advantage for reductive physicalism—namely, there are no longer problems with mental causation, downward causation, or the principle of causal exclusion. These difficulties are resolved because the mental *is* physical; a part of the physical world. According to Kim (1998, p. 120): "Reductive physicalism saves the mental but only as a part of the physical." Reductive physicalists agree, but would remove the words "but only" in Kim's sentence. Kim does acknowledge as much in a footnote (1998, p. 134 note 35): "The reductive physicalist would say that reductionism does retain mentality as a distinctive part of the physical domain, but its distinctiveness is physical distinctiveness, not some nonphysical distinctiveness."

The import of this particular advantage—removing all the problems associated with mental causation—is tremendous because it allows the strong commonsense view about the existence (and importance) of downward causation to prevail. Take this simple example: Given two cases of a pathologically similar (by biopsy) lung cancer. One cancer is caused by a number of spontaneous mutations in a nonsmoker. Let us represent this as:

Case One

$\text{Physical}_{\text{MU-1,2,3..n}} \rightarrow \text{Physical}_{\text{LC.}}$

Here MU-1,2, 3 . . . n stands for mutations 1, 2, 3 . . . n, and LC stands for lung cancer.

The second cancer is caused by similar mutations brought about by many instances of desiring and deciding to smoke. Let us represent this as:

Case Two

$\text{Mental}_{\text{DS-1, 2, 3 . . . 1,000 . . . n}} \rightarrow \text{Physical}_{\text{S-1, 2, 3 . . . 1,000. . .n''}}\ \text{Physical}_{\text{MU-1,2,3..n}} \rightarrow \text{Physical}_{\text{LC.}}$

Here, DS-1,2, 3, . . . 1,000 . . . n stands for the countless instances of desiring and deciding to smoke, and S-1, 2, 3 . . . 1,000 . . . n stands for that many instances of actually smoking.

Indeed, the many instances of the desire/decision to smoke, especially in light of the resultant episodes of smoking, seem best characterized as causally active, making Case One quite distinct from Case Two. Unlike Case One, in Case Two the *mental events* (the desires/decisions) cause (or at least causally contribute) to the physical events (acts of smoking), which in turn cause the physical cancer-causing mutations. But this is no problem for some reductive physicalists[44]—those for whom mental events *are* physical events. For these philosophers, there is just a different physical causal chain for cases one and two.

There are more advantages for reductive physicalism—in particular, a set of advantages that might best be categorized as demonstrating theoretical power. Hill (1991), for example, cites a philosophy of science rule, the *best explanation principle*, which he characterizes thus (p. 22): "If a theory provides a good explanation of a set of facts, and the explanation is better than any explanation provided by a competing theory,[45] there is good and sufficient reason for believing that the theory is true." He clearly believes that type reductionism offers just such a "best explanation" but does admit that the current state of mind/body identity theory needs the empirical support of psychophysical correlational studies (pp. 23–24).[46,47]

Another theoretical advantage for reductive physicalism is the matter of simplicity. Smart (1959, p. 156) ends his classic article, "Sensations and Brain Processes," by advocating for "the brain process [identity] theory" on the basis "of the principles of simplicity and parsimony." Here Smart points to a stark contrast between his brain process identity theory versus dualism,[48] wherein the latter has "a large number of irreducible psychophysical laws . . . of a queer sort . . . (whereby the nomological danglers dangle)" (p. 156). But Hill (1991) recognizes that, with respect to theoretical simplicity in this case, things are not so simple. Hill (p. 28) suggests that there are at least two kinds of simplicity relevant to reductive materialism: "*Formal simplicity* . . . when we say that a given theory is simpler than another because the former has a smaller number of primitive assumptions . . . and *ontological simplicity* . . . when. . .one theory is simpler than another because the former posits a . . . [smaller] . . .[49] number of mutually irreducible categories of entities." About formal simplicity, Hill admits that both dualism and reductive materialism have about the same number of primitive assumptions. But about ontological simplicity, Hill (p. 35) asserts: ". . . type materialism is simpler than dualism because it postulates fewer unreduced *events* . . .[and] type materialism is simpler than double-aspect theory [described as resembling some version of nonreductive physicalism][50] because it postulates fewer unreduced *facts*."

Finally, Hill (1991) points out one more theoretical advantage for reductive materialism—namely, that it allows a causal role for sensations and other mental events/states/properties insofar as these are reducible to the physical. He explains (p. 42): "In proposing a reduction of sensations to brain states, type materialism in effect proposes a reduction of psychophysical causal relations to neural causal relations . . . therefore type materialism is able to explain the causal roles of sensations."

***

Having listed some of the advantages of reductive materialism, let us turn now to multiple realization and the important and distinct effects this theory has for both type and token identity theorists.

Multiple Realization—A Problem for Type Physicalism

Kim (1993, p. 179) provides a succinct account of the Multiple Realization (MR) Argument and then its consequences. The argument advances the idea that "any mental state . . . can be 'physically realized' in many diverse types of organisms and physical structures (e.g., humans, mollusks, crustaceans, perhaps Martians and robots) so that, as a matter of empirical fact, it is extremely unlikely that some uniform physical state exists to serve as . . . physical correlate [to that mental state]." These various animals and machines, Kim continues (p. 179),

> . . . whose physiochemical structures are entirely different from our own, or from anything we know on this earth, may yet be "psychologically isomorphic" to us in the sense that . . . their observable behavior is best explained by imputing to them certain internal states which are connected among themselves, and to stimuli and behavior, in the way psychological states are so connected for humans. And yet the biochemistry of these creatures may be so different from ours that there is no sense in which we may speak of "the same physical" state underlying, say, pain for both humans and these creatures.

From the Multiple Realization Argument, according to Kim (1993, p. 272), it follows that:

> [Since] any psychological event-type can be "physically realized" or "instantiated" or "implemented" in endlessly diverse ways, depending on the physical-biological nature of the organism or system . . . it [is] highly implausible to expect the event[-type] to correlate uniformly with, and thus be identical with [or reducible to] some "single" type of neural or physical state.

This conclusion from the MR Argument made a deep impact upon those working on the mind/body question. Kim (1993) characterizes its effect as profound and devastating to type materialism (p. 309): "'[T]ype materialism' is standardly thought to have been definitively dispatched by MR to the heap of obsolete theories of mind." Indeed, because of this argument, type materialists seem to have retrenched. Certainly they limited their focus, as talk of type materialism narrowed to type materialism within a species. Thus, there would be human type pain ($Mental_{H\text{-}P}$) and human type brain circuits ($Physical_{H\text{-}BC}$); these not necessarily similar to mollusk type pain ($Mental_{Mol\text{-}P}$) and mollusk nervous tissue ($Physical_{Mol\text{-}NT}$); and Martian type pain ($Mental_{Mar\text{-}P}$) and Martian type physical pain realizer ($Physical_{Mar\text{-}PR}$); all of these also not necessarily similar to one another. Says Kim (1993, p. 274): "[T]he multiple realization argument . . . shows that the strong connectiblity of mental properties vis-à-vis physical properties does not obtain; however it *presupposes* that *species-specific strong connectibility* does hold." Kim goes onto say (1993, p. 274) that really all an argument against MR's antireductionism needs to hold is that the phenomenon of multiple realization is "*consistent* with . . . species-specific strong connectibility . . ."—something Kim (1993, p. 274) contends is "plainly true."

But there is more trouble for type physicalist, even species-specific type physicalists. Philosophers and neuroscientists alike have long known that different human beings may have different brain circuits involved in the same mental property, sometimes even gross differences in brain areas. Along with these micro- and even macro–brain differences across individuals, all realizing the same mental property/event, there is a still more problematic physical reality for the type physicalist. Consider variations even within a single individual. According to Bechtel and Mundale (1999, p. 176) within any one person ". . . the same psychological state can be realized by different brain states . . . a many-to-one mapping from brain states to psychological states." The term for this is "biological degeneracy," which Edelman and Gally (2001, p. 13763) define ". . . as the ability of elements that are structurally different to perform the same function or yield the same [contentful] output." Getting more specific, Figdor (2010) explains (p. 435): "On the neuroanatomical side, single cells, neuronal populations, anatomical areas, or anatomical networks are among the 'structural elements' that may appear in degenerate mappings." (See also Friston and Price, 2003; Noppeney, Friston, and Price, 2004; Price and Friston, 2002.) Even Kim (1993), while supporting local type reductions, acknowledges that (p. 273), ". . . given the phenomena of learning and maturation, and injuries to the brain, etc., the neural structure that subserves a psychological state or function may change for an individual over a lifetime." Noppeney, Friston, and Price (2004) characterize these sometimes dramatic, psychological function sparing, within-individual brain changes as follows (pp. 440–441):

> [M]aintenance and recovery of function in [neurologically damaged] patients can be explained by different neuronal mechanisms within the framework of degeneracy. First, maintenance and recovery of a particular cognitive function can be explained by degenerate functional neuroanatomy, i.e. degeneracy within subjects, because after lesions to one of multiple degenerate systems, the function can still be sustained by the remaining systems. In this case, plastic changes, induced by the lesion, are immediate and rely on unmasking of a pre-existing but functionally latent system . . . Second, recovery of function can be explained by degeneracy over subjects. In this case, only one system within a normal brain is capable of performing this particular task. However, an alternative system can emerge [in the injured brain] due to functional reorganization induced by the underlying pathological process . . . Plastic changes are then mediated by reorganization mechanisms with longer time-courses.

Clearly the brain's degeneracy and its plasticity are of great import for survival and for evolutionary success. Yet these current scientific developments severely compromise any type-physicalist view of the mind/body question. It becomes increasingly apparent that even the more limited local species-specific type physicalist cannot rely on type-type identity or type-type reduction, even within the brain of a single individual, much less across the brains of an entire species. No one-to-one physical type–to–mental type correlation can be found to exist.

The usual reaction among philosophers to this daunting challenge to type materialism has been to turn back to a nonreductive version of physicalism, neglecting token materialism, which in my view deserves much further investigation. Indeed, in the sections to follow token materialism will be explored in some depth. However and in any event, for now there is still more to say about type physicalism. Just below we take up two more type-materialist views, each adjusted in an attempt to deal with the damage inflicted upon type reductionism by the considerations multiple realization has necessitated.

First, there is disjunctive type materialism. On this account each mental type M is realized by a physical type P, where P actually consists of P_1 or P_2 or P_3 or P_n—that is, the disjunction of all of its physical realizers.[51] Kim

(1993, pp. 322–325) argues that this is unacceptable given that type materialists want to keep M as a unified non-wildly disjunctive non-heterogeneous mental type. So Kim asks and answers the following questions (p. 323):

> Why isn't pain's relationship to its [multiple disjunctive] realization bases . . . analogous to jade's relationship to jadeite and nephrite? If [i.e., since] jade turns out to be nonnomic on account of its dual "realizations" in distinct [chemical] microsturctures, why doesn't the same fate befall pain? . . . After all, the group of actual and nomologically possible realizations of pain, as they are described by the MR enthusiasts . . . , is far more motley than the two chemical kinds comprising jade.

The conclusion for Kim is that this type reductionism will not work: "We cannot hide the [unacceptable and wildly] disjunctive character of pain . . . [because] mental properties will . . . turn out to be disjunctions of their physical realization bases" (p. 324).

As for the second adjusted type materialism, it is Kim (1993) who offers his own solution, actually a hybrid type materialism. He asserts (pp. 364–366):

> [T]he standard type materialism is precluded; that is, we cannot identify mental properties of kinds with physical ones . . . However, any given *M*-instance must be either a P_1-instance or P_2-instance or . . . [P_n], where P_1, P_2, . . . [P_n] are realizers of *M*, and the set of all *M*-instances is the union of all of these P_i-instances. In this sense, we may say that mental kind *M* is *disjunctively identified* with physical kinds P_1, P_2, . . . [P_n]. Note that *M* is not identified with the *disjunction* of P_1, P_2, . . . [P_n]; nor is an *M*-instance identified with an instance of the disjunctive property *P_1 or P_2 or . . . [P_n]*.We may call this proposal "multiple-type physicalism."

Kim (1993, p. 366) characterizes his multiple-type physicalism as the view that "most proponents of token physicalism, especially those who have been moved to embrace it by considerations on multiple realization, have in mind."

But I hope that Kim is wrong about most token physicalists. Why? Because I intend to demonstrate below that a modern version of token physicalism is not only left unscathed by MR but can moreover do important work that Kim's multiple-type physicalism cannot. I have no argument with Kim's (1993, p. 366) claim that multiple-type physicalism is able to say ". . .something about how mental properties and kinds are related to physical kinds. It states that for an event, or object, to have a mental property is for it to have one or another of its realizing physical properties"—but in my view token physicalism can do even better.[52] A modern form of token physicalism can (at least in principle) specify *which* physical realizer is operant; and therefore an *M*-instance should be able to be identified with a particular *P*-instance of the disjunctive set of P_1 or P_2 or P_n physical realizers. Interestingly, Kim (2005)—in discussing a different matter in the passage to be quoted (namely, functional and local reduction)—gives a good account of just the sort of specificity that is plausible (p. 25):

> We may be interested in your pain now or my pain yesterday. Neural bases may differ for different instances of pain, but individual pains must nonetheless reduce to their respective neural/physical realizers . . . Suppose that pain has physical realizers, P_1, P_2, . . . Then, any given instance of pain is an instance of either P_1 or P_2 or . . . If you are in pain in virtue of being in state $P_{k,}$ there is nothing more, or less, to your being in pain than your being in state P_k.

***

We will return to multiple realization with a different emphasis—its advantages for token physicalism—in a section below. First, however, there is another problem with type materialism that proves important.

The Matter of Scale—A Related Problem for Type Physicalism

Restricting our inquiry to humans, and thereby restricting the physical realizers of mental properties and events to neuronal activities, it seems clear that there is a mismatch in scale between mental properties—for instance, belief or pain—and the brain processes underlying them. The brain processes are much more finely differentiated. Even more than forty years ago, Block and Fodor (1972) recognized that (p. 160) ". . .the central nervous system is highly labile and that a given type of psychological process is in fact often associated with a variety of distinct neurological structures." And Hill (1991), despite his intention to mount an argument in the opposite direction, that is in favor of type-type matching, allows that "Neuroscience is concerned with understanding the structure of single cells and the interaction of small assemblies of cells, but it also recognizes the existence of large-scale mechanisms that involve scattered and gerrymandered collections of cells" (p. 105). These statements taken together, along with the discussion of degeneracy and plasticity in the last section, can help demonstrate the scale problem when dealing with mental events/states/properties and their underlying physical realizers, determinants, and instantiations—that is, their supervenience bases.

Still, an analogy might be of some use. Suppose that one is flying from New York to Los Angeles but wants to make several stops in major U.S. cities along the way. There are many different routes that will all originate in New York and end in Los Angeles, each having different cities as stopovers. One can go from New York to Detroit to Chicago to Denver to Los

Angeles or from New York to Philadelphia to St. Louis to Salt Lake City to Los Angeles.

Applying this idea to the matter of interest, let's take a simple mental event like my current belief that dogs are wonderful. As is likely, let's stipulate that I will have this belief tomorrow too, and next week. Thus, in terms of content (dogs), evaluative judgment (positive), and cognitive attitude of an agent (a belief that I, LAWB, hold), one could consider these three occasions of a belief of mine—dogs are wonderful—as identical tokens[53] of a single mental type—LAWB's positive beliefs about dogs.

But when we shift to the neural circuitry, there are certainly three different cell assemblies neurochemically influenced by and recruited for each of these three instances of the same agent's belief. Furthermore, there are very likely three different electrophysiologic brain area activations and three different readings of oxygen uptake measures, each a distal reflection of not only the specific cell circuits but the adjacent brain structures (see Edelman and Gally, 2001; Friston and Price, 2003; Price and Friston, 2002.)

Maybe a gross anatomical pattern would be discernible—I would suspect that certain sectors of the brain would be activated in a similar interactive pattern during all three instances of my belief that dogs are wonderful—the frontal cortex, the occipital area, and the hippocampus; probably not the amygdala nor the cerebellum. But note that this very rough, rather than fine-grained. Particular brain area activation and interaction might well be true of many of my thoughts, hypotheses, fantasies, and other beliefs with varying contents. Perhaps there would be a certain LAWB electrophysiologic or oxygen uptake signature to mental events of which these three belief tokens would be examples. But even if there were such a signature, likely it would not be sufficiently fine-grained to pick out specific mental contents (about dogs) nor pick out a particular mental property type (e.g., a belief rather than a desire). And in fact, there is ample reason to have serious doubts about any such signature in the first place. Why? Because so much of the brain activity of those particular beliefs would be context dependent—contingent on what brain activities were occurring during my belief and, just as importantly, right before the belief, and so on (see Friston, 1997; Price and Friston, 1997).

The mismatch in scale between the very fine-grained physical brain events (consisting of neurochemicals, neuroanatomy, and neural connections) and the much coarser mental events they underlie is huge, even when the mental events are token beliefs of the same agent with the content held constant. The mismatch in scale is, of course, compounded exponentially when we consider attempting to match mental types (like beliefs in general or pains in general) with physical brain types.

Note that the current state of affairs regarding this mismatch does not in any way preclude future empirical findings allowing a better type-type match. And there is no reason why there could not be empirical findings in any one of several dimensions. Perhaps, for instance , there would be content matches rather than matches for cognitive attitudes—in other words, beliefs would not form a recognizable brain type, but beliefs, fantasies, desires, wishes, and intentions *about* a particular content would be categorized together by demonstrably similar underlying brain structures and processes. Or perhaps wrong ideas versus correct ones would be grouped together always with certain brain circuit regularities. Maybe attitudes marked by certain emotions would correlate with particular neural configurations in common brain areas. Perhaps pains would be grouped in brain registrations by body part, say with other discomforts (such as tickles or itches), and not with other pains, or by intensity, or some combination thereof.

If empirical data could reliably establish any of these patterns, then certain mental types could indeed be considered macroproperties micro based—novel mereological arrangements of their particular physical types, which would be capable of genuine and novel causal powers *as* mental events/states/properties. These sorts of research findings could in principle revive type materialism. But meanwhile, and especially if research findings do not go in this direction, we still have token physicalism!

TOKEN PHYSICALISM

Intrinsically free from the issues raised by the Causal Exclusion Argument (mental tokens *are* physical tokens providing causal efficacy and closure), token physicalism also remains unscathed both by the scale problem between mental and physical events/states/properties and the phenomenon of multiple realization.[54] In fact these issues, while highly problematic for type materialism, might actually be seen as helpful for modern token materialism. Thus, each identity between one instance of a mental event/state/property and one particular arrangement of a certain brain cell assembly not only fits the scale matching requirement, it can also provide confirming evidence for the scientific findings of degeneracy and multiple realization, in that separate but very similar mental events (two instances of a single agent's belief that X) are instantiated by different neuronal populations with different interactional patterns.

Moreover, in being a relationship of identity—that is, a relationship of an entity to itself, a unique singular event at a particular time, in which the mental event *m* and the physical event *p* are indiscernibles, with no property differences—one of the most vexing mind/body problem evaporates—there is no longer an ontological gap. Intuitively, this might seem wrong, as might the idea that a token mental event and its token physical configuration can be property-identical, sharing all properties and having no uniquely mental or uniquely physical properties. But this is exactly what token identity is, and in this way it is just like that of a water molecule being identical with its arrangement of hydrogen and oxygen as H_2O.

Admittedly, however, there is no denying the feeling that there *is* some important difference between token mental and physical events, on the one hand, and water and its molecular structure H_2O, on the other. One such difference is that, for the water case, the ontological gap is not only closed but also explained. The chemical knowledge of the structure of atoms and molecules, the proclivity of bonding between and among various atoms, and the structure and nature of these bonds allow a pretty thoroughgoing understanding of why water is identical to H_2O. We do not have this knowledge for token mental/physical events. At least we do not have this knowledge yet. But token physicalism can be highly compatible with scientific optimism. Thus, just as further scientific cataloging could lead from token physicalism to some sort of type physicalism (as discussed just above), another possibility (and one that is not mutually exclusive) is that future basic neuroscience investigations could provide an understanding for why and how token physical events are identical with, instantiate, and cause their mental tokens. These findings could be as revealing and compelling as are those in physical chemistry concerning the molecular structure of H_2O being identical with, and causing the properties of, water.

But even if these connections are discovered and understood, this will be at some time in the future. Let's take stock of the problems that remain for token materialism in our current understanding of the brain and the mind, and let us also assess issues unresolved for other mind/body positions.

A good part of the trouble for any mind/body theory is that, no matter what the particular view, there is so much to be taken into account. There are so many different relations between P (physical events/states/properties) and M (mental events/states/properties) to consider. And one must consider all of them, and simultaneously. For example, even if it is the case that the ontological gap has been closed because P = M, there are still *these* questions:

1. Are P and M like figure/ground?

   Could that be said of H_2O and water?

2. Does P cause M and provide an explanation for its nature?

   This would be true of H_2O and water—the chemical knowledge of atoms and so on does explain the nature of water. Regarding M and P, Searle (1992) suggests that Ms are emergent1 macroproperties, micro based,[55] whose nature can *in principle* be explained in the usual way of normal science, through understanding Ps. Yet does this understanding suffice? It might for me, but not for Searle (1992, 1995). Searle (1995, p. 226) reminds us that, "because the ontology of the mental is essentially a first person ontology, no third person account can capture the fully determinate aspectual [intentional] shapes in the mind of the agent." So, despite what I see as his optimism regarding scientific causal explanations of Ps causing Ms, Searle (1995) does say very clearly (p. 227), "Any description in purely third person terms always leaves the first person ontology underdetermined."

3. Do Ps mereologically constitute Ms?

If so, there is first the matter of scale that must be considered. Take even the simplest case, M. Is M at one particular instance, one mental event/state/property that is uniquely constituted by its P? In other words, is this M the composite result of all of the neurons and so on in a multi-neuronal assembly activated with the appropriate neurochemicals within a brain structure?

If yes, is this a Kim-sanctioned macroproperty micro-based mereological combination? Remember that, for Kim, these can include both:

a. uniform composites (except for unique individual instantiations at a time) like H_2 and $O_2 \rightarrow H_2O$ = water; and many H_2O molecules→ fluid or solid water (depending on the temperature and pressure) with the proper attendant properties;
b. much more diverse composites like baseballs and chairs—which, though composed of many diverse things, overall have constituents that are apparently similar enough for Kim. Or are Ms mereological combinations that are not sanctioned by Kim as macroproperties micro-based, this owing largely to multiple realization?

Furthermore, there are other gaps besides the ontological one. There is the causal gap, which, as can be seen just above, is embedded in the ontological/metaphysical questions raised, and there is also the epistemological gap. Note that both causal and epistemological gaps seem quite related to explanation. Kim (2010) contends that the identity relationship not only obviates any considerations of an ontological gap, holding that there just isn't one, but also renders questions such as: "'Why is heat identical with mke [molecular kinetic energy]?' . . . wrongheaded" (p. 219). He claims (2010, p. 232) that ". . . identities . . . eliminate the need for—indeed the possibility of—such explanations. Instead of 'closing' the explanatory gap, [identity] reductions . . . show that no such gaps exist in the first place."

Actually it is this conclusion that seems *wrongheaded* to me. Kim might be right in questioning the question "Why is P = M?", but this is far from the only question. Instead proper *how* questions seem as fitting as they are vexing, even with identity physicalist views. Thus, questions pertaining to the explanatory and epistemological gaps[56] such as: "How is it that P = M?"; "How is it that one gets from P to M?"; "How is it that Ms are caused by/constituted of/identical with Ps—what are the mechanisms?" are questions that ought not be precluded or dismissed. They could (and perhaps should) be questions that are as answerable (at least in principle) as are such questions regarding the identity relationship between water and H_2O.

Some philosophers agree with Kim. Block and Stalnaker (1999, p. 24) state that "Identities don't *have* explanations . . ." adding that "The role of identities is to disallow some questions [like the explanatory ones] and allow others." Papineau (1993, p. 180) colorfully claims that "Once we free ourselves from the seductive 'inner light' picture of consciousness, and take seriously the idea that being conscious may be literally identical with some physical A, then we should stop hankering for any further explanation of *why* physical state A yields consciousness." Other philosophers acknowledge the epistemological gap but attribute it to human cognitive limitations. So, for example, Jackson (2003, footnote 9), as cited above, characterizes the epistemic gap as "an illusion that fuels the epistemic intuition." Chalmers (2010, pp. 311–312) explains that philosophers like Jackson with this sort of account[57] use a strategy that ". . . involve[s] an attempted psychological explanation of why we think there is a epistemic gap between physical and phenomenal [mental] truths when [according to these philosophers] in fact there is none."

Still other philosophers do acknowledge that there is an epistemic/explanatory gap that is more than just a mere reflection of certain human psychological and/or cognitive limits. Levine (1993, p. 121) states that ". . . physicalist theories 'leave out' qualia in the epistemological sense, because they reveal our inability to explain qualitative character in terms of the physical properties of sensory states. The existence of this 'explanatory gap' constitutes a deep inadequacy in physicalist theories of the mind." Chalmers (2010, p. 244) weighs in on this side, too, asserting that those who hold the view that identities need and indeed admit of no explanation "conflate ontological and epistemological matters." Chalmers goes on to explain: "Identities are ontologically primitive, but they are not epistemologically primitive. Identities are typically implied by underlying truths that do not involve identities. The identities between . . . water and H_2O are implied by the underlying [physical chemistry] truths . . ." (p. 244).

And so now, fully realizing the continued existence of the epistemological and explanatory gaps in the mind/body problem, even on any identity theory account, I offer my own solution, with what I hope will be a small contribution:

TOWARD A SOLUTION FOR EPISTEMOLOGIC AND ONTOLOGIC GAPS

Reviewing the situation, token physicalism, ontologically, works well—and not just to fill in, but actually to obviate any ontological gap. Moreover, multiple realization of a mental property type does not threaten token physicalism. Thus, the fact that a singular earthly instance of a mental token of event/state/property type M, $m_{1\text{-earth}}$, is realized, constituted, and caused by[58] a particular collection of neurons activated by neurotransmitters,

$p_{\text{neurons-1}}$, at time t_1 is quite compatible with the fact that a specific Martian instance of a token of the type M, $m_{\text{1-mars}}$, is realized, constituted, and caused by vastly different physical materials, $p_{\text{mars-stuff-1}}$, also at t_1. More interesting and relevant, there is no problem for token physicalism when a distinctly different assembly of neurons, $p_{\text{neurons-2}}$, physically realizes, constitutes, and causes a subsequent mental token $m_{\text{2-earth}}$ of M on earth at time t_2. This is the case even when all of the mental tokens of M are identical[59] and belong to a single mental type. This is, of course, impossible and devastating for type reductive physicalism; there can be no type-type identity with such divergence between coarse-grained Ms and their fine-grained P realizers.

Thus, I will want to make token physicalism part of my solution to the ontologic and epistemologic gaps. However, before I present my account, it seems only fair to first discuss an important dissenting view—one that will enable a sharp contrast to be made. Hence, in the next subsection I will return to a particularly interesting sort of nonreductive physicalism—Pereboom's "robust nonreductivism."

Robust Nonreductivism due to Multiple Realization, Not Token Physicalism

Pereboom (2002), a nonreductive physicalist, looks at the situation presented above somewhat differently than I do, using multiple realization phenomena to advance his particular version of nonreductive physicalism—"robust nonreductivism." Introducing "higher-level token entities," Pereboom claims that these "are not typically identical with their realization bases" (p. 503). For his first example he offers (p. 503) that "The Ship of Thesus is not identical with its current token microphysical realization base, for it would have been the same token ship had the token microphysical realization been slightly different, and it will be the same ship when this microphysical realization in fact changes." Pereboom continues (p. 503):

> The same sort of argument can be run for token mental entities. Is token mental state M identical with P, its actual token microphysical realization base? . . . It is possible for M to be realized differently only in that a few neural pathways are used that are token distinct from those actually engaged . . . But it is evident that this alternative neural realization is itself realized by a microphysical state P* that is token-distinct from P.

Thus, the Ship of Thesus and M each provide Pereboom with an example of a "higher-level token multiply realizable" (p. 503). Continuing with regard to M, Pereboom states that, since M is identical neither with P nor with P*, M is not in causal competition with either P or P*, even though M's "causal powers are wholly constituted by token microphysical causal powers" (p. 504). Moreover, in terms of projectibility (quite important for any entity to be considered from a regular science viewpoint) Pereboom claims (p. 522) ". . . the projectibility-sustaining feature of a kind could be a structure [like a higher-level token] that is significantly homogeneous across its heterogeneous realizations, a structure that might instantiate a unitary causal power . . ."

Relatedly for Pereboom (2002, pp. 524–526) multiple realization can do the following very interesting nonreductive work: Because mental states can be realized in neural brain assemblies and in silicon structures, mental state kinds can be neither *essentially* brain based nor silicon based. Seemingly, then, the "essentialness" of Ms (along with their causal efficacy and projectibility) must be at the level of higher level tokens of a psychological/mental state kind.

TOKEN PHYSICALISM ONTOLOGICALLY

Derrick Pereboom and I have a different view of tokens. I am quite willing to admit that my notions might be idiosyncratic. I do, however, think my view allows a cleaner escape from frequent confounds between ontological and epistemological matters. With this in mind, let's examine one of Pereboom's own (2002, p. 529) "higher-level multiply realizable tokens"—his decision to ring the doorbell. Indeed, I agree with him that this *decision* "can plausibly survive changes in its realizing microphysical state" (p. 529). But I hold that it is the *decision* that would survive, not the unique mental event token—namely, *Pereboom's decision to ring the doorbell at time* t_1. His decision to ring the doorbell at t_1 is an individual token, caused and constituted by a particular arrangement of neurons and so on. The neuronal assembly (i.e., the physical tokening) will *necessarily* be different at time t_2,[60] when again Pereboom decides to ring that doorbell. Thus, on my account, the mental token that this second neural arrangement causes and constitutes will also be different. I want to make the claim that this is the ontological reality, even if the two decisions (or two decision events) are so similar that we humans are quite unable to discriminate Pereboom's mental state about the doorbell at t_1 from that at t_2. Our epistemological limits, however, are not determinative factors in what is ontologically the case.

There are two other factors operative here in our different understandings of "token." One concerns the issue of scale. Mental events/states/properties for Pereboom are regarded as higher-level tokens; for me, mental events/states/properties are picked out at a discrete time point, and in that way adjusted (at least somewhat) to the scale of the physical realizing tokens. The second issue is also of great interest—it is the issue of diachronic (over time) and synchronic (at a time) constitution of tokens and types. I turn to this matter now.

Diachronic/Epistemological and Synchronic/Ontological Considerations

Let's return to consider the Ship of Thesus. Suppose it is constituted by planks numbered 1 to 1,200 at the time of its completion, time t_1. Then at some later time, t_2, 200 planks need to be replaced. At t_2, the Ship of Thesus is thus constituted by 1,000 old planks and 200 new ones. And we can keep doing this (remembering that this "ship" is a famous sorites paradox example) until not one of the original planks remains. At various times, some portion of the planks will be original, some brand new, some in between. At any particular time, t_n, if the ship causes an accident—ramming into a much smaller vessel and damaging it, which entity (or group of entities) is causally efficacious—the Ship of Thesus, or all of its constituent parts at time t_n? On one understanding, it is the Ship of Thesus which has causal power, just as a mental property does, as long as one can consider such Ms macroproperties micro-based (or, in Searle's terms, emergent1). And that causal power is real and novel. For example, the shiplike arrangement of all of the Ship of Thesus's physical parts does not seem to inhere in any of the parts or even all of them together unless and until assembled in some composite notion of "ship." Further, as Pereboom suggests, different parts contribute to the Ship of Thesus at different time points, making it difficult to consider any parts or collections thereof as having causal powers.

However, looked at from a different perspective, at a particular time, t_n, it *is* instead the sum total of all of the physical parts constituting the Ship of Thesus *at that specific time point*; that sum which *is* causally efficacious—sufficient both for the arrangement and for the accident. True, if the accident had occurred at any different time, say at t_{n-1} or t_{n+100}, a somewhat different set of parts would have to be summed, each time slice having a different token Ship of Thesus. And, true, that even returning to just one particular time, t_n, to describe the total collection of parts would be horribly burdensome. But is that at all relevant to the ontology of the situation? And this question leads to my worry here: Should our ontological conclusions be based solely on what is human-sized and human-scaled, easily described by us, and readily seen as projectible by us? Do our epistemological limits and proclivities not only shape but confound our ontological convictions? Here is a silly example to help demonstrate this point. Suppose there is an ant on a smaller seagoing vessel when it is rammed into by the much larger Ship of Thesus. This ant is crushed by the impact of the crash. Next imagine that a close relative of this poor ant witnessed the fatal event and was then asked (by a journalist ant) to opine about the cause of his relative's death. From the surviving ant's point of view, because ants are so much smaller than humans, it is likely that something as large as the whole ship could not even be picked out as a single object. Hence, the witnessing ant would likely see just one little part as causally relevant—for example, a protruding nail as the cause of the crashing/crushing fatal blow.[61]

But, after all, we are human, and although I am friendly to the idea (as I in fact proposed it), that each Ship of Thesus examined at any particular time slice is a different Ship of Thesus token[62]—differently constituted (and not just by planks, but by nails, paint, rust, dust, and microbes, etc.)—I don't deny there is something else we need to consider. Namely, we need to take into account not just the time-slice entities or entities at any particular time that I've been championing, but also entities over time. Thus, there are differences between synchronic (at a specific time slice) versus diachronic (over time) Ship(s) of Thesus. Synchronically, at any one particular time, there is one Ship of Thesus token; viewed across many time slices, there are many different single Ship of Thesus tokens. But over time—that is, diachronically—there is a unified Ship of Thesus, no matter how many synchronic token ships there are, and no matter how many planks, nails, and so on are changed.[63]

Now maybe we can take this a step further. Is the diachronic view one that is essentially geared to our epistemological longings to know and understand, but also shaped and limited as well as facilitated by our cognitive capacities, including, most importantly, our human-scale time frame? Yes! Thus, I am proposing that analogous to the way we operate with spatial and material matters—seeing macroproperties as causally efficacious rather than dealing with their micro-based constituents (especially when they are perfectly well-behaved micro-based macroproperties)—we do likewise with time-slice constituents. Thus, we see the diachronic version—one Ship of Thesus, one decision on Pereboom's part to ring the doorbell, and one ongoing belief of mine about dogs—rather than several different time-slice versions (or tokens) of each event or entity. Importantly, when we do this—just as we spatially sum up micro-based parts to get causally effective macroproperties—we can understand diachronic mental tokens as *conjunctions* of their various synchronic physical-only token realizers—conjunctions that require no attribution of "essentialness" to some "higher-level" token mental state or kind. Clearly in this way, the version of token physicalism that I am here propounding is profoundly different from Pereboom's robust nonreductivism.[64]

DIACHRONIC CONJUNCTIVE TOKEN PHYSICALISM (DICOTOP): AN EPISTEMOLOGIC AND ONTOLOGIC SOLUTION

In light of the above, how can diachronic, across-time, "single" unified tokens—like one Ship of Thesus or one decision of Pereboom's to ring the doorbell (although it is the "same" decision made twice), or a particular belief about dogs that I hold over time—be properly characterized and understood? I propose that they be conceptualized as true macroproperties, indeed micro-based, but by the conjunctive constituent collections of their synchronic time-slice micro-based tokens. The sort of conjunction I have in mind here includes but is not limited to the physical mereological conjunctive constituents at any time slice: of the ship (planks, nails, paint, etc.); of all the physical components of Pereboom's decision at time t_1 (his brain network of neurons and neurotransmitters at that time); of the sum of all of the physical parts of my belief about dogs now (my brain's assembly of neurons, etc.). Yes, the conjunctions include these *plus* all the other mereological material constituents of *all the other relevant time-slice tokens* contributing to the "single" ship, decision, or belief.

To explore this, take for instance, Patient Z's fear of dogs, a mental event/state/ property that seems to have much psychological importance. He is afraid of dogs today; he was afraid of dogs yesterday; he's been afraid of dogs for years. Today he has encountered dogs named Bowie, Buddy, Xenia, and Henry; and Patient Z is afraid of Bowie, Buddy, Xenia, and Henry, each fear episode manifesting itself at a different time during the day. Thus, synchronically for each time slice occupied by each dog, he has been afraid. His fear is diachronic too—he is afraid of dogs generally, and his fear is also dispositional—he is disposed to feel fear upon seeing a dog or even thinking of one. To make things simple, let's suppose that his fear got triggered (as can happen with aversive conditioning) by a single frightening encounter with an angry-looking dog ten years ago, when Patient Z was ten years old. Now, as we saw in Chapter Two, we know that to deal with this phobia, to extinguish it as much as possible (though it can never be made extinct), many different nonaversive (safe-here and safe-now) conditioning trials will be needed. Furthermore, to be effective, these many different trials have to be in as many different contexts as possible, with as many different dogs, with as many different conditions as possible. Why? Along with the reasons given in Chapter Two, we can now add that the multiplicity of trials necessary toward the best approximation of extinction reflects two things:

1. Multiple realization—there are variations in neuronal assemblies and brain circuits—many *p*s (some only slightly different), all contributing in various combinations[65] conjunctively to the collective micro-bases of this important mental state—the macroproperty *M*, Patient Z's fear of dogs. Thus, if Henry is the dog used in a safe trial in a small green room, Patient Z may indeed register a diminished fear of Henry, but this improvement may be seen only in small green rooms, and Henry's appearance in a big red room may still be a source of fear for Patient Z. And, of course, Bowie in a small green room would still elicit fear. In both of these instances we can understand Z's fear not so much reinstituted as incompletely deconditioned, as different parts of the multiple realization base would not yet have been addressed.
2. The importance of synchronic tokens—each time-slice token of Patient Z's fear contributes conjunctively toward his diachronic fear of

> dogs. Hence, if Xenia is the dog in a number of safe trials for Patient Z today, at time t_1, not only will that not help his fear of Buddy, it may not even have much effect on his fear of Xenia later today at time t_2, or tomorrow at time t_3.

So the epistemologically relevant *M*, Patient Z's fear of dogs, consists of two sorts of ontological conjunctions: (1) synchronically, the sum of all of the physical constituents, realizers, and causes—for example, neurons, neurotransmitters, and so on at a single particular time slice; and (2) diachronically, the sum of all of these differently realized synchronic tokens—for example, fear of dog_1 at $t_1, t_2, \ldots t_n$; and fear of dog_2 at t_1, $t_2, \ldots t_n$.[66] Owing to these conjunctions of conjoints (compound conjunctions), we can consider Patient Z's fear of dogs, *M*, a diachronic, conjunctive macroproperty.

Similar reasoning obtains when we try to understand why psychoanalysis takes so long: Each M, where M is a troubling mental event/state/property consists conjunctively of both its synchronic, physically realized neuronal constituents operative at a particular time and its diachronic, differently realized synchronic time-slice tokens summed across time—all contributing to the single symptom experienced, M. Moreover, for each analytic patient, there are more than a few of these Ms—each one, a diachronic, conjunctive, problematic macroproperty.

***

So have we closed the gaps? There is no gap ontologically, not with token physicalism. And epistemologically, an aspect of the gap does seem less mysterious with the Diachronic Conjunctive Token Physicalism described. However, I have no illusions that any of this resolves the ever-mysterious *how* question—how does consciousness, its qualia and cognitive and conative attitudes with content—how does any of this arise from neuronal assemblies, neurotransmitters, and the like? That these physical processes *do cause* the mental properties, that is the simple yes answer applicable to questions regarding the causal gap. But as to *how*, although I think in principle we will sometime know (as we do with H_2O and water), for now this remains an unanswered question, and a deeply puzzling one at that.

REFERENCES

Anthony, L. (1999). Making room for the mental. *Philosophical Studies, 95*, 37–44.
Bechtel, W., & Mundale, J. (1999). Multiple realizability revisited: Linking cognitive and neural states. *Philosophy of Science, 66*, 175–207.
Bedau, M. (1997). Weak emergence. In J. Tomberlin (Ed.), *Philosophical Perspectives: Mind, Causation, and World* (pp.375-399). Malden, Mass: Blackwell.
Block, N. (2003). Do causal powers drain away? *Philosophy and Phenomenological Research, 67*, 133–150.

Block, N., & Fodor, J. (1972). What psychological states are not. *Psychological Review, 81*, 159–181.

Block, N., & Stalnaker, R. (1999). Conceptual analysis, dualism, and the explanatory gap. *The Philosophical Review, 108*, 1–46.

Brakel, L.A.W. (2010). *Unconscious knowing and other essays in psycho-philosophical analysis*. Oxford: Oxford University Press.

Brauer, J., Kaminski, J., Riedel, J., Call, J., & Tomasello, M. (2006). Making inferences about the location of hidden food: Social dog, causal ape. *Journal of Comparative Psychology, 120*, 38–47.

Calef, S. (2005). Dualism and mind. In J. Fieser & B. Dowden (Eds.), *The Internet encyclopedia of philosophy*. Accessed July 22, 2012. http:// www.iep.utm.edu/dualism/

Chalmers, D. (2006). Strong and weak emergence. In P. Clayton & P. Davies (Eds.), *The Re-emergence of emergence* (pp. 244–254). Oxford: Oxford University Press.

Chalmers, D. (2010). *The character of consciousness*. Oxford: Oxford University Press.

Davidson, D. (1970/1980). Mental events. In *Actions and events* (pp. 207–227). Oxford: Oxford University Press.

Dennett, D. (1979). On the absence of phenomenology. In D. Gustafson & B. Tapscott (Eds.), *Body, mind, and method* (pp. 93–113). Dordrecht: Kluwer.

Edelman, G,. & Gally, J. (2001). Degeneracy and complexity in biological systems. *Proceedings of the National Academy of Sciences, 98*, 13763–13768.

Figdor, C. (2010). Neuroscience and the multiple realization of cognitive functions. *Philosophy of Science, 77*, 419–456.

Fodor, J. (1974). Special sciences—or the disunity of science as a working hypothesis. *Synthese, 27*, 97–115.

Friston, K. (1997). Imaging cognitive anatomy. *Trends in Cognitive Science, 1*, 21–27.

Friston, K., & Price, C. (2003). Degeneracy and redundancy in cognitive anatomy. *Trends in Cognitive Science, 7*, 151–152.

Ganeri, J. (2011). Emergentisms, ancient and modern. *Mind, 120*, 671–703.

Gillett, C. (2006). Samuel Alexander's emergentism: Or higher causation for physicalists. *Synthese, 153*, 261–296.

Gillett, C., & Rives, B. (2001). Does the argument from realization generalize? Responses to Kim. *Southern Journal of Philosophy, 39*, 79–98.

Harman, G. (1966). The inference to the best explanation. *Philosophical Review, 74*, 88–95.

Hill, C. (1991). *Sensations: A defense of materialism*. Cambridge, UK: Cambridge University Press.

Hill, C. (1997). Imaginability, conceivability, possibility and the mind-body problem. *Philosophical Studies, 87*, 61–85.

Jackson, F. (1982). Epiphenomenal qualia. *Philosophical Quarterly, 32*, 127–136.

Jackson, F. (2003). Mind and illusion. In A. O'Hear (Ed.), *Minds and persons*. New York: Cambridge University Press.

Kim, J. (1993). *Supervenience and mind*. Cambridge, UK: Cambridge University Press.

Kim, J. (1998). *Mind in a physical world*. Cambridge, MA: MIT Press.

Kim, J. (1999a). Making sense of emergence. *Philosophical Studies, 95*, 3–36.

Kim, J. (1999b). Supervenient properties and micro-based properties: A reply to Noordhof. *Proceedings of the Aristotelian Society, 99*, 115–118.

Kim, J. (2002). Précis of *Mind in a Physical World*. *Philosophy and Phenomenological Research, 65*, 640–643.

Kim, J. (2005). *Physicalism or something near enough*. Princeton, NJ: Princeton University Press.

Kim, J. (2010). *Essays in the metaphysics of mind*. Oxford: Oxford University Press.

Kripke, S. (1972). *Naming and necessity*. Cambridge, MA: Harvard University Press.

Leuenberger, S. (2008). *Ceteris absentibus* physicalism. *Oxford Studies in Metaphysics, 4*, 145–170.

Levine, J. (1993). On leaving out what it's like. In M. Davies and G. Humpreys (Eds.), *Consciousness: Psychological and philosophical essays* (pp. 121–136). Oxford: Blackwell.

Levine, J. (1998). Conceivability and the metaphysics of mind. *Nous, 32*, 449–480.

Lewis, D. (1978/1983). Mad pain and Martian pain. In *Philosophical Papers* (Vol. 1, pp. 122–132). Oxford: Oxford University Press.

Lewis, D. (1983). New work for a theory of universals. *Australasian Journal of Philosophy, 61*, 343–377.

Lipton, P. (1991). *Inference to the best explanation*. London: Routledge.

Nagel, T. (1974). What is it like to be a bat? *Philosophical Review, 58*, 435–450.

Nagel, T. (1998). Conceiving the impossible and the mind-body problem. *Philosophy, 73*, 337–352.

Noppeney, U., Friston, K., & Price, C. (2004). Degenerate neuronal systems sustaining cognitive functions. *Journal of Anatomy, 205*, 433–442.

O'Connor, T (1994). Emergent properties. *American Philosophical Quarterly, 31*, 91–104.

O'Connor, T., & Churchill J. (2008). Nonreductive physicalism or emergent dualism? The argument from mental causation. In G. Bealer & R. Coons (Eds.), *The waning of materialism* (pp. 261–280). Oxford: Oxford University Press.

O'Connor, T., & Wong, H. (2005). The metaphysics of emergence. *Nous, 39*, 658–678.

Papineau, D. (1993). Physicalism, consciousness and the antipathetic fallacy. *Australasian Journal of Philosophy, 71*, 169–183.

Pereboom, D. (2002). Robust nonreductive materialism. *Journal of Philosophy, 99*, 499–531.

Price, C., & Friston, K. (1997). Cognitive conjunction; a new approach to brain activation experiments. *NeuroImage, 5*, 261–270.

Price, C., & Friston, K. (2002). Degeneracy and cognitive anatomy. *Trends in Cognitive Science, 6*, 416–421.

Putnam, H. (1967a/1975). The mental life of some machines. In *Mind, language, and reality: Philosophical papers* (Vol. 2, pp. 408–428). Cambridge, UK: Cambridge University Press.

Putnam, H. (1967b/1975). The nature of mental states. In *Mind, language, and reality: Philosophical papers* (Vol. 2, pp. 429–440). Cambridge, UK: Cambridge University Press.

Rueger, A. (2000). Robust supervenience and emergence. *Philosophy of Science, 67*, 466–489.

Salmon, W. (1984/1999). Causal connections. In J. Kim & E. Sosa (Eds.), *Metaphysics: An anthology* (pp. 444–457). Oxford: Blackwell.

Searle, J. (1992). *The rediscovery of the mind*. Cambridge, MA: MIT Press.

Searle, J. (1995). Consciousness, the brain and the connection principle: A reply. *Philosophy and Phenomenological Research, 55*, 217–232.

Shoemaker, S. (2007). *Physical realization*. Oxford: Oxford University Press.

Smart, J. J. (1959). Sensations and brain processes. *Philosophical Review, 68*, 141–156.

Sperry, R. (1969). A modified concept of consciousness. *Psychological Review, 76*, 532–536.

Strawson, G. (1994). *Mental reality*. Cambridge, MA: MIT Press.
Strawson, G. (2009). *Selves*. Oxford: Oxford University Press.
Van Gulick, R. (1992). Three bad arguments for intentional property epiphenomenalism. *Erkenntnis, 39*, 311–331.
Yablo, S. (1992). Mental causation. *Philosophical Review, 101*, 245–280.

Part IV

Uses and Abuses of Consistency

4 The Uses and Abuses of Consistency in Thought Experiments, Empirical Research, Experimental Philosophy, and Psychoanalysis

INTRODUCTION

We humans both love and crave consistency. We seek it out, find it, and we impart it. We criticize, reject, or try to ignore that which we find inconsistent or incongruous. Sometimes we go so far as to claim that whatever is inconsistent is incoherent or meaningless. Consistency is among the fundamental elements we use not only in organizing our world but also in experiencing it at all. We seek consistency at many levels, from the highly abstract structure of the theories we discover and construct to the very concrete stimuli we perceive (and also construct).

The purpose of the present chapter is to explore in depth (and at some length) the role of consistency in thought experiments, empirical research, experimental philosophy, and psychoanalysis. I begin gently and generally by providing first a few standard and very basic philosophical definitions of consistency, and then brief introductory comments about consistency from the three domains (of the four under consideration) in which this matter is explicitly addressed: thought experiments, empirical research, and psychoanalysis.

After that, the plan of the chapter is as follows. In Section One, "Common Goals, Different Paths," I advance the idea that these four domains, despite different routes, have a common aim: enhancing what is known and can be known through new findings that enlarge the realm of what is consistent and coheres with current knowledge. That consistency is the vehicle of these new discoveries in each of the four areas is taken up in Section Two, "The Uses of Consistency." Given that consistency plays this role, Section Three explores a somewhat surprising and paradoxical notion, "The Abuses of Consistency," focusing on specific examples from empirical research, experimental philosophy, psychoanalysis, and thought experiments. Section Four presents a solution to a particular type of consistency abuse problem prevalent in a number of seminal thought experiment cases. I term my solution "the method of intervening stepwise cases." A summary and conclusion close the chapter.

DEFINITIONS AND GENERAL COMMENTS

Standard Philosophical Definitions of Consistency

1. (From Wikipedia, 2011): "In logic, a *consistent* theory is one that does not contain a contradiction." Then Tarski (1946, p. 135) is quoted: "A . . . theory is called *consistent* or *non-contradictory* if no two asserted statements of this theory contradict each other . . ."
2. (From the entry Ethical Realism in *The Comprehensible Philosophy Dictionary, 2010-2013*): "Consistency: To be logically consistent is to have beliefs that all could be true. To have two beliefs that are mutually exclusive (only one could be true) is to be logically inconsistent."

Consistency and Thought Experiments

One of the most important functions of thought experiments is to explore intuitions, in fact one could say that thought experiments regularly take intuitions to their limits. Braddon-Mitchell (2003), a contemporary philosopher, defends the importance of intuition, taking issue with a certain type of critic who has doubts about any central role for intuitions at all: "The claim that intuition is no guide to possibility turns out to depend on intuitions about possibility, and thus is either *inconsistent* [LAWB's italics] or else open to the charge of choosing between intuitions arbitrarily" (p. 113).

Consistency in Empirical Research

From a classic empirical research article "On the Perception of Incongruity: A Paradigm," a work exploring the normal human quest for *consistency*, Bruner and Postman (1949, p. 208) assert:

> . . . for as long as possible and by whatever means available, the organism will ward off the perception of the unexpected, those things which do not fit his prevailing set. Our assumption, and it is hardly extravagant, is that most people come to depend upon a certain *consistency* [LAWB's italics] in their environment and, save under special conditions, attempt to ward off variations from this state of affairs.[1]

Consistency and Psychoanalysis

Regarding psychoanalysis, it is the case that in some important sense the whole enterprise, both its theory and clinical application, is predicated on consistency. Patients, for their part, feel compelled to cling to familiar neurotic ways, unconsciously forcing current goings-on to be *consistent* with (sometimes even congruent with) painful past histories, no matter how conflictual, disadvantageous, and downright strange their present behaviors may become. Meanwhile, analysts can find coherence in these symptomatic actions—actions that seem on the face of it not just slightly inconsistent but frankly contradictory and confounding. How can analysts do this? By drawing on the five basic presuppositions of psychoanalytic theory that hold that all sorts of symptomatic, nonrational behaviors can in fact be understood as *consistent*[2]—first by the analyst alone, and then through the analytic work made clearer to the patient. (This will be explained in the next section, specifically the subsection "Psychoanalysis/Psychoanalytic Interpretation." See also Brakel, 2009, pp. 4–8, for a fuller account of the five basic presuppositions of psychoanalysis.)

Consistency in This Chapter

As is probably already evident (and will become more so), the notions of *consistency* explored in this chapter are fluid and flexible, perhaps even vague and ambiguous. But this in itself is not problematic. There are no expectations that I, nor those whom I will criticize in the pages that follow, should be held to consistency as it is formally and logically defined. In fact the standards of consistency under discussion in this chapter will take many forms, including those I use to evaluate and sometimes challenge each conventional/foundational view. But, rather than undercut my criticisms, this highlights my main point—namely, that each author/theorist/researcher (myself included) cannot help but perform a selection, choosing the version of consistency most advantageous to his/her view. Knowing this, while perhaps difficult in the short run, can only prove helpful toward the broader goal: enlarging our capacity for genuine understanding.

***

While I hope that the importance of consistency in each area was at least hinted at in the few initial remarks above, in the next section I will present a straightforward case for consistency (in various forms) playing a vital and central role in thought experiments, empirical research, experimental philosophy, and psychoanalysis—this, despite serving different functions in each of these domains.

SECTION ONE: COMMON GOALS, DIFFERENT PATHS: THE ROLE OF CONSISTENCY IN THOUGHT EXPERIMENTS, EMPIRICAL RESEARCH, EXPERIMENTAL PHILOSOPHY, AND PSYCHOANALYSIS

Thought Experiments

After thoroughgoing agreement on two points about thought experiments—that they are (1) like empirical experiments in that they are devised to test hypotheses but (2) unlike empirical experiments since the experimental conditions are not put into action—writers on the subject have characterized thought experiments in a variety of ways. A general definition is given by Martin Cohen (2005, p. viii): "Thought experiments are that special kind of theory that predicts particular consequences given certain initial starting points and conditions. Like experiments in the laboratory, they are tests devised either to explore intuitions about how the world works—or to destroy them." Roy Sorensen (1992) provides a more technical view (p. 6): "The official role of thought experiment is to test modal consequences [in other words, necessities]." Lest we conclude that the function for thought experiments is thereby quite narrow, Sorensen (p. 6) quickly adds that ". . . there are many kinds of necessities: logical, physical, technological, moral." Sorensen (p. 6) continues by enumerating some "side tasks," clearly also of great importance in the use of thought experiments. Among them are ". . . concocting counterexamples to definitions and 'laws,' expanding the domain of theories, exhibiting modal fallacies, deriving astounding consequences, [and] suggesting impossibility proofs."

Elaborating on these views, it is important to highlight the particular modes by which thought experiments actually achieve the testing of hypotheses. These include the use of counterfactuals, counterexamples, and ideas and intuitions taken to their extremes, all toward one or more of the following goals: establishing whether a theory can continue to be explanatory under the pressure of unusual cases; discerning whether the questions being asked are really the questions at issue; and testing the limits under which particular definitions can hold. Some illustrative examples follow.

In his article "Is Justified True Belief Knowledge?" Edmund Gettier (1963) devised a thought experiment based on counterexamples, overturning what had become the standard epistemological definition of knowledge—namely, that it is justified true belief that constitutes knowledge. Here is a paraphrase of Gettier's (p. 122) first case. Smith and Jones are vying for a certain job. Smith has evidence for the proposition "Jones will get the job and the man who will get the job has ten coins in his pocket." Smith's evidence for the conjunction is another conjunction as follows: The boss recently told Smith that Jones would get the job, and Smith himself counted ten coins in Jones's pocket ten minutes ago. Smith then believes the entailed proposition, "The man who will get the job has ten coins in his pocket" and is clearly justified in so believing. But then, surprising Smith, the boss reverses himself and gives Smith the job. And further surprising to Smith, Smith, too, happens to have ten coins in his pocket. Can Smith be said to have *known* that "the man who will get the job has ten coins in his pocket"? How can this—Smith's justified true belief—count as knowledge for Smith when one of the evidence-conferring propositions from which he inferred the true content of the original proposition turns out to have been false? It would be *inconsistent* to consider Smith's attitude as knowledge.

In another example, Harry Frankfurt (1969/1988) uses a thought experiment that involves a counterfactual to demonstrate that it is *inconsistent* to consider "the principle of alternative possibilities" a necessary feature of the definition of responsibility. According to Frankfurt (p. 1), the principle in question states that "a person is morally responsible for what he has done only if he could have done otherwise." But Frankfurt (p. 8) shows that, "Even though the person was unable to do otherwise [,] . . . it may not be the case that he acted as he did because he could not have done otherwise." A very benign nonmoral case that I've constructed can quickly demonstrate Frankfurt's insight. Suppose an experimental participant is left in a room and told she can stay there for an hour or she can leave at any time before the hour is up. She chooses to stay for the full hour. But unbeknownst to her, she could not have left, because the door was locked from the outside. She chose to stay and is responsible for that action, even though she could not have done otherwise. Here is how Frankfurt sets it up with a much more sinister case. Black wants Jones to act in some morally reprehensible way. Black has coercive techniques he will employ, and he is

> . . . prepared to go to considerable lengths to get his way, but he prefers to avoid showing his hand . . . he waits until Jones is about to make up his mind . . . and he does nothing unless it is clear to him (Black is an excellent judge of such things) that Jones is going to decide to do something *other* than what he [Black] wants him to do. (p. 6)

Frankfurt continues: "Now suppose that Black never has to show his hand because Jones, for reasons of his own, decides to perform and does perform the very action Black wants him to perform. In that case, it seems clear, Jones will bear precisely the same moral responsibility for what he does as he would have borne if Black had not been ready to take steps to ensure that he would do it" (p. 7). From his thought experiment, Frankfurt concludes (1969/1988, p. 10): "The principle of alternative possibilities should be replaced by the following principle: a person is not morally responsible for what he has done if he did it *only* [LAWB's emphasis] because he could not have done otherwise." With this thought experiment argument, Frankfurt demonstrates that it is *inconsistent* to continue to consider "the principle of alternative possibilities" a necessary feature of the definition of responsibility.[3]

These few examples of the paths taken by thought experimenters demonstrate that thought experiments can lead to radical changes in central intuitions and definitions. Note that these important results take place outside of laboratories, without any of the real-world accoutrements of empirical experiments, and independent of the rigorous planned comparisons so central to empirical research. But although they do differ in these significant ways, thought experiments and empirical experiments alike are bound by the principles of the scientific method, and as such share the same basic goals. It is time to have a look at some of the goals of thought experiments—goals that actually have much in common with those most salient in empirical research.

For a first goal, the outcomes of good thought experiments, just like the results of successful empirical studies, should, guided by *consistency*, lead to more questions. This in turn leads to more research and experimentation, both in thought experiment and empirical research modes. In other words, thought experiment results should shape successive investigations. Take, for example, the Gettier thought experiment described just above. Since the Gettier cases establish that it can no longer be held to be *consistent* to properly define knowledge as justified true belief, just how should knowledge be defined? And going further, just what are the new relations between justified true belief and knowledge?

Then there is a second goal of thought experiments shared by their empirical research counterparts: that conclusions reached from good thought experiments, no less than from good empirical research studies, should point to changes in intuition, definition, and/or theory that will be more *consistent* (and/or avoid *inconsistency*) with other ideas and bodies of knowledge. Results from the Frankfurt cases, for instance, not only provide additional insight into age-old and ongoing questions of free will versus determinism, they also cohere well with modern views of moral responsibility and can potentially contribute to more enlightened theories of social justice.

Clearly, despite their very different paths, successful thought experiments and empirical research studies both share goals in which their findings and results ultimately aim at increasing *consistency* in our understanding of the world.

Empirical Research

Empirical research is done in many different ways, following a variety of paths. Perhaps the simplest, at least from a formal point of view, involves observation, correlation, and demonstration. When neuroanatomical (or neurophysiological) changes in a particular brain area are demonstrable in a great number of people with the same specific psychological and behavioral changes, it is *consistent* with the data to conclude that involvement of this brain area is significantly correlated with those psychological manifestations. But note that correlation is not the same as causation. Another factor, for example, could be causing both the brain and behavioral changes. More research will be required (and is in fact ongoing) not only in neuroanatomy but also in the related areas of neurophysiology, neurochemistry, and neuroendocrinology to address these sorts of causal questions empirically. (More will follow about empirical research and causality just below.)

Another instance of the observation, correlation, and demonstration path can be seen daily in the decisions made by clinicians dealing with infectious diseases. In deciding what antibiotic to give a patient with a recalcitrant bacterial infection, the bacteria from the patient (say in sputum, wound, blood, or urine) can be cultured in several growth media dishes, each with a different antibiotic present. This, after an appropriate number of hours, enables a clear presentation of the differential effectiveness of the various antibiotics in inhibiting the pathogenic bacterial growth.

But even in this straightforward example, there is a background causal inference that gains its warrant due to much prior basic research. Namely, it is assumed that the bacteria cultured are the causal agents in the infectious illness. But how was this piece of empirical research established? Was there a research path taken, more sophisticated from a theoretical viewpoint than mere observation and correlation? The answer is yes, because a causal link was established. Basically (and simplifying), the findings after a series of experiments were as follows: a particular set of signs and symptoms (1) always followed the introduction and proliferation of this particular infectious agent and (2) did not arise under other circumstances. Obviously, the two paths—observation/demonstration and causation—go together well, as the presence of recognizable, repeatable correlational patterns indicates possible causes, and the absence of such patterns allows some possibilities to be ruled out. This is all quite *consistent*, but also subject to further test.

Empirical experiments, whatever paths they follow, almost always employ (in some combination) observation, demonstration, correlation, and causation. They are all designed to increase *consistency* via: (1) testing hypotheses, and/or (2) generating more hypotheses needing additional tests, and/or (3) developing and testing theories. Sometimes an empirical experiment can test two competing hypotheses, gaining evidence for one and ruling out the other. More often, single experiments provide results that lend support to a particular hypothesis, with growing evidential weight accruing over a series of additional experiments testing related questions.

Although the categories may overlap, there are two other very broad types of empirical research paths. Empirical research experiments can take place naturalistically—as, for example, by watching the foraging strategies of a particular species under changing conditions, or they can take place in a controlled laboratory setting. In this latter case, findings from the experimental condition are compared with findings from the control conditions, and ideally there is only one difference between these the experimental and control conditions—the experimental variable being tested.

In the best controlled laboratory drug trials, for instance, there would be four groups of laboratory animals each with Disease Q induced so that all subjects would manifest (approximately) the same degree of pathology. Drug A, well known in its positive therapeutic ratio[4] for Disease Q, is given to one group; Drug B, a new drug, is given to a second group; the third group of animals receives a placebo drug (best formulated to have similar side effects to the active drugs); and a fourth group is not treated at all, so that the natural course of Disease Q can be taken into account.[5]

Turning to naturalistic empirical studies, let us examine an experiment that seems to involve only "simple" observation and demonstration, but which simultaneously illustrates another general feature of empirical research—the importance of paying attention to incidental findings. In 1654, Otto von Guericke showed that sound travels through water by ringing a bell just prior to feeding fish in a pond. After several repetitions, fish could be observed gathering as soon as the bell rang, whether or not food followed. This experiment is reported by Sorensen (1992, p. 133), who remarks that the very same experiment could be used to demonstrate an entirely different scientific phenomenon—namely, classical conditioning. Placebos have a similar history. When testing the comparative effects of different medications against supposed nonactive agents, researchers repeatedly found, quite incidental to the medications under direct test, that these nonactive agents, now widely known as placebos, can themselves sometimes have a pronounced therapeutic response. (For an overview account of the placebo effect, see Brakel, 2010, pp. 137–146.)

Observational data, in addition to demonstrating incidental findings, are often underdetermined, leading not only to different theoretical interpretations (as in the sound traveling through aqueous media/classical conditioning experiment), but in some cases to conflicting, mutually exclusive theories. For example, that the sun appears to rise and set every day is observational data seemingly *consistent* both with the Ptolemaic Earth-centered view and our current heliocentric theory. But these cannot both be correct. This, then, is another path for empirical research—organizing observations and/or constructing experiments to decide between two such theories. Of course, as has now been made clear through centuries of astronomical experimentation involving observations and calculations, the heliocentric view is accepted. But even before this could be empirically established, there were problems with the Ptolemaic geocentric theory that a philosopher of science might have appreciated. To make the geocentric theory *consistent* with the data and findings available at the time concerning all the heavenly bodies, many corrections—too many corrections—were required. Specifically, to adequately account for the orbits of the other planets around a stationary centrally placed Earth, complex additional retrograde motion epicycles had to be described and posited.

This example, along with the others above, shows, that, regardless of the type of empirical research embarked upon, and parallel with the particular goals of each experiment, there is a goal that is fundamental and general—namely, for the findings, results, and conclusions to be *consistent* not only within each experiment but across the range of evidence in that field, and even more broadly within the body of scientific knowledge generally. This is an important overarching aim of all empirical research, in fact its hallmark, and one that aligns it strongly with philosophy. (For a deeper understanding of the idea of science as an interconnected, interdependent, *consistent*, coherent network, see Quine, 1966, pp. 233–235.)

Experimental Philosophy

Known also as "x-phi," experimental philosophy combines some of the attributes of thought experiments with those of empirical research studies. This is the case even as some experimental philosophers make attempts to empirically investigate certain important thought experiment results. One major pathway for experimental philosophy studies, for instance, drawing largely on the research methods of survey data collection, challenges the "armchair" (thought experiment) intuitions of philosophers on matters of philosophical relevance—for example, free will versus determinism, the nature of intentional actions, and the extent of personal responsibility under various conditions (see, for example, Knobe, 2003; Petrinovich, O'Neill, and Jorgensen, 1993; Royzman and Baron, 2002; and Spranca, Minsk, and Baron, 1991). The findings reported in studies such as these suggest that the nature of folk intuitions about these matters is much more heterogeneous than expected—this arguably introducing doubt as to the *consistency* of armchair presuppositions that presume universality.

Relatedly, a number of x-phi studies using empirical survey methods to evaluate various armchair intuitions often occasion what can only be described as conflictual second-order armchair intuitions, in that two (or more) conclusions arise—equally data-derived but *inconsistent* with one another. Here is an example: Mikhail (2007, p. 143), on the basis of several reported x-phi survey data studies, proposes "a universal moral grammar" arguing for the central importance of intention and agential action with respect to responsibility for harm. This is consistent with the results reported in a study by Spranca et al. (1991).[6] However, Petrinovich et al. (1993), also on the basis of survey data, find the converse—that agency (action-inaction) is of but little significance in solving moral problems (p. 474). This group instead offers a theory of evolutionary ethics in which they suggest that moral dilemmas are largely decided on the basis of (1) utilitarian absolute number saved or harmed, (2) the social contract between people involved, and (3) choices that will enhance reproductive fitness and protect biological kin.

Another major path for experimental philosophy is one utilizing correlational brain studies in an attempt to understand human moral impulses, judgments, and intuitions. Contending that no single *consistent* moral principle can account for the different moral judgments the "folk" make on cases seemingly parallel—for example, it is deemed "good" to turn a runaway trolley from a track on which it will kill five people onto a track on which only one will be killed; but it is deemed "forbidden" to throw a fat man in the path of said runaway trolley, killing him but saving the same five[7]—a seminal study was conducted by Greene, Sommerville, Nystrom, Darley, and Cohen (2001) to address this matter.[8] First, the researchers (neuroscientists and experimental philosophers) posited that moral judgments that are more "emotional" are treated in a different way than moral decisions that are not emotional. They defined emotional as "up close and personal" (p. 2106), including such factors as direct agency and immediacy/nearness to the event in question. Then, they predicted that judgments made about the more emotional/personal type of moral dilemmas would activate brain areas associated with emotion more than judgments made on moral dilemmas that were less emotional/personal (p. 2106). To test their hypothesis, fMRI brain scans were done on participants who made judgments on dilemmas from three categories: moral-personal, moral-impersonal, and nonmoral (and impersonal). The researchers' hypothesis was supported as (1) brain areas associated with emotion[9] were more activated in the moral-personal dilemma category than in the other two category types; and (2) brain areas known to be less active during emotional processing[10] were less active in decisions about the moral-personal dilemmas than they were in decisions about the other dilemma categories (see Greene et al., 2001, pp. 2106–2107).[11]

With these results, some experimental philosophy proponents claim that empirical research methods can lead to a clearer, more *consistent* explanation for perplexing *inconsistencies* in moral judgment dilemmas than can any conclusions resulting from philosophical thought experiments. But this particular experiment is not without its flaws (see, for example, the serious problem raised in endnote 11 and discussed just below). And, as will be discussed later (Section Five), the apparent *inconsistencies* in dealing with seemingly parallel moral judgment dilemmas might, after all, be better reconciled with novel thought experiment approaches. And yet, these important considerations notwithstanding, what is incontrovertible is that for experimental philosophy—no less than for its two parent disciplines, standard philosophical thought experiment and empirical research—the most important goals are realized in not only providing new findings but developing more questions and testable hypotheses. The aim in all these disciplines is to promote better integration with results from other studies, including those from related fields, allowing increased *consistency* in our overall understanding of the world.

Psychoanalysis/Psychoanalytic Interpretation

Psychoanalysis (like empirical research, thought experiments, and experimental philosophy) relies on consistency and attempts to increase consistent understanding. In one important respect, psychoanalytic interpretation most closely resembles experimental philosophy in that it, too, can be considered a blend of thought experiment and empirical research features. This can best be illustrated by considering almost every interpretation offered by a psychoanalyst to an analytic patient as a type of pilot experiment. But this is obviously an idea that cannot begin to be adequately addressed until some preliminary information about psychoanalytic theory is provided. In several steps to follow I hope to accomplish this task.

First, as with any experiment that utilizes a particular scientific theory, several background assumptions are in place whenever a psychoanalytic clinical interpretation is in the foreground. The undertaking of every clinical psychoanalysis entails psychoanalytic theory as its underpinning, with psychoanalytic theory functioning both as a general theory of mind and as a clinical theory more specific to psychopathology and the clinical situation.

General Psychoanalytic Theory of Mind

Because I have in prior work (Brakel, 2009, esp. pp. 4–8) discussed in some detail the fundamental assumptions of the general psychoanalytic theory of mind, I will but briefly summarize them here. The first and second assumptions, those of *psychic (psychological) continuity* and *psychic (psychological) determinism*, belong together and link psychoanalysis to other normal scientific endeavors. They claim that the phenomena under study (mental states, attitudes, and their contents) have features that demonstrate particular sorts of regularities and continuities, and, as such, they can be accounted for under the application of particular laws, lawlike structures, or rules, including, importantly, the law of cause and effect.

The third assumption, best appreciated when there is a seeming break or gap in psychological continuity, posits that there exists a *dynamic psychological unconscious*, replete with unconscious conflicts. When there is such a continuity break—say, in a person's conscious attempt to express some thought—the positing of a dynamic unconscious with meaningful contentful mentation not only allows the gap to be filled in but does so in a way that demonstrates that psychological continuity was in fact ongoing. In other words, the assumption of a contentful dynamic unconscious facilitates meaningful explanation for the frequent "inconsistencies" seen in mental life. This is hard to explain and probably even harder to understand without a real-life example, and so I offer the following simple demonstration in which I am the subject.

> I am reading a text orally, and lose my place at a particular word. Why should I lose the capacity to read fluidly? What has caused this inconsistent break in my psychological continuity? When I later see that the word in question was *leopard* and I remember that my good friend Leo just died, we can understand that I have a content-laden unconscious conflict: I am unconsciously in conflict with the reality of my friend's death, fending off these painful thoughts by refusing (for a moment) to read a word that contains his name. Fueled by my unconscious conflict, this unconsciously motivated act caused (or at least causally contributed to) my reading problem, and thereby to the seeming inconsistency of my behavior. With this knowledge, my behavior now can be understood as having been psychologically continuous all along, despite the symptomatic act.

The fourth assumption is that of *free association*. Different from the other assumptions, free association is a method that is presumed to reveal the unconscious contents that "solve" the inconsistencies. In the above example, for instance, upon seeing that the problematic word was *leopard*, I could immediately associate to my friend named Leo, his death, and my wish to deny this part of reality.

The fifth and final assumption is really a corollary in that its existence is predicated on the other four. It consists in the positing of two types of mentation, each organized according to different principles—the primary and secondary processes. Secondary processes predominate in the types of thinking we see in our ordinary rational goings-on, whereas primary process mentation can be seen in somewhat more unusual situations, including dreams, psychological symptoms, the thought processes of very young children, and particularly when one free-associates to seeming breaks in psychological continuity. To illustrate this in action, I return to my reading problem. Although the word *leopard* is like the word *Leo*, the animal with spots is really quite different from my friend whose name was Leo. Yet the primary process similarity between *Leo* and *leopard* registered unconsciously. Therefore, at that particular time, I unconsciously categorized the word *leopard* as a word to avoid, as something painful. In this way, the primary process categorization was the cause (at least a cause) of my momentarily disrupted reading.

These, then, are the fundamental assumptions of psychoanalysis as a general theory of mind. Importantly, they show considerable overlap with Freud's famous[12] five metapsychological principles or viewpoints. Together, these five principles can describe any psychological event. And they provide a link between the general psychoanalytic theory of mind and psychoanalytic clinical theory. The metapsychological principles include viewpoints known as the *economic*, *topographic*, *dynamic* (Freud 1915b/1953), *developmental* or *genetic* (Freud 1900/1953), and *structural* (Freud 1923/1953, 1926/1953). The economic viewpoint refers to the energy balance among (a) the drives underlying our desires, (b) the emotions so associated, and (c) the modulating effects needed to regulate both—including defenses that can be both adaptive and pathological. The topographic viewpoint considers that all psychological events have both conscious and unconscious aspects. Conflicts often arise between what is conscious and what is unconscious as well as among the drives/desires, attendant emotions, and the modulating processes. The existence and nature of these conflicts comprise the dynamic viewpoint. Similarly, there are often dynamic conflicts between mature attitudes and desires versus those conflicts and desires that are more drive-centered originating in an individual's early life. These phase-of-life-relevant attitudes represent aspects of the developmental or genetic principle, as do the well-known psychosexual stages of development—oral, anal, phallic, Oedipal, post-Oedipal, and so on. Finally, the structural viewpoint concerns various mental functional capacities, which are categorized (for heuristic purposes) into three basic compartments: *id*, seat of drives/wishes/desires; *superego*, representing all manner of one's self-assessments, including one's conscience; and *ego*, referring to the myriad of functions necessary for registering and dealing most effectively with reality, operating in conflict and cooperation with one's drives and desires and with one's superego.

Psychoanalytic Clinical Theory

Whereas there is but one general psychoanalytic theory of mind, there are different schools of clinical psychoanalysis, each with a somewhat different set of clinical psychoanalytic *theories*. There are, for example, analysts who would be described as ego psychologists or structuralists, focusing on the interplay of ego defenses and capacities, affects, id strivings, and superego pressures. Another group of analysts, the relationalists, focus mainly on their patients' current relationships with people, including, importantly, all aspects of their interactions with their analysts. There is a third group of psychoanalysts who embrace early internalized relationships as central—those in the so-called object relations school. And then there are the Kleinians, who, among other ideas, posit affectively charged positive and negative attitudes directed at very primitive internal objects, where "object" refers both to whole persons and parts thereof. Note that this is not an exhaustive list.

This plethora of clinical theories should not be taken to imply that there are no essential components to any clinical theory properly described as "psychoanalytic." There are such minimum requirements common to all branches and schools. Thus, for any clinical theory to be psychoanalytic: (1) it must be predicated upon the background general theory assumptions (including the method of free association); (2) it must recognize the dynamic, developmental, and topographic principles in so far as these represent, respectively, the importance of conflict, the influential nature of the past upon the present, and the shaping of conscious thought and behavior by unconscious mentation; and (3) it must entail the central role of transference in the clinical situation. Let us turn next to the concept of transference.

Transference, the experiencing of a past situation in the present, often inappropriately although not without cause,[13] is vital to the clinical psychoanalytic endeavor (see Freud, 1905/1953; 1912/1953; 1915a/1953). Transference to the person of the analyst—along with the analyst's function, the physical environment of the analysis, and the therapeutic nature of the treatment—all of this is invited, indeed encouraged, in the clinical psychoanalytic setting. Already different from almost any other situation in a person's life (in most of which transferences certainly exist but are ignored, repressed, or acted out) in psychoanalysis, patients' transferences to their analysts is just the beginning (see Brenner, 1976; 1982, esp. pp. 195, 208).

In psychoanalysis analysts and patients examine, understand, and work through transferences, so as to resolve them to the degree that patients no longer automatically suffer their consequences.[14]

With the assumptions of the general psychoanalytic theory and those common to any clinical psychoanalytic theory outlined, we are now ready to proceed to the next step concerning the claim that psychoanalytic interpretations are pilot experiments.

Interpretations as Pilot Experiments

Much as scientists who, when testing hypotheses related to a particular theory, perform each of their experiments with background assumptions both about a particular theory and the testing methods in place, psychoanalysts listen to their patients with two levels of assumptions (the general theory of mind assumptions and those of the particular clinical theory) at least tacitly in mind. Each patient brings in a highly detailed and variegated account of his/her life, mind, desires, aims, and conflicts, describing and explaining things from many angles. And then, often enough—arguably whenever an interpretation is made—the analyst sees something in the particulars of the patient that he/she hypothesizes can be illuminated when understood in terms of one or more of the psychoanalytic assumptions. Minimally, a slip of the tongue or another sort of parapraxis (mistake in action) will have been understood by the analyst after associations render *consistent* what otherwise would have seemed incoherent or contradictory. Here is an example:

> Patient Z says to his analyst whose air-conditioning system has just broken, "It is suddenly hate in here," an almost unintelligible sentence as it stands, but one that, given the temperature, is obviously an attempt to say, "It is suddenly hot in here." When Patient Z is asked for associations (as would be the case whether or not the patient had been aware of his mistake), he admits that the warmth of the room is annoying. He continues, "But that's not all . . ." launching first into a tirade of hateful complaints about the analyst and his office and then, surprising himself, remembering something he had not before discussed with his analyst.[15] As a young boy, Patient Z had had an experience of sudden fear, anger, and *hate* when undergoing a medical procedure that concluded with a subjective sensation of heat accompanying the injection of dye.

Understanding Patient Z's slip of the tongue and his associations enable the patient and analyst together to make a preliminary interpretation about Z's hatred and some of its origins. This interpretation as a pilot experiment both employs and tests many of the fundamental assumptions of psychoanalysis. Thus, insofar as the pilot experiment is successful and the assumptions hold, the patient should (a) feel an increased sense of *consistency*,

(b) produce more analytic material that converges, and (c) offer new data for additional testing. These positive outcomes, indeed experienced by Patient Z after the interpretation, are quite analogous to those of a successful empirical experiment that has gained evidence for (or even confirmed) a particular hypothesis as *consistent*.

A more involved interpretation, one testing aspects of the clinical theory too, can be used to demonstrate the claim that interpretative interventions are a type of pilot experiment. Patient X had just finished a very successful big project. Strangely, though, she felt dejected, unable to carry on, and terribly anxious. She felt that future ventures, although very much like the one she had just completed, would be "way too much for her," a phrase she often used. Interestingly, she could not specify why she imagined that further successes would be so frightening. She had no detailed picture, no particulars; she "just knew" that she "couldn't handle it—whatever 'it' was." At precisely this point in the analysis, she returned to familiar material about her parents' bad marriage, specifically her notion (and unconscious Oedipal-level wish) that her father would prefer her to her mother. The analyst pointed out that her father never made any overtures to Patient X, even when he was divorcing her mother. Patient X, who had been in analysis many years, could agree with this, and, further, she acknowledged her own unconscious wish to be preferred. This was not new. What was new was the analyst's next interpretation that Patient X's fear and anxiety about further professional advances—a fear that was at once totally unfounded, distressingly acute, and inchoately vague—was a current-day version of the sort of anxiety a child would have if her Oedipal wishes were fulfilled and she *were in fact* the partner to her father, a grown-up adult. "What does go on there?" "What is required?" "What do I have to handle?" It would indeed be, for any child, "way too much."

Patient X felt very relieved by this interpretation almost as soon as it was presented. It immediately explained what had before been incoherent—the sense of overwhelming anxiety and especially the bewildering vagueness. Soon she was able to resume productive work, as her work realm had been successfully disentangled from her childhood Oedipal wishes and her fantasy of their fulfillment. If we consider this interpretation as a pilot experiment testing a particular instantiation of an aspect of clinical psychoanalytic theory, then it was a successful experiment indeed—the patient felt increased consistency, and new and convergent material emerged. In succeeding sessions, she realized that this pattern in regard to adult achievements had obtained before, and not only in work-related matters.

Quite different from the typical outcome measures employed in empirical research studies, or even those used to assess thought experiments, with psychoanalytic interpretation it is the patients' subsequent responses (oral and behavioral) that determine whether the pilot experiment can confirm (or more modestly provide evidence for) the specific hypothesis under test. But, just like empirical research investigations and thought experiments, the ultimate success of an interpretation/pilot experiment can only be evaluated in terms of *consistency*—successful pilot interpretations, like the successful thought experiments and empirical studies, increase consistency. In the psychoanalytic cases, such an increase can manifest itself in at least two ways: first, an enlarging of the patient's self-understanding, often showing a convergence with other data already known to patient and/or analyst; and, second, the emergence of new material, in any of a number of forms—new questions, new hypotheses to test, new memories, and new behaviors and activities.

***

In the foregoing discussion, I have held and argued for the claim that empirical research, thought experiments, and the two hybrids—experimental philosophy and psychoanalytic interpretation/pilot experiments—although all quite distinct, have much that is similar. I have shown how each takes different routes to a common goal: increasing knowledge of the world—through the integration of convergent findings and the emergence of new data, new questions, and new hypotheses, all toward discovering (and effecting) more coherence and greater consistency.

In the next section I will elaborate upon the mechanisms of the uses of consistency in empirical research, experimental philosophy, thought experiments, and the psychoanalytic pilot experiments known as interpretations.

SECTION TWO: THE USES OF CONSISTENCY

Empirical Research

The role of consistency in empirical experiments is both necessary and essential. In fact, it is no exaggeration to claim that there could be no empirical investigations at all if consistency did not play a central role in the inquiries. To illustrate this point, let us return to the area of empirical tests of new therapeutic drugs. In the gold standard set-up, the performance of a new drug (drug N) will be compared with both a currently effective active drug (drug E) and a placebo substance (drug P). Consistency comes into play in several key ways.

1. Assuming a large pool of study participants, each is randomly assigned to one of the three medications such that there are no features distinguishing one group from the other two. Random assignment allows that there be *consistency* (no bias) with respect to gender, age, symptom severity, general health, and socioeconomic factors across all three groups of participants.[16] Random assignment also obviates any self-selection biases, either those of the participants or those of the researchers.

2. Both experimenters and participants are blind as to whether particular subjects are in the group receiving N, E, or P, so that reasonable baseline expectations are relatively *consistent*.[17] If participant X knew that he would be getting the placebo drug, and participant Y knew that she was in the group receiving drug E, these two subjects would be likely to have markedly different expectations. Likewise, if a researcher knew that participant A was to get the potent new drug, and participant B the placebo, the researcher's expectations and subsequent behavior toward these two subjects might be quite different. That these differing behaviors and attitudes can themselves influence drug response has been widely established (for references, see Stewart-Williams and Podd, 2004; and see Amanzio, Pollo, Maggi, and Benedetti, 2001; Benedetti, Arduino, Costa, Vighetti, Tarenzi, Rainero, and Asteggiano, 2009; Moerman, 2002, p. 81). Thus, controlling for these differing expectations is necessary in the service of *consistency*.
3. Drugs N, E, and P are not only delivered in the same manner, they are manufactured to have side effects *consistent* with one another,[18] and to look alike (see Moerman and Wayne, 2002, for an account of how important this last factor can be).
4. Finally, follow-up appointments with participants in each of the three groups are uniform. Every participant receives the same number of visits, at which identical questions are asked, questionnaires delivered, clinical progress assessed, and technical measurements made, all at the same time intervals. And, of course, the data from all three groups are evaluated using the same statistical tests. *Consistency* is essential in the accurate evaluation of the dependent variable—the relative effectiveness of drug N as compared with both drug E and the active placebo P.

We see in the above paradigm of a controlled empirical study an idealized research criterion realized—namely, everything is held as *consistent* as possible in order to assess with the most precision possible, the measure of interest: How well does drug N perform versus drug E and versus the placebo? The three drugs are different. Demonstrating their relative effectiveness is the purpose of the study. This goal is best fulfilled by performing tests of all three drugs under consistent conditions.

With this example in mind, another aspect of consistency in empirical research can be shown. Based on the results of a particular experiment (or set of experiments), new experiments are designed. For example, suppose in the study above, drug N does significantly better in halting the symptom than either drug E or the placebo. A follow-up set of studies first verifies that the findings can be replicated in different laboratories. Next, drug N's performance is measured in different population types. Another set of experiments, perhaps now looking just at the N arm of the original study, determines what dose of drug N achieves the very best therapeutic-to-toxic ratio. Additional studies might explore the efficacy of various vehicles for drug delivery. And following this, experiments may even be run to determine whether certain nonspecific factors like color of pill, number of pills, and brand and logo can add to the drug's success. Moerman and Wayne (2002, p. 472) assert that these factors can be quite significant.

In each of these many types of follow-up studies, only one factor is changed while everything else is held *consistent*. In the replication trials with different populations, only the character of the population is changed. In the dosage studies, all but the amount of drug is held constant. And in the vehicle experiments, all is consistent with the prior study, save different delivery vehicles—for example, intramuscular versus intravenous versus oral. Then, if the oral vehicle works, studies pitting liquid versus one big pill versus two smaller ones can be done, as well as those testing differently colored medications.

I hope to have shown that, at least in the idealized case of regular normal science, consistency is the cornerstone of success. Within each experiment, everything is held as constant as possible, except the measure of interest. And new studies mark their progress by varying only one factor at a time. This sort of consistency is what allows interpretative elegance in empirical research, even if it is the case that in actual practice such elegance can only be approximated.

Experimental Philosophy

As discussed above, experimental philosophy studies, insofar as they are well-designed empirical research experiments, make use of consistency in the ways just described. Two such studies, both examining moral judgments and the assignment of responsibility, tested two closely related hypotheses concerning the familiar "omission bias" and the newer "indirect harm bias." (Both of these hypotheses and the particular experiments will be described briefly just below.)

In the Spranca et al. (1991) study, the researchers found that subjects judged harms caused by *omission* as less blameworthy than those caused directly by *commission*. In a within-subjects design, participants read pairs of hypothetical scenarios that varied only in the omission/commission dimension,[19] while the motives and intentions of the characters within each scenario pair and the consequences of their actions were all held *consistent* with one another (p. 76). Here is a sample scenario pair (pp. 82–83): Ivan and John will be playing an important tennis match after a shared dinner. John knows that Ivan is allergic to red pepper, and John also knows that the house dressing has much red pepper. Ivan, of course, knows of his own allergy, but he is not aware of the presence of red pepper among the ingredients in the house dressing. In the omission version of the story, Ivan orders the house dressing, John says nothing, Ivan gets a stomachache, and John wins the match. In the commission version of the story, Ivan orders the

Italian dressing, John suggests the house dressing instead, Ivan has the house dressing, gets a stomachache, and John wins the match. Subjects judged John in the omission version as significantly less blameworthy than John in the commission version.

Similarly, Royzman and Baron (2002), in their within-subjects experiment, found that subjects evaluated actions causing *indirect harm* as less objectionable than actions causing *direct harm* when judging two versions of eight scenario pairs differing only on this dimension. Here is a sample item pair from this study (p. 169):

> The subject . . . notices that someone is about to shoot at him. In the direct [harm] action, the subject can position himself behind someone else who will take the bullet. In the indirect [harm] action, the subject can leap aside, in which someone else . . . will take the bullet.

Participants in this experiment judged the direct harm cases as significantly more objectionable than the indirect harm cases. This was despite the fact, as the researchers noted (p. 165), that the ". . . result could not be . . . explained in terms of difference in judgments about which option was more active, more intentional, more likely to cause harm, or more subject to disapproval of others," because these factors were *consistent* across the pairs presented.

Two other experimental philosophy investigations followed a similar pattern—a within-subjects design study of pairs of moral dilemma vignettes—with an additional aim in mind. Cushman, Young, and Hauser (2006) and Hauser, Cushman, Young, Jin, and Mikhail (2007) wanted to ascertain whether participants' moral judgments were predicated on conscious reasoning and could thereby be sufficiently justified. They reported on two sets of findings. First, Cushman et.al. (2006, p. 1082) reported three results. Replicating the findings of Spranca et al. (1991) and Royzman and Baron (2002), they found that participants evaluated (a) harm caused by action as worse than harm caused by omission; and (b) harm intended as the means to an end as worse than harm as an anticipated side effect of another means to a goal. Further, these researchers found that their participants judged (c) harm involving physical contact as worse than harm not involving physical contact. Second, Cushman et al. (2006, p. 1082) and Hauser et al. (2007, p. 1) found that subjects could not justify their harsher judgments of harm as the means to an end versus harm as the anticipated side effect of another means. Thus, the researchers concluded that this moral principle was not consciously evoked as explanatory.

What is of particular interest about the extra aim of these last two studies for our purposes is that one of the measures of proper justification was whether subjects could provide a *consistent* account of the moral intuitions underlying their different judgments on seemingly parallel cases. Hauser et al. (2007) deemed a justification "insufficient" when a subject (pp. 13–14):

> . . . explicitly expressed an inability to account for their contrasting judgments . . . [or left off] without offering any further explanation of how they reasoned . . . [or] . . . explained their judgment of one case using utilitarian reasoning . . . and their judgment of the other using deontological reasoning . . . without resolving their conflicting responses.

In other words, the subjects were not consistent in their moral reasoning.

***

These experimental philosophers are not alone in seeking consistency, particularly as pertains to moral judgments. Other philosophers, such as Zangwill (2011, p. 466), hold that the drive for consistency in normative matters is separate from logical consistency. For Zangwill, the latter derives from our aspirations for correctness; whereas, with respect to the former, he holds: "[t]he requirement of consistency is an essential part of our moral thought. It is partly constitutive of it" (p. 5). Knobe and Doris (2010, p. 322) claim that ". . . almost all philosophical discussions of moral responsibility [have assumed] . . . that people should apply the *same* criteria in *all* of their moral responsibility judgments." They continue (p. 322): "This assumption is so basic that it has never been given a name. We will refer to it as the assumption of *invariance*."[20]

Are things similar with respect to consistency in the realm of thought experiments? Let's explore that next.

Thought Experiments

Consistency is, in some important sense, at the heart of most thought experiments, too. Many (indeed most) thought experiments are constructed in such a way as to rely on consistent parallels in order to: (a) promote reconsideration of seemingly obvious conclusions; (b) find the limits of our views, positions, and understandings toward their possible revision; and (c) question whether the very questions we deem important are indeed important.

To illustrate this, let me first properly present a thought experiment briefly alluded to above that will be much discussed throughout the rest of this chapter. It is called the Trolley Case. Introduced by Philippa Foot (1967) originally as the Tram Case, it was constructed as an explicit parallel paired with the Judge Case, which Foot describes as follows (p. 8):

> Suppose that a judge . . . is faced with rioters demanding that a culprit be found for a certain crime and threatening otherwise to take their own bloody revenge . . . The real culprit being unknown, the judge sees himself as able to prevent the bloodshed only by framing some innocent person and having him executed.

Presuming that the judge would not be justified in doing this, Foot sets up the parallel case (p. 8):

> [There is] the driver of a runaway tram which he can only steer from one narrow track on to another . . . five men are working on one track and one man on the other; anyone on the track . . . [that the tram] enters is bound to be killed.

Foot then observes that, although the cases are parallel and *consistent* with each another, they lead to radically *inconsistent* ethical judgments (p. 8): "The question is why we should say, without hesitation, that the driver should steer for the less occupied track, while most of us would be appalled at the idea that the innocent man [in the Judge Case] could be framed."

In attempting to solve this thought experiment problem, Foot (1967, p. 9) constructs another pair of cases, congruent with the two above. Each case in this pair, too, seems parallel to the other, and yet an ethical judgment consistent for both of these new cases would be, Foot recognized, morally repugnant to most people. Here is the new pair of cases. First, there is a drug in short supply, all about to be given to Patient 1, whose illness requires a massive dose. Suddenly Patients 2, 3, 4, 5, and 6 present themselves, all needing the same drug, but each requiring only one-fifth the dose Patient 1 needs. Foot asserts (p. 9) that most people would have no trouble in giving the drug to Patients 2 through 6, and not to Patient 1—having one die instead of five. And yet she points out that most people would find the same judgment morally abhorrent in the second new case, in which one is asked if it is acceptable to (p. 9) ". . . kill a certain [healthy] individual and make serum from his dead body" even if this were the only way to save ". . . several dangerously ill people."

On reflection, perhaps we can appreciate closer (or deeper or better) parallels both between the pair of allowable situations—(1) turning the runaway tram and (2) providing the drug to the five in the short-supply drug case—and between the pair of forbidden cases—(1) framing the innocent man for execution in the Judge Case and (2) the killing of one person for serum—than between the two cases in each of the original pairs—judge and trolley and short-supply drug and killing for serum. If so, then at least with respect to these four situations as imagined by Foot, *consistent* moral reasoning might in fact be possible, but only if one can discern the deeper/closer/better parallels.

Using this sort of refinement in the need for consistency (along with other diverse and interesting moves), Foot, along with many other philosophers and practitioners of experimental philosophy (and of thought experiments), deal with these and other apparent inconsistencies in several different and intriguing ways. Indeed, the tradition will be continued here. Much more will be discussed about the Trolley Case and its various parallels in

Section Three, "Abuses of Consistency," and Section Four, "Solving the False Parallel Problem."

Meanwhile, however, let us leave the trolleys for now and examine another type of thought experiment—one designed to raise serious doubts about the viability of a set of questions whose consistence and coherence had been very much taken for granted previously. Derek Parfit (1984, pp. 236–243), in discussing aspects of "teletransporting," provides an opportunity to investigate the coherence/consistency of our standard conception of personal identity.

My brief (and somewhat altered for ease of exposition) summary of the pertinent facts is as follows: Earthly person X (hereafter Earth-X), steps into a teletransporter. After pressing a button signaling his readiness, Earth-X is destroyed but quickly reconstituted in the teletransporter on Mars as Mars-X. The Martian replica is constituted of human biological material, including human brain material (neurons and their connections, etc.) such that Parfit stipulates that all of X's body and all of his psychology too can be replicated. Indeed, on Mars, Mars-X experiences himself as X, much as Earth-X experienced himself as X on Earth. When the process is reversed—that is, when Mars-X is teletransported back to Earth as Earth-X, X experiences no differences in himself, other than the new adventures he had (as himself) on Mars.

Now suppose something goes wrong with the teletransporter such that Earth-X cannot be reconstituted. Is Mars-X X, or has X stopped existing? What if another type of teletransporter malfunction causes Earth-X and Mars-X to coexist for a time? Are they both X? If not, which one is X? Will one's identification of X as X change if one of them dies? Should a contingent fact like that matter in the determination of X's identity?

Parfit uses these situations (and various analogues) to explore the question of what constitutes X's continued personal identity as X.[21] Here is another example. Taking up what he calls the "Combined Spectrum," which ". . . involve[s] all of the possible variations in the degrees of *both* physical *and* psychological connectedness . . ." (p. 236), Parfit holds: "At the near end of the spectrum is the normal case in which a future person would be fully continuous with me as I am now, both physically and psychologically . . . At the far end of the spectrum the resulting person would have no continuity with me as I am now, either physically or psychologically" (pp. 236–237). Thus, at the farthest point of the far end, Parfit describes the scientists destroying his own (Derek Parfit's) brain and body and building "out of new organic matter, a perfect replica of someone else" (p. 237)—someone who is not recognizable at all as Derek Parfit and is not Derek Parfit. At the other extreme, at the near end, the scientists are using Parfit's own organic matter to construct a replica of Parfit. In this case, especially as the building materials are entirely Parfit's own, one would be tempted to say (and perhaps Parfit would agree), "that replica is Parfit." Returning now to the far end of the spectrum, but with just a bit of Parfit's own brain and body material and a little of his psychology, one would likely hold that the resultant replica would not be Parfit. This seems clear, but a problem arises with the middle-spectrum cases. Just how much non-Parfit organic material, constituting how much of a different person, will be tolerated before one says, "no, that's not Parfit"? Can there be 5 percent different organic materials, with 5 percent non-Parfit memories and other psychological processes in the Parfit replica, with this still being Parfit? But what about if 37 percent (or 54 percent) of the organic material is different from Parfit's biological matter, and the new replica has 37 percent (or 54 percent) of his memories different from Parfit's memories?

Even with this dilemma of the middle cases, Parfit offers (p. 238): "We might continue to believe that, to the question 'Would the resulting person be me?' there must always be an answer . . . simply Yes or No." He continues (p. 238): "We would then be forced to accept the following claims: Somewhere in this Spectrum, there is a sharp borderline." But this is, of course, absurd, as Parfit well knows. It is a sorites paradox problem, the type of problem in which one tries in vain, through consistency and logic, to render precise a concept that is hopelessly vague.[22] One is left with a paradox and/or an empty (worthless) question. Parfit says as much (p. 239): "In the central cases of the Combined Spectrum, it would be an empty question whether the resulting person would be me."

Now, because the question is empty in the central cases of the Combined Spectrum, Parfit realizes that the question is empty in general! He goes on to make the following recommendation (p. 241): ". . . we should not try to decide between the different criteria of personal identity. One reason is that personal identity is not what matters [even when one is concerned with one's own survival]." Parfit does describe at some length what does matter in his view.[23] But most important for our purposes is Parfit's use of the sorites paradox, with its essential reliance on *consistency*—the similarity (in terms of baldness) of a man with one million hairs to a man with 999,999 hairs, itself predicated on the similarity of one iterated single unit subtraction to the next—to construct his thought experiment study, one which concludes that perfectly ordinary and natural questions about continuity in personal identity are in fact exactly the wrong questions to ask! Parfit's teletransporter/Combined Spectrum thought experiment, via consistency, arrives at the very surprising conclusion that when I'm concerned about my future survival as "me," my personal identity is not at all at issue. His thought experiment is an interesting one in that he uses consistency to successfully question the very question of personal identity.

As is the case with empirical research, and as is demonstrated by these last two emblematic examples, consistency is a necessary and essential aspect of thought experiments. What about consistency in psychoanalysis?

Psychoanalysis

There are (at least) two very different ways in which the use of consistency figures centrally in psychoanalysts' endeavors to understand and help patients. First, following Freud (1900/1953, 1905/1953, 1909a/1953, 1909b/1953, 1915a/1953, 1926/1953), psychoanalysts hold that psychological symptoms, symptom clusters, and even entire neuroses, no matter how incoherent they seem, are meaningful psychological structures constructed by patients as the best and most *consistent* (least inconsistent) adaptation they can manage at a particular time. What follows just below is an example from an ordinary psychoanalysis demonstrating how such symptomatic manifestations can be understood as intelligible, coherent, and consistent.

Patient A, a lifelong but recovering hypochondriac, developed a puzzling new symptom in the final phase of his psychoanalytic treatment. He would be feeling quite well until one hour prior to his analytic appointment, at which time he would start to feel "woozy, sick in some unspecified way, and worried." During the hour, he would feel fine, even better than fine; and yet each day, the pre-session hypochondria returned. This continued for several sessions, until one day, as he was lamenting about his self-described "symptomatic and incoherent behavior," he reported that he was suddenly aware of a song going through his head with lyrics slightly altered from the real version. The actual words were "My world is empty without you babe"; but in Mr. A's version they were changed to something phonologically similar: "My world is MD without you babe." With these associations it was easy for both patient and analyst to grasp that his latest hypochondriacal symptom was devised to stay in treatment with me, his MD psychoanalyst. True, feeling less than well was not great, but in Patient A's mind, it was quite a bit better to stay in the "MD world" as opposed to the "empty world."

Mr. A and I together could come to understand this symptom because we initially assumed that the new bout of hypochondria was representative of something meaningfully consistent that we had not yet grasped. Then, in following his associations, we found that embedded in the symptom was an important contentful unconscious conflict about ending his psychoanalysis. We were able to use Mr. A's primary process associations to understand the underlying unconscious content of his psychological symptom, thereby restoring our appreciation of the consistency and coherence of what had heretofore been his puzzling behavior.[24]

Patient A's symptom can help illuminate another aspect of this first use of consistency in psychoanalysis. Again following Freud (1905/1953, 1909a/1953, 1912/1953, 1915b/1953, 1940/1953), psychoanalysts have found that, although the great majority of neurotic people mature (for the most part) quite normally, the structure of their neuroses retains a consistent core throughout life. Often first constituted as a neurosis in childhood, and termed "the infantile neurosis,"[25] as we shall see below, the adult neurosis is usually a recognizable version thereof. Moreover, aspects of both the infantile neurosis and the adult neurosis are (unconsciously) re-created in the treatment as the "the transference neurosis." In the transference neurosis, the person of the analyst is experienced as a transference version of crucial persons from the past. These consistencies can be seen quite clearly in Patient A's case. In fact so clearly it is almost as though we had an equation, with everything remaining constant (*consistent*) save for the value of one variable. The information relevant to this claim follows.

Mr. A's father, an MD, was for the most part remote, distant, and preoccupied. But he was different with his own patients. A pediatrician, he treated the children in his practice in a way that Mr. A described as "tenderhearted." Interestingly, when Mr. A had an illness or a somatic complaint, his father treated him with kindness, moreover with true concern beyond just the medical situation. Unfortunately, Dr. A's attention and interest in his son lasted only as long as a particular bout of illness. It is from this behavior that Mr. A formed one of the core features of his neurosis—the repeated expectation that father types would be emotionally engaged with him only when he (Mr. A) was sick. In this way Mr. A kept the pathological equation intact, endlessly plugging in various different people in the "cold father" variable slot. In the course of his analysis we could see (and experience) this particular father transference with many father figures (of course including powerful women) such as coaches, bosses, his wife's parents, doctors, lawyers, accountants, and, not surprisingly, me, his "MD analyst" (a phrase he often used in referring to me). Starting in childhood and continuing until he could effect a change consistent with his psychoanalytic progress, Mr. A's tactics for dealing with people came in two stages: Initially, Mr. A would behave in a fashion designed (consciously or unconsciously) to get a father figure's involvement with him. This was often through illness or some other sort of problem, but could sometimes be achieved through good work. The second stage consisted of Mr. A quickly (and sometimes suddenly) disappearing, so that he would be the one to withdraw. Mr. A would do this before the father figure had a chance to lose interest in him, as Mr. A, under the sway of the father transference, "knew" would happen.[26]

The second use of consistency in psychoanalysis concerns a particular kind of clinical intervention—indeed, the kind most routinely employed. Here is an example, in abstract form: A patient seems to be behaving inconsistently—speaking in a less than rational (maybe even incoherent) fashion, performing contradictory actions based on contradictory beliefs, clearly not acting in his/her best interest. Although the analyst fully believes that consistency lies behind such behavior (and perhaps could even understand the patient's neurosis without the patient's associations), the analyst brings the patient's *apparent inconsistency* to his/her attention. Sometimes this will surprise the patient. Sometimes the patient will defend against the observation. And sometimes the patient will even feel offended or just plain bad. Less often a patient will find such an observation pleasing. In any case, having the patient associate to the observation of inconsistency is the next step. Often the patient will begin to associate spontaneously. If not, he/she will be invited to do so. As we've seen (for instance in Mr. A's case), free associations with much primary process material often do follow. These associations allow the analyst (and patient) to understand the symptom or slip of the tongue from a novel perspective, thereby reducing, if not obviating, the apparent inconsistency and its attendant dysphoria.

Thus, what I am terming the second use of consistency in psychoanalysis amounts simply to employing one of the most basic of psychoanalytic techniques—observing the inconsistency and then asking for associations. This type of intervention is not only among the most frequent, it is among the most critical in every analysis. Its success is due both to the assumptions of general psychoanalytic theory discussed in Section Two above and to the overriding need we humans have for consistency in general, and particularly as we evaluate our own psychology, ethics, and behavior. But this tendency can sometimes lead to problems, as I shall illustrate in the next section.

SECTION THREE: THE ABUSES OF CONSISTENCY

Psychoanalysis

Not surprisingly, the human hunger for consistency can have its downsides. In psychoanalysis, for instance, most analysts find the experience of making an interpretation that seems to solve a puzzle and restore recognizable consistency very gratifying. So much so that analysts can become enamored of their interpretations—including those that are not quite right or even wrong—sticking to them, evidence to the contrary from their patients' further associations notwithstanding. Worse still, analysts can feel so satisfied with what appears a consistency-restoring interpretation that they do not even listen for their patient's responses.[27] After all, psychoanalysts are human and humans crave consistency.

There are other abuses of consistency in psychoanalysis. Much as any theory is underdetermined by the available data—the same data can often be adequately accounted for by more than one theory—it is the case that for any patient a particular state of consistency is not a determinate matter. In other words, the specifics that constitute the patient's history, transference state—and associations up to and including that point at which consistency seems to be lost—can admit of different interpretative solutions, seemingly equivalent in terms of their consistency-restoring capacities. To give an example, let us return to Patient A, but add some fictional (but not at all implausible) data. Suppose that, along with the struggles already outlined, he was also coping with a miscarriage recently suffered by his wife. Then his pre-session hypochondriacal symptom and the song's refrain "My world is empty without you babe"—along with the distortion from "empty" to "MD"—might well refer not primarily to his feelings about his analyst and losing her but instead to his feeling that the world is empty without his baby, and perhaps also to fears about his wife's well-being. This last would especially be the case if the miscarriage had involved medical problems occasioning intense contact with physicians—contact that itself might feel emotionally painful to Mr. A. Interpretation about losing the analyst, were these last described fictional events to have actually taken place, would still have resolved the inconsistency but would not have been useful or empathic.

Overvaluing the first interpretation that appears to resolve a particular inconsistency inhibits the analyst's sensitivity to his/her patient. Also, it stifles the analyst's creativity regarding alternatives. Interestingly, adhering to first solutions is quite similar to the processes employed (mostly unconsciously) by patients both in neurosis formation and in neurosis maintenance. There, creativity is curtailed as central and important aspects of life are inhibited, or at least prevented from progressing, as the neurotic compromises hold sway. While it is the case that neurotic solutions are not good solutions (and in some cases they are obviously bad), it should be kept in mind that, to the extent that they are first-line inconsistency removers, they, like wrong first interpretations, are hard to give up.

Continuing with the theme that consistency can be a problem from the side of the patient, I have heard a psychoanalyst describe neurosis as an ailment in which the sufferer has managed to get everything in life to go together, consistently, but not at all in a good way.[28] In other words, this analyst characterized neurosis as a very bad set of attitudes, behaviors, compromises, feelings, and desires, but a consistent set nonetheless, with no obvious conscious contradictions, all arranged in a manner such that most things seem at least stable and coherent. The organized consistency of a neurosis contributes to its being hard to change and harder to give up. Mr. A's neurosis demonstrates these features. We see a remarkable stability from childhood to adulthood in his neurotic reactions, first to a father who was cold except when Mr. A was sick, and then in his active re-creation of this painful and pathological relationship with a myriad of father figures all through his life. To this Mr. A also added hypochondria, chronic underachievement, and provocation, these quite consistent with his original neurotic conflicts, in fact exacerbating them.

Indeed, there are a number of factors that contribute to the refractory nature of neurotic psychopathology. Among them are:

1. That the symptom provides unconscious gratification via the satisfaction (in fantasy) of unacceptable impulses. At the same time, the superego (conscience) reacts to this harshly, adding unconscious sadistic pleasure to the masochistic suffering most neurotic symptoms occasion.

2. That there is the so-called secondary gain phenomenon, whereby people with neurotic symptoms often garner sympathy from others or at least are able to legitimize getting off from work.
3. That related to both of the above, neuroses are constituted partly to deny reality and its difficult tasks.

And yet the stability, and even more so the consistence, of a neurosis is arguably one of the most important elements in understanding why successful treatment is so arduous and often takes so long. The patient integrates his/her neurotic solutions into every stage of his/her life,[29] thereby "fixing" what is unstable, shoring up the conflicts that can threaten his/her very coherence with symptoms that bind them together so that life is at least predictable—if not all that good. In this way it becomes clear that the recalcitrance of analytic patients to address their symptoms and improve their lives comes in large part from the importance of consistency in human life—in this case, its abuses more than its uses.

Empirical Research

In the realm of empirical research there is but one *obvious* downside to consistency, a single trend that one could regard as an abuse of consistency. This concerns the slow stepwise progress of much empirical research in general, and perhaps in particular (especially these days) most federally funded research. Because research budgets and research grants are enormous, one can certainly understand that sure-thing outcomes receive priority; but there is a loss—more creative projects, those with a higher risk of failure but also the possibility for more profound gain, are often not funded. Does this trend relate to empirical research as an endeavor that has become largely findings-driven rather than a theory-driven? Some sort of balance would, of course, be ideal. But I am on speculative grounds here. And since I am, let me get even more speculative.

In the opening sentences of this subsection I alluded to there being only one "obvious" downside to the use of consistency in empirical research. Let me now present a less obvious, but equally pervasive, downside—one that may be due not only to our cravings for consistency but also to our desires for striking findings. This combination contributes to an overreliance on between-subject designs and what we make of their results, at least in some major psychology experiments. I will use as my paradigm example an experiment that I love—one conducted by Medin, Goldstone, and Gentner (1990): "Similarity involving attributes and relations: judgments of similarity and difference are not inverses."

In this study participants made forced choices on a number of stimulus items consisting of three figures. On each item the participants had to decide which of two alternative figures was either "more similar" (for those subjects in the similarity judgment condition) or which was "more different" (for those in the difference judgment condition) to a target figure. The same stimulus items were used for participants in both groups. For each stimulus item, one of the choices was like the target in terms of a matching unique "attribute," while the other choice shared a unique "relation" with the target stimulus. Attributes, in this study, referred to primitive (not decomposable) constituent properties or features of a stimulus—for example, shading (e.g., checkered), shape, size. Relations connected two or more attributes within a stimulus (from Medin et al., 1990, pp. 65–66). All of this is made much clearer with an example. See Figure 4.1:

In Figure 4.1, an actual item from the study, A, the attributionally similar item shares checkered shading with T, the target stimulus. B, the relational choice, does not have any checkered shaded figures but illustrates its relational similarity to T because all the figures in B have the same shading as one another (they are all white), just as all the figures in T have the same shading as one another (checkered). The shadings of the figures in A are not uniform and therefore not relationally similar to T.

In the first study,[30] thirty-six sets of geometric stimuli were used. Presentation order and left-right positioning of attributional and relational choices were both counterbalanced across participants. The design was a between-subjects (or participants) design, in which the twenty-three participants who were asked to make similarity judgments were not the same subjects as the

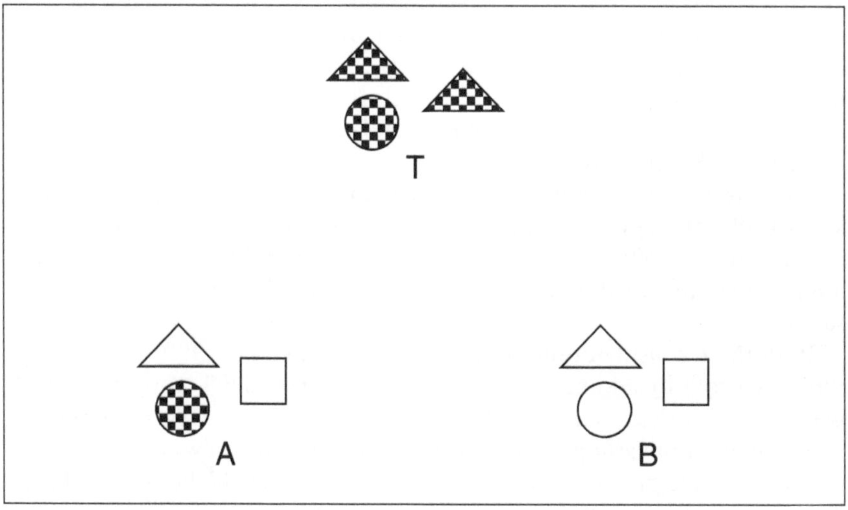

Figure 4.1 Sample stimulus: T, the standard, is attributionally similar to A because they both have a checkered circle. B does not contain this attributional similarity to T; instead, B has a matching relation, "same-shading," with T.

(This figure appears in "Similarities Involving Attributes and Relations: Judgments of Similarity and Difference Are Not Inverses," by D. Medin, R. Goldstone, and D. Gentner, 1990, *Psychological Science, 1*, p. 66. Copyright 1990 by Sage Publications.)

forty-five subjects who made difference judgments (pp. 65–66). The findings were surprising and striking. As the authors put it (p. 66): These sets of ". . . similarity and difference judgments show clear departures from [the expected] complementarity." They continue (p. 66) reporting ". . . [a] systematic pattern of the relational alternative being selected [significantly more often] for both similarity and dissimilarity judgments." From this they conclude both that (p. 69) "similarity and difference judgments are not necessarily inverse to one another . . ." and that "attributes and relations are psychologically distinct" (p. 68). Their conclusions seem both sound and warranted.

So what is the trouble? I maintain that the between-subjects design is problematic in this case and in many like it. Predicated on the need to obviate what the researchers presumed would be the natural participant tendency toward consistent responses—that is, the assumption was that subjects would ensure that similarity and difference judgments about the same items would be inverse—the cost is a lack of knowledge, potentially obtainable, about participant judgments in a natural context, one in which judgments of similarity and difference would not be artificially separated.

On the positive side, the between-subjects design in this study does facilitate a certain cleanness of response; a particular participant's similarity judgment about an item does not influence his/her difference judgment about the same item. And indeed, anyone (this author included) who has ever embarked on empirical research investigations is sympathetic to the attempt to hold as much as possible constant and consistent, allowing only one element to vary, assessing the matter of interest under test as simply as possible and eliminating everything else. Some would even consider this methodological approach the very essence of empirical science. But the pro-natural context editors of a volume titled *The Mind in Context* (Mesquita, Barrett, and Smith 2010) are less understanding and far more critical. They claim there is a significant price to pay because (p. 342): "[s]cience is well known for valuing elegance, parsimony, and power in theoretical and empirical research. When possible scientists like to avoid messy complexity, imprecision, and weak effects." These authors imply that truth and reality suffer.

With these considerations in mind, the Medin et al. (1990) study would certainly profit by adding a more naturalistic within-subjects portion. And, in fact, it is not clear that such an addition would actually weaken the effects and/or make things imprecise and messy. For on my view, the separation of similarity judgments from difference judgments in the between-subjects design was not the most desirable even on scientific grounds, beyond merely sacrificing natural context knowledge concerning similarity *and* difference judgments about the same items. Let me illustrate this with an imagined "replication with extension" revision of the Medin et al. (1990) work.

Suppose that the same participants made both similarity judgments and difference judgments, in a blocked design. That is, half the subjects would make their similarity judgments first, and then their difference judgments, on the same items in randomized orders. The other half of the participants would make their difference judgments first with their similarity judgments in the second block. Now the two sets of first blocks (similarity judgments versus difference judgments) could be compared between subjects, replicating the Medin et al. (1990) experiment exactly.

Additionally, with attributional similarity responses expected to rise in the second block of both between-subject groups (assuming that the finding that relational similarity predominated in initial judgments of both similarity and difference would still obtain), a within-subjects calculation of similarity/difference complementarity—that is, how much the first block influenced the second block toward the expected (*consistent*) notion of similarity and difference as inverses—could be obtained. Specifically, the increases in attributional responses in second-block similarity judgments and second-block difference judgments could be measured against the baselines of attributional responses in first-block similarity judgments and first-block difference judgments, respectively.

Were all to go well, at the completion of this imagined replication-with-extension study, the researchers could have two good effects:

1. Replication results drawn from the between-subject comparisons of the first-block similarity judgments with the first-block difference judgments, presumably strengthening the two conclusions of the first study: (a) that judgments of similarity and difference are not necessarily inverses and (b) that attributional and relational processes are psychologically distinct.

And then another finding, also potentially of great importance:

2. A way to index and then quantify the need for consistency, which the researchers had initially just assumed and then controlled for. How could this be done? By measuring the similarity/difference complementarity in the within-subjects portion of the experiment. This would be reflected in increases in attributional responses in both similarity and difference judgments in second blocks as compared with their first-block baseline norms.

Admittedly, although the above replication with extension might well have proved revealing, the drive toward consistency was not the topic Medin and colleagues were investigating. Indeed, *pace* my own criticism, the between-subjects design employed to control for the pressure subjects feel to make consistent responses, did not vitiate the Medin et.al. (1990) results nor invalidate their conclusions. Unfortunately, I suspect this is not always the case in some important experiments in the world of experimental philosophy. Let me turn to this now.

Experimental Philosophy

As discussed above, there is a branch of experimental philosophy that can be considered a special case of empirical research in that its practitioners carry out empirical tests of hypotheses derived from thought experiments and from the intuitions of armchair philosophers. It is a seminal experiment from this group that I choose as an exemplar to continue the exploration of the abuses of consistency. Here again I find that some of the most serious problems are occasioned by a between-subjects experimental design. Let me now turn to the famous Chairman Case (Knobe, 2003).

In Knobe's (2003) attempt to understand the intuitions people have about intentionality, particularly whether side effects are viewed as being brought about intentionally, he conducted an elegant[31] experiment based on the following story (p. 190):

> The chairman of the board of a company has decided to implement a new program. He believes 1) that the program will make a lot of money for his company and 2) that the program will also produce some other effect x. But the chairman doesn't care at all about effect x. His sole reason for implementing the new program is that he believes it will make a lot of money for the company. In the end, everything proceeds as anticipated: the program makes a lot of money for the company and also produces effect x.

Knobe hypothesized that, whether or not people think that an agent intentionally brought about some side effect x, varies as a function of the nature of x. "In particular," he asserted (p. 191), "it makes a great deal of difference whether they think that x is something good or something bad" with bad side effects regarded as intended significantly more often.

Knobe tested this hypothesis in a between-subjects design experiment in which half of the seventy-eight subjects were assigned to the "harm" condition and half to the "help" condition. The two groups of subjects received vignettes that were consistent with each another, actually identical, except that the three times in which the harm condition subjects saw the word *harm*, the help condition subjects saw the word *help* (p. 191).[32] Also, the task each group received was slightly different. Below are the two vignettes and two task versions.

The harm condition subjects read (p. 191):

> The vice president of a company went to the chairman of the board and said, "We are thinking of starting a new program. It will help us increase profits, but it will also harm the environment." The chairman of the board answered, "I don't care at all about harming the environment. I just want to make as much profit as I can. Let's start the new

> program." They started the new program. Sure enough, the environment was harmed.

These participants were then asked to rate, on a scale from one to six, ". . . how much blame the chairman deserved for what he did . . ." and to indicate "whether they thought the chairman *intentionally* harmed the environment" (p. 191).

The help condition subjects read this version (p. 191):

> The vice president of a company went to the chairman of the board and said, "We are thinking of starting a new program. It will help us increase profits, and it will also help the environment." The chairman of the board answered, "I don't care at all about helping the environment. I just want to make as much profit as I can. Let's start the new program." They started the new program. Sure enough, the environment was helped.

This group of participants was then asked to rate, on a scale from one to six, ". . . how much praise the chairman deserved for what he did . . ." and to indicate "whether they thought the chairman *intentionally* helped the environment" (p. 192).

The results were as Knobe (2003) predicted (p. 192): The two conditions ". . . elicited two radically different patterns of response. In the harm condition, most subjects (82%) said that the agent brought about the side-effect intentionally, whereas in the help condition, most subjects (77%) said that the agent did not bring about the side-effect intentionally. This difference was highly statistically significant."

That the experiment utilized a between-subjects design was not discussed by the author. It seems, however, fairly safe to conclude that the experimenter was trying to circumvent and control for the natural human proclivity in his subjects to provide consistent responses to closely parallel situations. But note, the parallel between these two vignettes is more apparent than real, as one chairman is quite a bit more fictional than the other. Interestingly, the chairman who doesn't care at all about harming the environment is not the unrealistic figure—his sort of blind arrogance is (all too readily) imaginable. Instead, the fanciful portrayal is that of his counterpart who says "I don't care at all about helping the environment." What chairman would not be pleased to get something like helping the environment for free, even if the environment is not something about which he particularly cares? Helping the environment, particularly as a side effect, would have to delight even the crassest corporate capitalist, as he would realize it would aid his own project, enhance his company's image, and further his own self-interested goals.

Given this subtle asymmetry, I am claiming that the results of Knobe's experiment[33] are a lot less interesting than they look, owing to the fact that many (perhaps the majority) of subjects (correctly if unconsciously) perceived that this "help" chairman is out of his mind and in no way worthy of credit or intentionality in achieving a good anticipated side effect. As it stands, half of the participants are evaluating whether selfish chairmen should be blamed for intending anticipated bad side effects, while the other half of participants are asked whether crazy selfish chairmen should be credited with intending anticipated good side effects. A truer test of Knobe's hypothesis requires more natural vignettes, even if a between-subjects design is retained, to more accurately evaluate the contrasts Knobe seeks. I propose, for example, a sequence involving these four different chairmen:

1. A chairman knows the environment will be harmed. He says, "I don't care at all that the environment will be harmed, *because* I just want to make as much profit as possible. Let's start the project." The environment is harmed.
2. A chairman knows the environment will be harmed. He says, "I think it is a shame that the environment will be harmed, *but* I just want to make as much profit as possible. Let's start the project." The environment is harmed.
3. A chairman knows the environment will be helped. He says, "It is OK that the environment is helped, *because* I just want to make as much profit as possible. Let's start the project." The environment is helped.
4. A chairman knows the environment will be helped. He says, "I think it is great that the environment is helped, *but* I just want to make as much profit as possible. Let's start the project." The environment is helped.

Knobe's contrast cases are most like my Cases 1 and 3. My Case 3 is a more natural reading of the chairman who doesn't care at all about the environment, because my uncaring chairman will take for free the environment-helping side effect as furthering the likely success of his own program.[34] So now there are two crucial questions for Knobe's result and his conclusion. First, with this more natural reading of the uncaring chairman whose program will nonetheless produce good side effects, will Knobe's initial finding hold—that the uncaring chairman is given no credit for intending to help? If this finding does stand up, still we should consider these questions: Will the contrast between my Cases 2 and 4—still designed to measure differences in intuitions about intentionality with good versus bad side effects—be markedly less significant than Cases 1 and 3? Will there be a significant difference at all between Cases 2 and 4? Remember that, given Knobe's hypothesis, the significant difference between cases with good versus bad side effects should hold up. But I hope I have introduced room for doubt, and therefore motive for someone to run the revised experiment!

And yet, even my suggested changes to the Chairman Case experiment operate within the response isolation afforded in a between-subjects design. Indeed, while some of my criticisms would be addressed by making the statements from the lucky chairman receiving incidental environmental benefits more natural, circumventing the human penchant for consistency through the experiment's between-subjects design may well preclude a deeper understanding of the matter of interest. My worry and critique can be concisely summarized: Should an assessment of human judgment about intentionality, blame, credit, really be done without regard to *consistency*, and out of context? What if, for instance, consistency over a variety of judgments about several types of actions is essential to the very application of the concept of intention? In other words, could Knobe's (2003) striking findings actually disappear in a within-subjects design, especially with my additional cases? And if they did, should we, along with the researchers, still conclude that, with respect to our evaluation of one another's intentionality, our human propensity for consistency is just a contingent coincidental feature, one to be controlled for experimentally? Clearly, I think we should not conclude this, not were we to be concluding properly. Thus, my claim is that this experiment both (1) in its very attempt to control for consistency and (2) in its design that is superficially parallel (and consistent) but deeply asymmetric, demonstrates a subtle abuse (or at least a misuse) of the type of consistency routinely applied in experimental designs.[35]

***

I will now turn to another type of abuse of consistency problem in another important experimental philosophy study of a different type. The experiment is that of Greene, Sommerville, Nystrom, Darley, and Cohen, (2001), discussed above (see also Greene and Haidt, 2002, for an article that, among other things, comments on the Greene et al., 2001, findings and conclusions). Remember that the experiment was constructed as follows: Subjects were presented dilemmas (in a within-subjects design) from three categories: (1) emotional/personal moral dilemmas; (2) nonemotional/nonpersonal moral dilemmas; (3) dilemmas that were not of a moral or emotional/personal nature. The experimenters hypothesized (p. 2106) that judgments made about the emotional/personal moral dilemmas would activate brain areas associated with emotion more so than judgments made on dilemmas from the other two categories, as would be evidenced by fMRI brain scans done on the participants making these judgments. The hypothesis was supported (pp. 2106–2107): (1) brain areas associated with emotion were more activated in the emotional/personal moral dilemma category than in the other two categories, and (2) brain areas found to be less active during emotional processing were less active in decisions about the emotional/personal moral dilemmas than in decisions in the other two categories.

But there was no test of a fourth group of dilemmas: those that are emotional and personal but not of a moral nature. There are a lot of problems that fall into this fourth class. One example is a problem many women face who are positive for deleterious mutations in the BRCA-1 or BRCA-2 gene and who have a strong family history of breast cancer. These women are far more susceptible to breast cancer than is average, and of a virulent and early-striking type. Should such a woman submit to prophylactic double mastectomy before there is any evidence of a breast tumor?

Since there was no test of dilemmas of this type, what did this study actually discover? Suppose, for example, that the findings with emotional/personal nonmoral dilemmas were just like the findings for the emotional/personal moral dilemmas. This would be reasonable to hypothesize. But if these *were* the results, then the study would have found that emotional dilemmas of all sorts activate emotional brain areas and show less activity in areas less associated with emotion. So what would this tell us about moral judgments, the putative point of the Greene et al. (2001) study?

Here in attempting to highlight sharply the contrast of most importance to the investigators, Greene and his colleagues designed the experiment with consistent controls—but only those that would highlight their hypothesized finding. Thus, while it is consistent to contrast *nonmoral* nonemotional/nonpersonal dilemmas with *moral* nonemotional/nonpersonal dilemmas and to contrast such moral *nonemotional/nonpersonal* dilemmas with moral *emotional/personal* dilemmas, one type of dilemma was omitted—there was no study of *emotional/personal nonmoral dilemmas*. Obviously these are capable researchers. They could have provided the other vital control condition. Since the problem with this experiment thus reveals what can only be considered a lapse in the researchers' consistency capacity, I feel justified in classifying the situation as one that illustrates another type of abuse of consistency.

Thought Experiments

By far the biggest problem with the abuse of consistency in the realm of (philosophical) thought experiments is the problem of false parallels. I addressed this problem in some detail above with respect to the Chairman Case, a seminal empirical experimental philosophy study done by Knobe (2003). I claimed that in this work parallels that were only superficially consistent were used to facilitate more striking findings. Let's return now to the matter of false parallel as a particular type of abuse of consistency as we consider some classic philosophical thought experiments.

Judith Jarvis Thomson's (1971) Violinist Case, proposed as a defense of abortion, is a good place to start. The thought experiment is set up simply as follows (pp. 48–49): What if you, against your will, were rendered unconscious, kidnapped, and then hooked up to a famous but desperately ailing violinist (whose blood and tissue type matched yours extremely well) in order for your kidney function to aid his for nine months? The analogue to an unwillingly pregnant woman with a totally dependent fetus is unmistakable. Regarding just such aesthetically pleasing and clever parallels as this one, Roy Sorensen (1992), in *Thought Experiments*, warns (p. 266), "When irony or absurdity requires a surprising symmetry between cases, we nurse the analogy by suppressing differences and exaggerating similarities." Indeed for both apt and false parallels, the logic is simple and appealing. Given that you think A is the case, and A* is constructed expressly to be consistent with A, how can you not also think that A* is the case? How could A* not be the case when A is the case?

So, with respect to the Violinist Case, are the parallels between the desperately ill violinist and the unborn infant, and that between you as hostage and the unwillingly pregnant woman consistent (noncontradictory), or are they false constructions, only seemingly parallel? If false, where do they become false? As with a pregnancy, the nine months "obligation" matches; so does the unique position of helpless dependence, and there is even biological compatibility. But, regardless of one's views of abortion (and with full disclosure I state that I am pro-choice), one must admit that, other than in relatively rare criminal and/or perverse instances, most women do not engage in sex when they are unconscious. Nor do many acts take place (even rapes) in which the victim is totally unaware that pregnancy is a possible outcome. The situations of a woman with an unwanted pregnancy and that of a person kidnapped in order to physiologically service a stranger over an extended period of time are not actually all that congruent. Thus, while the parallels drawn *seem* to be consistent, they are clearly problematic. The Violinist Case, therefore, provides us with another instance of abuse of consistency via false parallels.

***

Next I return to the famous and important Tram Case (or, as it is better known, the Trolley Case), a thought experiment that lends itself to so many *different* parallels—some of them false—that they make one's head spin.[36] The Trolley Case (which was presented briefly above) basically concerns a runaway trolley that will hit and kill five people on the track at which it is headed unless it is turned to another track, where on impact it will kill one person. Should the driver turn the trolley? Yes, most think. But then why do most people choose not to save the five and sacrifice one in the Killing for Serum Case (also alluded to above)—that is, kill one healthy individual in order to produce a special serum to save five? And along these lines, let's consider the Transplant Case. Sometime in the future when transplant technology is amazingly successful, why not cause the death of one healthy donor by transplanting five of his/her excellent organs to save five people who are healthy except for the dire need each has for one of these five organs? At least as strongly as most people think the runaway trolley should be turned, most individuals are appalled at the Transplant and Killing for Serum Cases. With these last two examples in mind, we can begin to entertain the notion that perhaps the problem lies with the Trolley Case being *falsely* parallel (i.e., inconsistent) both with the Killing for Serum and the Transplant Cases, while the latter two are more consistent and parallel with each another.

Foot (1967, pp. 8–9), originator of the Trolley Case along with some of its falsely consistent parallels, was quite aware that one could not reasonably argue directly from one of these situations to the other, no matter how consistent the constructed parallels appeared to be. She sought to explain the deeper divergences in the cases like Transplant versus Trolley as those concerning negative versus positive duties, with the negative duties obligating us more (pp. 11–12). Thus, the negative duty not to kill (even) one person in the Serum and Transplant Cases obligates us more than the positive duty to prevent five from dying; whereas in the Trolley Case, the negative duty not to kill five outweighs the negative duty not to kill one.

But the story does not end here; far from it. Thomson (1976, pp. 207–208) constructs another parallel to the Trolley Case, the Fat Man on the Footbridge Case, in which killing one versus letting five die once again does not seem acceptable. This is so even though in this example the parallel to the Trolley Case appears in some sense more consistent, closer, as more of the elements match than do in the Serum and Transplant Cases. In the Fat Man on the Footbridge Case, the trolley is again speeding toward the five people. The driver is unconscious. George, a bystander on a footbridge overlooking the tracks, sees that the only way to prevent the death of five is to drop a heavy weight onto the path of the onrushing trolley. A fat man is also on the footbridge overlooking the tracks in question, and his weight would suffice. Should George push the fat man onto the trolley track? Most people, including Thomson herself, would say no. Is her reasoning the same as Foot's regarding negative versus positive duties? Or is Thomson alluding to a different distinction—that between passive inactions and active actions, in which case passively allowing the five to die would be judged as more morally acceptable than actively killing the fat man.

Regarding this sort of passivity and activity in moral behaviors, Michael Tooley (1974/1980) offers a thought experiment proving quite devastating to the moral force of the active/passive distinction, at least in its most basic form. He says (p. 60): "Imagine a machine containing two children, John and Mary. If one pushes a button, John will be killed, but Mary will emerge unharmed. If one does not push the button, John will emerge unharmed, but Mary will be killed. In the first case one kills John, while in the second case one merely lets Mary die."[37] And indeed Thomson (1976), perhaps aware of Tooley's argument,[38] does offer another explanation entirely. Discussing the difference between the sanctioned turning of the runaway trolley to kill one versus letting it kill five, as opposed to the unacceptable throwing of the fat man to save the five, Thomson asserts (p. 208): ". . . what is in question is deflecting a threat from a larger group onto a smaller group [i.e., turning the trolley to kill one instead of five] . . . [versus] . . . bringing a different threat to bear on the smaller group [i.e., throwing the fat man off the footbridge]." She then refines this further, wondering if (p. 216) ". . . what matters in these cases in which a threat is to be distributed is whether the agent distributes it by doing something to it [i.e., to the threat, by turning the trolley], or whether he distributes it by doing something to a person [i.e., throwing the fat man off the footbridge]."

From here there are a great many possible parallels, all *appearing* consistent, but with some *actually* more consistent than others. Let's take, for instance, the issue of manipulating the threat rather than a person. Suppose that the trolley company, aware of the risk posed by runaway trolleys, especially to trolley company employees fixing the track, devised a new mechanism that works as follows. A button could be pressed that would activate a catapult mechanism preloaded with a heavy weight. This weighted catapult would be strategically placed on the footbridge overlooking the track such that, when activated, the catapulted weight would stop such errant trolleys. A good solution, except that the new mechanism was known to have one serious engineering problem: if anyone happened to be at the catapult area on the footbridge at the time when the mechanism activated, that person would also be catapulted down, and killed. But mostly no one would be there, with the exception of the occasional trolley company worker adjusting and fine-tuning the catapult mechanism. Therefore, such an untoward event would be very unlikely since it would require a high degree of coincidence.

So now I have created the Trolley Company Catapult Case. The runaway trolley is about to kill five workers on its track, but it could be diverted to a different track with only one worker on it, simply by activating the weighted catapult. Should George the bystander push the button to activate the mechanism? Yes, in the usual (unpeopled catapult) case, because one will be lost but five will be saved. But what if, in a slightly different version, George sees with relief that there is an empty alternative track but soon notes with horror that there is a trolley company man at the exact spot of the catapult on the footbridge? Clearly this man will plunge to his death along with the diverting weight if George activates the catapult. Should George push the button? Is this situation analogous to simply turning the trolley, in that George would be doing something to the trolley company's mechanism, killing one worker instead of five? Or is this case more like the fat man on the footbridge? In other words, would George (just) be manipulating the threat itself—killing, albeit incidentally, one trolley company employee working on the catapult mechanism, but saving five trolley company track workers? Or would George be manipulating a person, bringing to bear a new threat to the man unfortunately positioned within the catapult mechanism?

Now, suppose we change the case just a bit. The trolley company has been remiss in reloading the heavy weight. Again we have the speeding runaway trolley about to kill five people. George sees an empty alternative track and the trolley catapult button. But he quickly notices two things: (1) there is no trolley company weight in place, but (2) there happens to be a fat man at the catapult spot on the footbridge whose weight looks to be at least that of the usual catapult weight. However, since in this version, the only mass stopping the trolley would be that of the fat man, his death would not be incidental. Should George push the button in this Remiss Trolley Company

Catapult Case? Should it matter to George whether the regular catapult weight is also in place? Should it matter if the fat man happens to be a trolley company worker, and, for that matter, whether the five on the tracks are or are not trolley company employees working on the track? One thing is clear: In this set-up we have George manipulating the person (the fat man) directly as well as manipulating the threat (the trolley company's mechanism) in redistributing that threat to a smaller group (i.e., the fat man).[39] Are there false and inconsistent parallels here somewhere, accounting for our perplexed state over these examples? What are they? And where do the consistent parallels break down?

Thomson (1985) tackles these problems again, returning to variations on the Trolley Case—both to contest Foot's original conclusions and to refine her earlier views. In this work, instead of a driver who can turn the trolley onto one track, killing one person instead of killing five people, Thomson sets forth the Bystander at the Switch Case, in which a bystander can either cause the trolley to turn, killing one person, or do nothing, allowing five to die. Thompson believes most people would think that the bystander should throw the switch. But if Foot's view is correct about negative versus positive duties, and/or if the active/passive distinction is important, Thomson points out that the Bystander at the Switch Case should not seem all that different from the impermissible Fat Man on the Footbridge or the Transplant Cases, where the killing of one is not allowed even though five would be saved. But Thomson (1985, p. 1408) explains (much as she had previously) that what sanctions the action in the Bystander at the Switch Case is that: (1) the agent is permissibly manipulating the threat rather than manipulating a person (whereas throwing the fat man from the bridge certainly is manipulating that person), and (2) the agent does not violate a person's rights.[40] Thus, for Thomson, when dealing with persons in both tracks, all under the same chance of the runaway trolley threat, it is preferable that one person be killed rather than five be allowed to die. But this is not the situation for the Transplant Case or the Fat Man on the Footbridge Case. In the former, the five people needing a transplant are seriously ill and under a serious threat. The healthy would-be donor, on the other hand, if unimpeded, is under no threat and has proprietary rights to his/her own organs that no agent can violate. (This last is not unlike the reasoning in the Violinist Case, where the kidnapped renal helper was under no preexisting threat and has the right to his/her freedom along with his/her own renal functions.) Likewise, it is implied on Thomson's view that the fat man on the footbridge is not under the same threat as the people on the tracks, and therefore an agent would be violating the rights of the fat man were he to be sacrificed.

With Thomson's (1985) explanation, the uncomplicated Trolley Company Catapult Case, in which no workers are in the catapult area and the catapult is properly loaded, can be easily decided in favor of the observing agent pressing the button and activating the mechanism, so that one worker on the alternate track will be killed instead of the five on the original track. The agent in so doing would be manipulating the threat present to all the people on the tracks, not manipulating their persons, and thus would not be violating anyone's rights. This case is a consistent parallel with the Bystander at the Switch and the Turn the Trolley Cases. But not so with the two complicated versions of the Trolley Company Catapult Case—one in which a person (either a trolley company worker or a passerby) just happens to be present within the company's mechanism, and the other, the Remiss Trolley Company Catapult Case, in which a fat man is the only weight present because the company failed to load the catapult mechanism. These cases are not consistent parallels with the Turn the Trolley or the Bystander at the Switch Cases, in that a person's rights are certainly being violated.

And yet, in both of these Complicated Trolley Company Catapult Cases, too, much as is true with the six people on the two tracks in the uncomplicated versions, various pieces of trolley company equipment—the runaway trolleys, the tracks, and also the catapult mechanism—represent known potential (albeit unlikely) threats, both to the general public and especially to trolley company workers. From this point of view, the following two cases are hard to distinguish:

1. A bystander pushing the trolley company's button to activate the trolley company's accidently manned catapult mechanism, plunging one to a painful death to save five.
2. A bystander at the trolley company's switch, turning the trolley company's trolley so that one person on a nearby track is painfully killed to save five.

Both cases manipulate trolley company devices rather than directly manipulating persons or personal rights.

Pursuing this consistent/inconsistent dilemma further toward a potentially helpful new set of questions, let me introduce the views of James Montmarquet (1982) and Robert Hanna (1991). Montmarquet (1982, p. 454) states his principle that harming (even killing) is allowable to save [more] lives if and only if ". . . the persons killed are co-threatened with those we save" and "we do not inflict more harm on that person than that with which he was already threatened." Thus, Montmarquet (p. 446) permits the driver of a runaway train to steer it onto a side track so as to kill one worker rather than to passively allow five to be killed. But he does not sanction a surgeon operating in the following case (pp. 446–447): "Three patients (who cannot be moved) need an emergency operation to live. Because of a malfunction, though, performance of this operation would leak deadly gas into the next room, where it would kill its lone inhabitant (who also cannot be moved). The latter is a relatively healthy person . . ."[41]

Similarly, Hanna (1991, p. 331) holds:

> In cases in which there is the option of either a) harming one bystander by forcing him into the threat-situation, or b) harming one or five participants [already] in the same threat-situation only in order to bring about the best possible distribution of the threat, it is impermissible to do a) but sometimes permissible to do b).

Thus, for Hanna (p. 331): "[I]t is permissible to bring about the death of the one in order to save the five in *The Trolley Driver* [Turn the Trolley Case], but not in *The Spectator on the Bridge* [Fat Man on the Footbridge Case]."

Although these are familiar views, they are stated in such a way that they encourage three new questions: (1) How far can one go in defining those who are "co-threatened"? Relatedly: (2) How does one decide the extension of those who are participants in some threat event, and who are the bystanders? And, perhaps most deeply: (3) What constitutes the boundaries of the physico-causal (Hanna's term) composition of any particular event relevant to an extant threat? As my Complicated Trolley Company Catapult Cases suggest, there is a plausible case to be made in which the Fat Man is, in walking in an area with trolley company devices, a co-threatened participant rather than a bystander, with status no different from the people on the tracks. Furthermore, in cases such as these, it is clear that the fat man, along with a particular area of the footbridge and the trolley company's catapult apparatus, are all as much a part of the trolley event as are the trolleys, tracks, and the people on them.

John Harris (1975, esp. p. 83) pushes this line of argument even further, as he examines the issue of killing versus letting die with his "survival lottery." Here is how his thought experiment goes: Given that transplant surgery is perfected and optimal age considerations have been worked out, when two or more people could survive with a transplant, one person from those whose tissues are compatible is drawn from the lottery and sacrificed. In the world of the survival lottery, *everyone* in a particular society is part of a lottery for organ donation, and therefore absolutely *everyone* is a *co-threatened* participant.

Certainly the three questions alluded to just above—concerning (1) the ontological boundaries of an event and its threat, (2) the constitution of participants versus bystanders, and (3) the defining features of the co-threatened—are all deep metaphysical issues. Each of these was raised directly or indirectly in consideration of parallels to the classic Trolley Case thought experiment. As such one has to be impressed with the variety, creativity, and richness of the models devised and examples utilized.

And yet what we have is a myriad of *unreliable* parallels—some superficial and some faulty—each, however, seemingly consistent with an aspect of the Trolley Case and thus contributing to the sense that these important metaphysical problems seem unsolvable. Can we work out better solutions? I propose one method for doing just that in the next section.

SECTION FOUR: SOLVING THE PARADOX OF FALSE PARALLELS: THE METHOD OF INTERVENING STEPWISE CASES

False parallel cases, as demonstrated in the examples above, are an interesting blend of the consistent and inconsistent. They *are* parallels and so there is the inclination to treat the situations described in a consistent manner, and yet there is something amiss, something inconsistent. I am going to suggest that some of the problems with these false parallel paradox cases—both in the realm of the thought experiments we've been exploring and in experimental philosophy cases—can be resolved using a method derived from sorites paradox cases and vague concepts, but with an outcome much more successful than in these actual sorites cases.

Thus, employing a technique much like that used in trying to get a grip on the vague concept of baldness—that is, having a look at sequential cases in between someone clearly bald and someone clearly not bald—the method of intervening stepwise cases attempts to solve false parallel paradox cases by developing cases that are middle steps between two problematic parallels of interest. For instance (as I will take up at length in the subsection below), cases can be devised that are in between the sanctioned Turn the Trolley Case and the seemingly parallel (in that both kill one person to save five) but impermissible Transplant Case. The intermediate cases mitigate the jarring false parallel, and instead allow a more genuine consistency to be appreciated.

Interestingly, the method of intervening stepwise cases is likely quietly operative in much empirical research. Consider, for example, the multitude of studies necessary to determine drug dosages. Empirical investigations are necessary to establish the best therapeutic-to-toxic ratios possible for patients of various ages, weights, and metabolic rates. Thus, starting out with a dose that is toxic but efficacious at one extreme and safe but ineffective on the other, researchers must manipulate both conditions in various experimental trials using intermediate amounts of the drug being tested, often in a stepwise manner. Further and in related fashion, all kinds of empirical experiments require a sort of pre-study stepwise calibration of instruments to find the right technical settings allowing the measures of interest to be best appreciated.

Even in psychoanalysis the development of the transference neurosis[42] is a sort of intermediate step. Located between the infantile neurosis and the adult neurosis, the transference neurosis focuses all the problematic transferences of the patient's life upon the person of the analyst. The transference neurosis is a shared construction, serving as a living (in vivo) model of the patient's problems so that they can be worked out, not in absentia, but in the vivid present.

But I am getting way ahead of the story. I need to provide examples that demonstrate the method in detail. But even before describing the experimental philosophy studies and thought experiments that might benefit by employing the method of sorites-like intervening cases, I want to make it totally clear that in certain instances this process will not be useful—sometimes even when it appears that intermediate cases could help. I offer the following important negative example from Thomas Nagel's (1974) famous thoughts about the mysterious nature of bat-hood. Without using the exact term, Nagel (p. 439) asserts on no uncertain terms that intervening stepwise cases could not help him to understand what it would be like to be a bat. He explains that he does not mean that he could not imagine what it would be like for him, Thomas Nagel, to be a bat. That, he implies, he could conceivably accomplish. Rather, he means that he has no way to fathom what it would be like for the bat-he-would-be to be a bat—in other words, what being a bat would be like. He states (p. 439): "Even if I could by gradual degrees be transformed into a bat, nothing in my present constitution enables me to imagine what the experiences of such a future stage of myself thus metamorphosed would be like." Clearly, then, in Nagel's view, the sorites-like intermediate stepwise approach could bring him no closer to approximating a bat's experience as a bat.

Acknowledging the limitations of its applicability, let us proceed to a demonstration of the method of intervening cases in the type of studies for which constructing such stepwise cases can ameliorate some of the problems wrought by the paradox of faulty parallels—parallels that are consistent but inconsistent, superficial, or false.

Experimental Philosophy

Returning again to Knobe's Chairman Case experiment, let's see if what I'm calling the method of intervening stepwise cases can temper some of my own criticisms of his study. As I said above, the findings of the Chairman Case as presented may in fact be mediated by the "not-caring-at-all" attitude of the chairmen. But what if Knobe were willing to expand his stimulus items to include the sort of chairmen who did care a lot about the environment, keeping everything else in the experiment constant? On my view, he could in fact construct intervening stepwise cases merely by adding the same two conditions I discussed above:

1. A chairman who knew about the anticipated good side effects, did care about the environment, and whose program led to good side effects.
2. A chairman who knew about the anticipated bad side effects, did care about the environment, *but* whose program led to bad side effects.

These additional chairman conditions would (I predict) have an effect on the study's findings. The results would likely be far less striking than those of the original study. But on the plus side, the results would likely be more accurate: It is not unreasonable to speculate that the use of these additional cases, even in a simple between-subjects design extension, could reveal both that the chairman *who cared* and whose project had the expected good side effects might be credited with some intentional responsibility for them. And, more importantly for Knobe's interests, the chairman *who cared but* whose program had the expected bad side effects might be let off the hook a bit with respect to intentional responsibility for them. (After all, they were bad *side* effects; they weren't the main effects at which he was aiming.)

In a more ideal experimental world, two within-subjects design studies, one using Knobe's original study items only and one with the additional caring chairmen items I proposed just above, would be run in addition to the between-subjects extension experiment with more realistic chairmen I suggested earlier in the chapter. The aim of all of these additional experiments—each constituting a sort of intervening stepwise case—would be toward making Knobe's original Chairman Case experiment more realistic in assessing the matters of interest—even if the findings were less dramatic and striking.[43]

Thought Experiments

When dealing with certain problematic thought experiments, let me propose outright the following potential remedy. Wherever there exist parallels that seem consistent but nonetheless just don't work, their paradoxical inconsistency may be resolved by constructing a sorites-type series of intervening cases. Minimally the intermediate cases can clarify whether the question at issue might best be reframed. More interestingly, the intervening stepwise method can modify the falseness of the parallels, providing cases that enable one to see how the two members of the original problematic pair might move closer to each another, achieving a sort of topological congruence. This sounds mysterious but will become clearer with some examples.

First, take the paradoxically inconsistent parallel between the Turn the Trolley Case and the Transplant Case. In both, one person is killed to save five. This is the single, but highly salient, parallel. But then there are significant differences in the actions taken. In the Trolley Case, the trolley is merely rerouted from potentially killing five to actually killing one, whereas in the Transplant Case five organs of a healthy person are removed, killing this donor in order to save five people who need these transplants. And indeed these behaviors are seen as inconsistent—the actions specified in the Trolley Case are allowable, maybe even ethically obligatory, while the activities outlined in the Transplant Case are impermissible, reprehensible. This is the typical stalemate end point of these inconsistently parallel cases.

So next, let us devise and consider intermediate cases between these two extremes. This can be done, perhaps most simply, by changing certain quantitative facts. Suppose first, that the putative transplant donor is found unconscious, and, second, that parts of several of his organs, but not entire organs, will, if removed and transplanted suffice to save many people.

Suppose further that, although using *parts* of his organs will put him at *some* risk, it is not the case that the partial removal of his organs will surely kill him.

Let us imagine, as our starting condition, that the baseline risk is 50 percent for the donor, and twenty other people will be saved. Now vary the risk so that it is lower and the number of people so that it is higher. Do this several times until we have created the Low-ish Risk/Many Saved Transplant Case. Probably there will be some point at which most people queried, including those who had held the typical majority intuitions when presented only the two original extreme cases—Turn the Trolley and Transplant—find that action in the Low-ish Risk/Many Saved Transplant Case is now at least as acceptable as that in the Turn the Trolley Case. This will be especially likely if the respondents are made aware of the stepwise intervening cases insofar as these cases provide a context for reevaluating initial judgments.[44]

But some will object to this move, claiming that these changes have had the effect of destroying the strict parallel with the original Trolley and Transplant Cases. For instance, no longer is it certain that one will be killed in order to save many others. Responding to this, let's increase the mortality risk for the organ donor in the Many Saved Transplant Case in a series of steps. First to 60 percent, then 75 percent until it is back up to nearly 100 percent, just as it is for the donor in the original Transplant Case and for the person in the side track in the Turn the Trolley Case. Meanwhile, keeping the number equal for both the New Transplant Case and the New Trolley Case, let's increase this number substantially from the five originally specified. Particularly if aware of all the intervening steps, it is likely that many people will find some instantiation of these revised paired cases, Certain Death/Great Many Saved Transplant Case and One Dead/Great Many Saved Turn the Trolley Case, much more in line with one another than was true of the originals. This is likely to be so even when people plainly see that each of the members of the final pair is not dissimilar from its complement member in the very first original pair! In fact there are only quantitative differences. (Spelling this out: The Certain Death/Great Many Saved Transplant Case is just like the original Transplant Case, except that in the new quantitatively changed version one is killed so that a great number of others can live. Likewise, the One Dead/Great Many Saved Turn the Trolley Case is just like the original Turn the Trolley Case, except that one is killed in order to save some number of people greater than five.)

So what have we accomplished? The claim is that the sorites-like intervening case method utilizes intermediate steps to allow two original cases—seen as paradoxically far apart despite superficially parallel consistency—to be brought closer together, appreciated as more genuinely in line with one another. And that is indeed all this method promises. It argues neither for consequentialism (end/means justifications), deontological rule-based ethics, nor utilitarianism. In fact, it provides no evidence for or against any of the general theories of moral judgments proposed in regard to these thought experiment puzzles. Thus, it favors neither the doctrine of double effect nor its negation. It does not suggest that passive activities are more allowable than active (or vice versa), nor does it maintain that manipulating a threat is more sanctioned than manipulating a person and his/her rights. The method does not differentiate between agent- and victim-focused principles of harm, nor does it weigh in favor of condemning acts that are up close and personal more than more distant ones. In short, the method of intervening stepwise cases proposed is one employed simply to help resolve cases of paradoxically consistent yet inconsistent parallels.

So how well can the method of intervening steps fare with another, perhaps more difficult, pair of consistent/inconsistent paradoxically parallel cases—the standard Turn the Trolley Case versus the Fat Man on the Footbridge Case? Here increasing the numbers saved while still actively pushing the fat man may not suffice to make the intuitions about the two cases congruent. But there are other possibilities. Imagine, for example, stepwise intervening cases where simultaneously one's own active agency decreases and the fat man's *participant-hood* (rather than *bystander-ness*) in the threat event increases. Let's take Z, a person who is observing the scene from near the footbridge.

1. In Case 1, Z arranges for the fat man to slip and fall to his death.
2. In Case 2, noting the fat man's trolley company uniform, Z throws a switch activating the trolley company's catapult mechanism. Z does this, even though Z can see that the fat catapult inspector is either the only weight in place or is within the mechanism's perimeter. In either case, Z correctly reasons that the fat man will surely be catapulted to his death.
3. In Case 3, Z reports the situation to a nearby trolley official who Z has reason to believe will either (a) push the fat inspector to the tracks, or (b) throw the switch activating the manned-catapult mechanism. Again, this trolley company worker's death is close to certain.
4. And in Case 4, Z pushes a button alerting the trolley company's surveillance system to check out the potential accident. Z does this despite realizing that the company, hoping to lessen its liability, will almost surely choose to activate the catapult mechanism—indeed killing one versus five of its own workers.

Z might find this last situation acceptable, given the combination of (1) Z's low level of *direct* activity and his remove from the mortal event, (2) the fat man's trolley company association, and, finally, (3) the utilitarian results. If most people, like our man Z, find Case 4 acceptable, especially after considering the sequential steps leading to step four—steps that include Cases 2, 3 (3a; 3b), and 4, all of which show the fat man to be every bit as susceptible to the trolley company's threatening risks as are the people (especially workers) on the tracks—they may well conclude that the Turn the Trolley and Fat

Man on the Footbridge cases are not so inconsistent after all. This, despite the fact that the two cases were initially framed as very paradoxically parallel indeed; consistent yet very inconsistent.

Of course there is another consideration. It is conceivable that presenting people with the original pair of cases along with intermediate intervening-step cases may actually have the opposite effect. It may cause people to think more deliberately about the *principles* involved in their various moral judgments, no matter how the particulars are manipulated. So, for example, looking at the *principle(s)* involved in *actively* harming the fat man—a person who could be thought of as a mere bystander and therefore putatively a *more innocent victim*—subjects might insist that, regardless of the pull of the intermediate cases, their initial intuitions were correct: that the permissible Turn the Trolley Case and the prohibited Fat Man on the Footbridge Case are radically different on principle.

But against this objection Peter Unger (1996, p. 98) presents The Yard, a case in which he is able to demonstrate that all innocent victims are equally innocent. In The Yard, a runaway trolley can either (a) be left on its course by an onlooking agent such that it will kill six innocents, or (b) the agent can "flip a remote control toggle" activating a switch that will engage and enable another empty trolley to collide with the first one. Option (b) leads to derailing both trolleys, sending them careening "down a hill and across a road into someone's yard, where they will wreak fatal havoc on the yard's owner, asleep in his hammock." Should the six on the track die, or should the so-called *more* innocent bystander—the man in his hammock become the only casualty? (All quotations in this paragraph are from Unger, 1996, p. 98.)

Although Unger has convinced me of his point, he himself is not confident that most people would see the seven potential victims as equally innocent—that is, that the six on the track are no less innocent than the man in his yard.[45] All Unger would need to make his claim even stronger would be the addition of one intervening intermediate stepwise case. Let's construct such a case and call it The Two Yards. Suppose now that the runaway trolley had enough momentum to jump its own track and crash through all the other tracks and barriers to the yard adjacent to the tracks around 200 feet away. Suppose there were six innocents in that adjacent yard. Now confront the following choices: (a) do nothing, whereby the six from the adjacent yard will be killed, or (b) flip the toggle, which would clearly result in track switching such that the runaway trolley would collide with another trolley ending in one innocent being killed—a man in his hammock in *his* yard 400 feet away, not adjacent to the tracks but in a direction that would result from the vector formed by the speeding trolley and its collision with the second trolley. Should six in the adjacent yard die rather than the man in his hammock in the nonadjacent yard 400 feet away? Which of the yard dwellers is most innocent? In this example, with the employment of a sorites-type progression of cases—comparing 200 feet with 400 feet, and "directly adjacent" with "not directly adjacent," the bystander relationship takes on a different character for Unger than for Montmarquet and Hanna as discussed above. Unger's slogan might well be something like: We are all equally participants (or bystanders) in the set of events in the world, all equally involved; or at least we should be.[46]

* * *

Still, despite full deployment of the method of intervening stepwise cases, there may be another difficulty in seeing the original Turn the Trolley Case and the Fat Man on the Footbridge Cases as meaningfully congruent. After all, in every version of the latter there is an active, agent-initiated, direct, and very serious harm visited upon an innocent person; whereas in Unger's case of The Yard (and in my slightly altered version, The Two Yards) the agent's activity in causing the death of the man in his hammock is obscured by the chaotic sequence—so much so that his death seems almost random. Moreover, in the Fat Man on the Footbridge Cases the agent and (often) the victim are fully alert and aware of the choices and the consequences. Not so for either The Yard or The Two Yards Cases. On a natural reading of these cases, only an omniscient agent could anticipate that all of that toggling, switching, colliding, and careening would lead to a trolley traveling along a vector with sufficient momentum to kill a person, especially someone at the nonadjacent and more remote yard. Also the man in the hammock and the people in the yard have no idea what will befall them.[47]

Thus, it is instructive to see that even the use of the intervening case method—including presenting subjects with the stepwise options at once (within-subjects design style as Unger, 1996, pp. 88–92 also recommends)[48]—will not always suffice to bring a pair of parallel but paradoxically consistent/inconsistent thought experiment exemplars together. Sometimes such an impasse indicates that the question under study is incoherent or at least in need of reframing. This is the type of claim Parfit (1984, pp. 236–237) makes as he offers the sorites series discussed earlier in the chapter with respect to the Combined Spectrum Cases. He uses what amounts to the method of intervening stepwise cases to convincingly demonstrate that attempts to establish "personal identity" are wrongheaded attempts.

Other paradoxically consistent/inconsistent cases can be refractory to the stepwise intervening case method approach when they are incongruent in one or more of the following four matters taken up at length by Unger (1996, pp. 28, 33–36, 76–81): (1) personal connection between the agent and the subject harmed, (2) proximity of the agent to the action and to the subject harmed, (3) emotion, stirred by the action itself and/or concerning the subject harmed, and (4) salience. Salience is obviously related to the other three in a myriad of ways and can also involve some other contrasts—dramatic acts and interventions versus those that are inconspicuous, as well as hopeless situations versus those about which one believes some actions on one's part could be effective.[49]

***

It is clear that the method of intervening stepwise cases is applicable only to some thought experiment puzzles, and of these it can only resolve some of the paradoxes. And yet this method does allow a simpler, if less exciting, understanding of the radically divergent moral intuitions evoked in paradoxically consistent/inconsistent versions of seminal experimental philosophy and thought experiment cases.

SUMMARY AND CONCLUSION

In the introduction to this chapter, I made the claim that consistency is a major element in human understanding. We not only appreciate a great variety of consistent aspects in the world we explore, we also organize our investigations of the world using consistency as a criterion and a tool. This is one important way in which we contribute to the shape of the world we discover.

As such I asserted in the section titled "Common Goals, Different Paths" that four different human endeavors—empirical research, thought experiments, experimental philosophy, and psychoanalysis—use consistency in diverse ways to accomplish a common basic aim: to further knowledge and understanding. The advance of knowledge is measured in terms of consistency, too, as new results from one discipline cohere with findings from related areas, raising new questions and pointing the way for further investigations.

In the section called "The Uses of Consistency," I filled out the claims of the prior section by demonstrating different mechanisms in the use of consistency in each of the disciplines under study. I presented paradigm examples from various types of empirical research, thought experiments, experimental philosophy studies, and psychoanalytic investigations, showing that, in each of these four areas, the aim of increasing consistent, coherent, convergent general understanding is crucial. Indeed, to my mind this sort of understanding is their central goal.

The section on "The Abuses of Consistency" explored the darker side of our desire for consistency. I began with psychoanalytic patients, explaining how the quest for consistency contributes to neurosis formation and maintenance. I continued with psychoanalysts themselves, demonstrating that an analogous overvaluing of consistency can lead to a sense of complacency with initial interpretations. Next I presented a critique of the use of consistency in two seminal studies, one from the domain of empirical research and the other an experimental philosophy study. I made the claim that the use of between-subjects designs in both of these cases—employed to control for consistency—was problematic insofar as consistency might have been better considered integral to the matters under study. True, it is quite possible that substituting within-subject design experiments for the between-subject studies run might have resulted in less surprising and striking findings. But perhaps the gain in greater accuracy would have been worth that cost. Also, I raised the possibility of running these studies in both within-subject and between-subject versions. This would minimize the loss of striking findings from the between-subjects version as well as enable a comparison of the two types of design, with the within-subject version providing a natural context for measuring, assessing, and indexing (rather than controlling for) the pressure toward consistent response felt by the subjects.

Continuing with the abuses of consistency, I took up a problem evident both in some important experimental philosophy studies and in a great many thought experiments—a problem I term "the paradox of false parallels." Here parallels are set up in such a manner that two or more exemplar cases are devised precisely to seem consistent with each another. And yet something does not work. The seemingly consistent parallel cases are paradoxically inconsistent, falsely parallel—this, as is evidenced by the fact that in each case of these pairs, people (i.e., subjects) are led to radically different conclusions and moral judgments of the matters and issues at hand.

I addressed this problem in the final section of this work, "Solving the Paradox of False Parallels: The Method of Intervening Stepwise Cases." Here I introduced a technique for diagnosing and treating *some* cases of false parallels in important experimental philosophy studies and in well-known thought experiments. In a sorites-like stepwise manner, intervening cases are developed. These cases are still parallel to the originals, but intermediate between the two initial consistent but inconsistent extremes. These intervening cases sometimes are helpful in revealing that the question at hand needs reframing. More promising, the intervening stepwise case method offers to explain and resolve problematic divergent moral intuitions in a sparer fashion than heretofore. How? Simply by iteratively replacing apparent parallels that are actually inconsistent and faulty with those that are more deeply parallel and convergent. While this solution may be less dazzling, it is more elegant and should for this reason take its place as a welcome, if small, addition to our continued quest to accrue consistent knowledge.

***

A final note: In case it is not abundantly clear, just like every one of the researchers and thinkers I have criticized, I have traded on the flexible nature of consistency. Like them, in order to highlight the findings and conclusions presented in this chapter, I have chosen from among various versions of consistency, selecting in each case the version whose standards could best accommodate *my* main point. That my main point concerns the abuses of consistency is, of course, deeply and unavoidably paradoxical.

REFERENCES

Amanzio, M., Pollo, A., Maggi, G., & Benedetti, F. (2001). Response variability to analgesics. *Pain, 90*, 205–215.

Benedetti, F., Arduino, C., Costa, S., Vighetti, S., Tarenzi, L., Rainero, I., & Asteggiano, G. (2009). Loss of expectation-related mechanisms in Alzheimer's disease makes analgesic therapies less effective. *Pain, 121*, 133–144.

Braddon-Mitchell, D. (2003). Qualia and analytic conditionals. *Journal of Philosophy, 100*, 111–135.

Brakel, L.A.W. (2009). *Philosophy, psychoanalysis, and the a-rational mind*. Oxford: Oxford University Press.

Brakel, L.A.W. (2010). *Unconscious knowing and other essays in psycho-philosophical analysis*. Oxford: Oxford University Press.

Brenner, C. (1976). *Psychoanalytic technique and psychic conflict*. New York: International Universities Press.

Brenner, C. (1982). *The mind in conflict*. New York: International Universities Press.

Bruner, J., & Postman, L. (1949). On the perception of incongruity: A paradigm. *Journal of Personality, 18*, 206–223.

Cohen, M. (2005). *Wittgenstein's beetle and other classic thought experiments*. Oxford: Blackwell.

Cushman, F., Young, L., & Hauser, M. (2006). The role of conscious reasoning and intuition in moral judgment. *Psychological Science, 17*, 1082–1089.

Foot, P. (1967). The problem of abortion and the doctrine of the double effect. *The Oxford Review, 5*, 5–15.

Frankfurt, H. (1969/1988). Alternative possibilities and moral responsibility. In *The importance of what we care about* (pp. 1–10). Cambridge, UK: Cambridge University Press.

Freud, S. (1900/1953). *The interpretation of dreams*. In J. Strachey (Ed. & Trans.), *The standard edition of the complete psychological works of Sigmund Freud* (Vols. 4 and 5, pp. 1–627). London: Hogarth Press.

Freud, S. (1905/1953). Fragment of an analysis of a case of hysteria. In J. Strachey (Ed. & Trans.), *The standard edition of the complete psychological works of Sigmund Freud* (Vol. 7, pp. 1–122). London: Hogarth Press.

Freud, S. (1909a/1953). Analysis of a phobia in a five-year-old boy. In J. Strachey (Ed. & Trans.), *The standard edition of the complete psychological works of Sigmund Freud* (Vol. 10, pp. 1–149). London: Hogarth Press.

Freud, S. (1909b/1953). Notes upon a case of obsessional neurosis. In J. Strachey (Ed. & Trans.), *The standard edition of the complete psychological works of Sigmund Freud* (Vol. 10, pp. 151–318). London: Hogarth Press.

Freud, S. (1912/1953). The dynamics of transference. In J. Strachey (Ed. & Trans.), *The standard edition of the complete psychological works of Sigmund Freud* (Vol. 12, pp. 97–108). London: Hogarth Press.

Freud, S. (1915a/1953). Observations on transference-love. In J. Strachey (Ed. & Trans.), *The standard edition of the complete psychological works of Sigmund Freud* (Vol. 12, pp. 157–171). London: Hogarth Press.

Freud, S. (1915b/1953). The unconscious. In J. Strachey (Ed. & Trans.), *The standard edition of the complete psychological works of Sigmund Freud* (Vol. 14, pp. 159–215). London: Hogarth Press.

Freud, S. (1923/1953). The ego and the id. In J. Strachey (Ed. & Trans.), *The standard edition of the complete psychological works of Sigmund Freud* (Vol. 19, pp. 1–66). London: Hogarth Press.

Freud, S. (1926 [1925]/1953). *Inhibitions, symptoms and anxiety*. In J. Strachey (Ed. & Trans.), *The standard edition of the complete psychological works of Sigmund Freud* (Vol. 20, pp. 75–174). London: Hogarth Press.

Freud, S. (1940 [1938]/1953). An outline of psychoanalysis. In J. Strachey (Ed. & Trans.), *The standard edition of the complete psychological works of Sigmund Freud* (Vol. 23, pp. 139–207). London: Hogarth Press.

Gettier, E. (1963). Is justified true belief knowledge? *Analysis, 23*, 121–123.

Gray, J. W. (2010-2013). *The Comprehensible Philosophy Dictionary*. Ethical Realism. Accessed July 22, 2011. http://www.ethicalrealism.wordpress.com/philosophy-dictionary-glossary/.

Greene, J. (2003). From neural "is" to moral "ought": What are the moral implications of neuroscientific moral psychology? *Nature Reviews, Neuroscience, 4*, 847–850.

Greene, J., & Haidt, J. (2002). How and where does moral judgment work? *Trends Cognitive Science, 6*, 517–523.

Greene, J., Sommerville, R., Nystrom, L., Darley, J., & Cohen, J. (2001). An fMRI investigation of emotional engagement in moral judgment. *Science, 293*, 2105–2108.

Hanna, R. (1991). Morality *de re*: Reflections on the trolley problem. In J. Fisher (Ed.), *Ethics: Problems and principles* (pp. 318–336). Fort Worth, TX: Harcourt Brace Jovanovich.

Harris, J. (1975). The survival lottery. *Philosophy, 50*, 81–87.

Hauser, M., Cushman, F., Young, L., Jin, R., & Mikhail, J. (2007). A dissociation between moral judgments and justifications. *Mind and Language, 22*, 1–21.

Kamm, F. (1989). Harming some to save others. *Philosophical Studies, 57*, 227–260.

Knobe, J. (2003). Intentional action and side effects in ordinary language. *Analysis, 63*, 190–193.

Knobe, J., and Doris, J. (2010). Responsibility. In J. Doris (Ed.), *The handbook of moral psychology* (pp. 321–354). Oxford: Oxford University Press.

Kuhn, T. (1964/1977). A function for thought experiments. In *The essential tension* (pp. 240–265). Chicago: University of Chicago Press.

Medin, D., Goldstone, R., & Gentner, D. (1990). Similarity involving attributes and relations: Judgments of similarity and difference are not inverses. *Psychological Science, 1*, 64–69.

Mesquita, B., Barrett, L., & Smith, E. (Eds.). (2010). *The mind in context*. New York: Guilford Press.

Mikhail, J. (2007). Universal moral grammar: Theory, evidence and the future. *Trends in Cognitive Sciences, 11*, 143–152.

Moerman, D. (2002). Explanatory mechanisms for placebo effects: Cultural influences and the meaning response. In H. Guess, A. Kleinman, J. Kusek, & L. Engel (Eds.), *The science of the placebo: Toward an interdisciplinary research agenda* (pp.77–107). London: BMJ Books.

Moerman, D., & Wayne J. (2002). Deconstructing the placebo effect and finding the meaning response. *Annals of Internal Medicine, 136*, 471–476.

Montmarquet, J. (1982). On doing good: The right and the wrong way. *Journal of Philosophy, 79*, 439–455.

Nagel, T. (1974). What is it like to be a bat? *Philosophical Review, 83*, 435–450.

Nagera, H. (1966). *Early childhood disturbances, the infantile neurosis, and the adult disturbances: Problems of a developmental psychoanalytic psychology*. Monograph Series of the Psychoanalytic Study of the Child, No. 2. New York: International Universities Press.

Parfit, D. (1984). *Reasons and persons*. Oxford: Oxford University Press.

Petrinovich, L., O'Neill, P., & Jorgensen, M. (1993). An empirical study of moral intuitions: Toward an evolutionary ethics. *Journal of Personality and Social Psychology, 64*, 467–478.

Quine, W. V. (1966). *The ways of paradox and other essays*. Cambridge, MA: Harvard University Press.

Rachels, J. (1975). Active and passive euthanasia. *New England Journal of Medicine, 292*, 78–80.

Royzman, E., & Baron, J. (2002). The preference for indirect harm. *Social Justice Research, 15*, 165–183.

Schlesinger, H. (1995). Interpretation and change. *Journal of the American Psychoanalytic Association, 43*, 663–688.

Sorensen, R. (1992). *Thought experiments*. Oxford: Oxford University Press.

Spranca, M., Minsk, E., & Baron, J. (1991). Omission and commission in judgment and choice. *Journal of Experimental Social Psychology, 27*, 76–105.

Stewart-Williams, S., & Podd, J. (2004). The placebo effect: Dissolving the expectancy versus conditioning debate. *Psychological Bulletin, 130*, 324–340.

Tarski, A. (1946). *Introduction to logic and to the methodologies of deductive sciences*. New York: Dover Publications.

Thomson, J. (1971). A defense of abortion. *Philosophy and Public Affairs, 1*, 47–66.

Thomson, J. (1976). Killing, letting die, and the trolley problem. *The Monist, 59*, 204–217.

Thomson, J. (1985). The trolley problem. *Yale Law Journal, 94*, 1395–1415.

Tooley, M. (1974/1980). An irrelevant consideration: Killing versus letting die. In B. Steinbock (Ed.), *Killing and letting die* (pp. 56–62). Englewood Cliffs, NJ: Prentice-Hall.

Unger, P. (1996). *Living high and letting die: Our illusion of innocence*. Oxford: Oxford University Press.

Wikipedia. (2011). Consistency. Accessed July 22, 2011. http://www.en.wikipedia.org/wiki/Consistency

Zangwill, N. (2011). Non-cognitivism and consistency. *Zeitschrift fur Philosophisce Forschung, 65*, 465-484.

Part V

Conclusion

5 Summary and Conclusions

INTRODUCTION TO THIS FINAL CHAPTER

Any typical approach to concluding this book is complicated. This is indeed my own fault and owes to the fact that in many of this book's pages I have suggested, recommended, and then practiced various intellectual stances, all of which weigh against exciting conclusions. Therefore, and precisely to the extent that I have been successful in making this case, I run the risk of being self-contradictory here as I proclaim the importance of my own results and findings in this summary and conclusions chapter. But reassuring myself with the idea that contradictions can be instructive, and (as was discussed in Chapter Four) often more so than false consistencies, I will next present my view of the advantages of this volume.

METHOD, TECHNIQUES, AND TOOL

In this book I advocate a method that is thoroughly interdisciplinary in approaching the disciplines devoted to the study of the mind. From within the mainstream of psychoanalysis, or the philosophy of mind, or the philosophy of action, or experimental philosophy, or any particular branch of empirical psychological research, the currents can be so swift and so unidirectional, with the pressing issues so specific and specialized, that communications become restricted to other mainstreamers only. In more extreme circumstances, communications (and particularly the understandings thereof) may be limited to only those in the same boat. This has the unhappy consequence that other equally important problems go by the wayside, totally missed. This book, then, has among its aims, to provide a corrective to this mainstream tendency.

At the same time, I hope that it is understood tacitly, if not always stated explicitly throughout these pages, that the techniques of each discipline involved in the study of mind have much to offer in regard to the content of the others. Thus, the concision of philosophical definition and argumentation, the rigor of empirical experimentation, the inventiveness of thought experiments, and the breadth of psychoanalytic understanding can—perhaps must—operate together. They must respect and utilize (rather than ignore or disparage) the concepts and conventions of the other cognate disciplines in order to gain a better appreciation of the mental and the mind.

Alongside this general interdisciplinary approach, which can perhaps be loosely regarded as a method, this volume is just as much the product of a more specific interdisciplinary tool, a sort of starting point I have used to initiate the investigations embarked upon here. I have given several names to this tool—which operates as a point of departure: epistemological queasiness, epistemological unease, epistemological disorientation, epistemological discomfort, and epistemological distress—but in any case the function is the same. Namely, to provide a signal that something incoherent, or paradoxically too consistent, or not quite right, or way too striking and therefore too good to be true lurks behind some experimental result, patient report, or philosophical argument and conclusion. This sense or signal is familiar to mainstream contributors in each of the fields of mental studies considered in this book. It is the sense that:

1. leads psychoanalysts to make trial interpretations and/or to ask questions of their patients;
2. causes researchers to run replication or contrastive studies;
3. motivates various philosophical articles contesting the conclusions and arguments of other philosophers; and
4. initiates many thought experiments.

With respect to the foundational matters challenged in each of the chapters of this volume, it is the use of this tool—registering the signal of epistemological disorder—that led directly to the application of the interdisciplinary method, questioning conventions and studying alternatives. I turn now to summarize the high points of these explorations in each of the chapters.

SUMMARY OF PART TWO/CHAPTER TWO: BIOLOGICAL PSYCHOLOGY

Part Two consists only of Chapter Two, which is titled "Extinction Phenomena: A Biologic Perspective on How and Why Psychoanalysis Works." It begins by recognizing a new trend. Namely, that psychoanalysts trying to modernize our field while maximizing opportunity for increasing the population of patients, reasoned that some of the classic technical aspects of psychoanalysis could be jettisoned. The frequency of psychoanalytic appointments and the patient reclining on a couch with the analyst out of sight were the two matters many psychoanalysts thought most dispensable. Sessions over the phone and particularly sessions using Skype software became widely popular, in some cases replacing the standard consulting room sessions. Busy patients overseas could now communicate with their analysts, and new markets on every continent became available to psychoanalysts. And yet something seemed unsound, at least to some analysts, I among them. Beginning with my epistemological unease, I investigated the matter, and, surprising to me no less than to my colleagues, I arrived at the following conclusion: psychoanalysis works because of its great biological effectiveness with respect to reversing classically conditioned aversive symptoms. Success in psychoanalytic treatment—that intrinsically, essentially, paradigmatically *psychological* procedure—is predicated on a basic biological process (and a biological process orthogonal to the necessary neuroscience brain/mind correlational studies important and in vogue).

The argument proceeded in several steps. First, I needed to establish that the types of psychopathological symptoms seen in nearly all psychoanalytic patients could (and likely do) involve complicated aversive conditioning. Next, I amassed recent biological-psychology research that demonstrates that aversively conditioned responses could never be entirely extinguished, but that extinction of such symptoms could be approximated by many different contexts of safe-here and safe-now extinction trials. Then in the next step, I showed that classical psychoanalysis affords a unique advantage in producing the many and diverse contexts needed to approximate extinction, this through the development of multiple, intensely felt transference experiences. In the final stage of the argument, I provided evidence that there are requirements for these variegated intense transferences to develop—requirements that Skype inhibits, while frequent sessions of imaginative relivings on an analytic couch promote.

PART THREE/CHAPTER THREE: PSYCHOLOGICAL BIOLOGY

This part of the book also consists of a single chapter, Chapter Three, "The Ontology of Psychology." This, the central chapter, and the one for which the volume is named, is the most ambitious. Only many bouts of acute epistemological disorientation along with a long background of chronic epistemological queasiness would induce someone, even an outsider/insider such as I am, to even contemplate, much less engage in, an exploration of the mind/body problem. But with psychiatry becoming more biological, psychoanalysis less theoretical, and the philosophy of mind more technical, I gave in to this investigatory compulsion. What this chapter offers, I hope, is, first, an evenhanded view of this age-old problem, and then a small original contribution to the solution.

I say evenhanded as I had taken no previous position concerning the ever-vexing mind/body problem. First, I reviewed what I considered the most interesting (and in my view the best arguments) for dualism. I examined the Zombie Conceivability Argument and various versions of the Knowledge Argument. I then presented some problems with each of them. From there

I admitted my own greater comfort with physicalism and explored in some detail and depth several important nonreductive physicalist views. Advantages and disadvantages of each point of view were taken up; in the process, emergentism and the intertwined problems of mental causation, downward causation, and the Causal Exclusion Argument were discussed, followed by the Generalization Argument and other arguments directed against causal closure/exclusion. Next I reviewed reductive physicalism. Here I put much emphasis on the importance of multiple realization, both as a philosophical view profoundly wounding to type physicalism, and perhaps even more importantly, as a biologically sophisticated view—compatible with the redundancy, plasticity, and particularly the degeneracy so advantageous in the brain and other biological structures—thereby allowing a new token physicalism.

Derived from this new view of token physicalism, I offered what I propose as a modest contribution to the mind/body problem solution. The very opposite of an elegant name, I term it Diachronic Conjunctive Token Physicalism (or DiCoToP).[1] And although its full name sounds more like a disease than any kind of solution, it essentially advances the following idea: Each instance of what we would consider a single mental event/state/property—take, for example, my emotional thought "I love my dog"—is variously realized by different neuronal assemblies as it occurs in my brain at different times. This is the case although it is a singular thought and one that lasts over time. Looked at synchronically, at any particular time (t_1), my mental state in thinking "I love my dog" is identical with its particular neuronal network[2] realizer (i.e., *this specific* assembly of neurons is ontologically constitutive of my mental state). Over time—that is, diachronically ($t_1 \rightarrow t_2 \rightarrow t_n$)—there is no one neuronal group to do the constituting/realizing work for *all the instances* of my singular[3] mental state characterized each time and over time as my emotional thought, "I love my dog." Thus, only the conjunctive group of neuronal assemblies—the total amalgam—can fully constitute and thereby specify the identity of this one mental state, LAWB's emotional thought, "I love my dog." Moreover, and of at least equal importance, any mental event/state/property like my emotional thought about my dog—e.g., X's desire to eat jelly beans or Y's fear of dogs—itself now has real ontological standing (and can be considered causally effective). This, even as its physical underpinnings are shifting, with no neural assembly realizer alone ontologically constitutive, and no neural assembly realizer excluded from the conjunctive amalgam.

I will make one more point about the importance of the diachronic as well as the synchronic understanding of the mental that I posit. My version of token physicalism, DiCoToP, allows an initially unintended, but totally welcomed additional result. The account in Chapter Three fits remarkably well with the findings of Chapter Two! If, indeed, as I have argued, any given psychological event/state/property—let's say a phobic fear state—must consist *diachronically* of many different instantiations of neuronal arrangements,[4] no wonder the multiple contexts of deconditioning (described in Chapter Two) will be necessary to even begin to approximate extinction.

Clearly, even were this modest solution found helpful, much about the mind/body problem must properly be classified as unresolved. I end this chapter pointing out that, while ontological questions may find certain answers, and while most may be convinced that physical brain processes indeed cause all that we identify as mental, the *how* of this process—how our consciousness, our qualia, our sense of first-person agency, our beliefs, desires, and contents thereof *derive* from our neuronal collections and other neuroanatomical, neurophysiologic, and neurochemical structures and processes—this remains a challenging puzzle.

PART FOUR/CHAPTER FOUR: USES AND ABUSES OF CONSISTENCY

This part consists also of a single chapter, "The Uses and Abuses of Consistency in Thought Experiments, Empirical Research, Experimental Philosophy, and Psychoanalysis." It starts innocently enough by showing that the aims of the four disciplines under discussion are similar. All four disciplines seek consistency in their goal of increasing knowledge, albeit with each discipline's goal taking different forms. But this chapter is actually *the* troublemaking chapter in a volume of full of gadfly-like troublemakers. Not only do the works scrutinized use the notion of consistency in a flexible and fluid manner without certain constraints, thereby subject to my critical comments; this is no less true of my own work, in the current volume generally and the fourth chapter in particular. Here I, too, bend consistency to highlight my views, which, of course, happen to be the critiques at hand. Further, particularly insofar as I advocate more modest, if less exciting, findings, proposing that it is often the case that the less striking results represent reality more accurately, I cannot then turn around and present my own positive contributions in a bright spotlight.

That said, there are a number of things of interest to recommend this chapter. First, I have presented both the commonalities and the differences among the four disciplines. I have done this to enable a better appreciation of how they each strive to participate in the larger framework of the study of the mind and the understanding the mental realm. Second, I have pointed to consistency-related problems, not only in specific seminal experiments but also in the very fundamentals of a basic experimental design—the between-subjects design type. While I hope this is refreshing and evocative, it has to be at least provocative.

Finally, this chapter also contains a modest original contribution. It can be presented in two parts: First, I recognized and diagnosed a problem particularly prevalent in certain experimental philosophy and thought experiment cases—those that play on inconsistently consistent parallel constructions. I call the problem the paradox of the false parallel. Second, I proposed a treatment—the method of intervening stepwise cases. This is a method, related to within-subjects designs, in which contexts are rendered more natural, and our human desire for consistency is respected (rather than controlled for and removed from experimental consideration), as less problematic middle-ground parallels are devised. Through the development of such stepwise intervening cases, findings are sometimes rendered less exciting but often more realistic.

CONCLUSIONS

1. Foundations in the study of mind can and should be challenged.
2. An interdisciplinary approach both allows for the discovery of problems not appreciated within a single domain and promotes even-handed accounts and solutions.
3. Epistemological queasiness is a feeling and intuition experienced by researchers, practitioners, and theorists in all disciplines. It can signal that a challenge to received knowledge or common assumptions is appropriate.
4. Modest, less striking findings can result, but these can be more realistic. And reality can be exciting enough—actually quite exciting.

Notes

NOTES TO CHAPTER 1

1. The assumptions of psychoanalysis as a theory and as a method are taken up in great detail in Brakel (2009, chap. 1).
2. Deconditioning trials are those trials in which the noxious stimulus is rendered "safe here" and "safe now."
3. I am assuming here that time itself has ontologic, not merely epistemologic, standing. This topic is beyond the scope of this volume, but it is something I hope to explore in the future.
4. This follows from the work of Jaegwon Kim (particularly 1993, 1998, 2005, 2010) on causal exclusion, a topic that will be discussed at length in Chapter Three.

NOTES TO CHAPTER 2

1. As is true for all outcome research in psychoanalysis, the efficacy of analyses conducted by Skype would not be an easy matter to study. Perhaps, however, an initial study could be as follows: neutral analysts, blind to the type of analysis received by each patient, could evaluate an equal number of both sorts of patients at various intervals after their treatments. Self-reports from patients and the treating analysts would also be of use. But this question arises: Would the research analysts conduct at least some of their interviews using Skype technology?
2. Although a bit awkward, I suppose an analytic patient could recline on a couch during a Skype analytic session.
3. This is not to say that therapies aimed at this higher level are ineffective. In fact, classical psychoanalysis is, in my view, uniquely effective precisely because it alone, unlike the other treatments, operates on *both* higher-level human autobiographical psychological learning and on the more basic biological level I intend to outline.
4. While there is no contesting conditioning in creatures as simple as aplysia, there is some debate as to whether or not single celled organisms can undergo true conditioning. Those who doubt conditioning in one-celled organisms hold the view that a nervous system, however primitive, is necessary for associative learning. Recent work by Fernando, Liekens, Bingle, Beck, Lenser, Stekel, and Rowe (2009) however, suggests that under certain circumstances (at least in principle) even single celled organisms can undergo associative learning, i.e., true conditioning.

5. This quote is from a personal e-mail communication on January 5, 2011.
6. In naturalistic cases like this, the boundary between context and conditioned stimulus proper is not nearly as clear as it is in laboratory experiments.
7. This account raises the possibility that some sort of aversive conditioning causes, or at least causally contributes to, the development of many (if not most) phobic symptoms.
8. These generalizations often demonstrate a particular type of similarity—similarity based on primary process (emotional and a-rational) categories rather than secondary process (rational) categories. For more on primary process a-rational categories, see Brakel (2009, esp. pp. 7–8; and 2010, esp. pp. 59–62).
9. Further, as almost goes without saying, when human beliefs, desires, fantasies, and behaviors are at issue, there are almost always other more complex functions/structures (such as those involved with language, conscious and unconscious autobiographical memories, and deliberate agential goals) that operate in addition to underlying conditioning mechanisms. (See, for example, Rangel, Camerer, and Montague, 2008, for a review article concerning the interplay of three levels—that which has been conditioned, the habitual level, and the level of goal-directed and autobiographically relevant behavior.) Clearly for the heuristic purposes of this chapter, the role of conditioning has been highlighted, but the multilevel nature of psychopathology not denied. In fact, my own view is that there is always an interaction causally and constitutively in terms of the structure, function, and content in human desires, beliefs, fantasies, and behavior (see Brakel, 2009, particularly chaps. 6, 7, and 8). In this regard it is interesting to note that even Rangel, Camerer, and Montague (2008, p. 554) do place singular emphasis on the conditioning level for some psychological maladies: ". . . [R]einforcement-learning models predict the existence of valuation malfunctions, in which a drug, a disease or a *developmental event* [Brakel's emphasis] perturbs the brain's capacity to assign appropriate value to behavioural acts or mental states."
10. See Bouton (1988, 1993, 2004); Bouton and Swartzentruber (1991); Bouton, Westbrook, Corcoran, and Maren (2006); Chang, Knapska, Orsini, Rabinak, Zimmerman, and Maren (2009); Ji and Maren (2007); Quirk (2002).
11. For a review article, see Hermans, Craske, Mineka, and Lovibond (2006). For reports on laboratory-induced human fear conditioning and extinction, see Vansteenwegen, Hermans, Vervliet, Francken, Beckers, Baeyens, and Eelen (2005); Vervliet, Vansteenwegen, Baeyens, Hermans, and Eelen (2005). For extinction of fears in the clinic, see Mineka, Mystkowski, Hladek, and Rodriguez (1999); Mystkowski, Craske, and Echiverri (2002); Mystkowski and Mineka (2007).
12. To use the terminology of the conditioning researchers, only A-B-B contexts preserve extinction, whereas contexts A-B-A and A-B-C (where C is any new context) do not. Moreover in A-A-B contexts, where the fear conditioning and extinction occur in the same context A, but the testing is in any different context, represented here by B, extinction is again lost in favor of renewal effects.
13. A particularly potent variant of reinstatement is described in Hermans et al. (2006, p. 363) in which trials of the US without the CS are presented in the same area (Context A) in which the original conditioning took place. Here, when the CS is later presented again in this same Context A area, the CR is reestablished with extreme ease and rapidity. This clearly indicates that conditioning of Context A itself—where Context A stands for the entire context of the original conditioning event—has taken place.
14. He refers here to Bouton, Woods, and Pinero (2004) and to unpublished studies of Woods and Bouton. I introduce the rather complicated matter of this

procedure only because it will prove relevant in the next section, where the efficacy of psychoanalytic techniques toward achieving extinction is taken up.

15. Thinking along similar lines, given that many of the various physical characteristics of the conditioned stimulus (CS) can provide different contexts, Mystkowski, Craske, and Echiverri (2002, p. 414) proposed that ". . . exposure with as many different alterations of the phobic stimulus as possible would be beneficial when the stimulus is confronted in a new situation." For people with spider phobia, for instance, extinction with different types of spiders—those with hairy long legs, those with thick bodies, those small and large—would most likely include whatever ". . . pertinent features that a person has stored in their fear memory structure" (p. 414).

    Note that along with the multiple contexts suggested here, these authors touch upon an interesting point recognized by psychoanalysts. Namely, a spider phobia might well be a conscious representation of any one of a number of different unconscious conflicts. Hence the unconscious representations of spiders may vary considerably among a group of people with spider phobia. (This is currently being explored in a study underway at the University of Michigan. See Finn, Shevrin, Brakel, and Snodgrass, 2013.)

16. These difficulties with extinction have much to do with the limitations of cognitive-behavioral therapies (CBTs), in which there are indeed (1) multiple contexts and (2) benign therapists. Psychoanalytic treatment is different from CBT (and other treatments) in both respects. First, as will become clearer in the text of the chapter, psychoanalysis allows (perhaps even promotes) many contexts in the form of unconsciously meditated transferences. Transferences (which are explained more fully in the section on "Classical Psychoanalytic Technique and Extinction") are psychological attitudes (both cognitive and conative) that are not only deeply held but of long duration, providing the type of multiple contexts that do seem more successful in approximating longer-term extinction. Second, whatever variegated transferences arise, they are always within the overarching context of a good therapeutic alliance, a working relationship in which the patient and analyst are striving together toward the patient's best interests. (As a patient of mine recently put it: "You are always on *my* side, where the 'my' means my healthiest self.") This particular overarching positive transference can also be seen as providing a baseline "safe-here" type of context to whatever else goes on in the treatment.
17. Transference is an important concept, central to psychoanalysis. For more on the concept of transference within this volume, see Chapter Four, pp. 107–108, including notes 13 and 14; and pp. 118–119, including notes 25 and 26.
18. The participants who imagined three repetitions of eating some particular food did not differ significantly from the control participants, suggesting that the appetitive sensitization did not occur.
19. Renewal is the most common type of reappearance of aversively conditioned symptoms. In any psychoanalysis, although the great preponderance of transference experiences (extinction trials) are CS-no US, there are always a few intermittent CS-US. (This will be very clear in the case material that follows in the text.) This is important because, according to Bouton et al. (2006, p. 353), in cases subject to renewal, very few aversive conditioning trials in the midst of many extinction trials actually facilitate a more robust extinction (see this volume, p. 26).
20. Briefly, this work was done in several ways. First, experiencing me in a father transference, Mr. H worried that his accomplishments would result in my failures. He observed instead that his achievements were co-occurrent with some important publications of mine. Relatedly, Mr. H gradually became aware

that his children's successes were not inversely correlated with, nor did they negate or challenge, his own achievements. He had worried about that, and had become concerned that he was either undermining his own progress or that of his children, making him a not-successful father. By confirming on several occasions that his own achievements, and those of his children and analyst, could indeed all vary independently, another aspect of the CS-US underwent a set of extinction trials (CS-no US), all according to these various (but specific) transference situations.

In general, much work was done throughout the analysis on Mr. H's lifelong avoidance of success. We could see the avoidance in almost every developmental phase, with many such situations re-experienced in transference versions. All to the good, those that could be re-experienced in that way in effect constituted specific context extinction trials.

21. Interestingly, without thinking explicitly in this way at all, he observed the "safe-here" multiple contexts aspect of extinction in that he only very slowly allowed first different locations for lovemaking and then different sexual positions.
22. During Mr. H's several years of psychoanalysis at my office in my house, he had the opportunity to see me interact briefly and infrequently with (1) other male patients, (2) my husband, (3) a handful of different workmen, and (4) a male neighbor.
23. This quotation is from Moore and Fine's (1990, p. 210) *Psychoanalytic Terms and Concepts*. I use these words because they indeed pertain to Mr. H, but also because the passage appears in an entry in Moore and Fine's work explaining the general need for "working through," which in turn is defined as a "a crucial part of the analytic process" involving multiple interpretations of the same problem again and again. This quotation highlights the prototypical nature of Mr. H's psychopathology.
24. Subliminal presentations of a stimulus may have a related effect, because people, unaware of the origin of subliminal stimuli, can experience them as coming from any one of a number of sources. Consider the following situation potentially available with subliminal exposure treatments designed for people with phobias: It is possible that early subliminal trials could be assimilated to the patient's internal representation of the feared phobic object, whereas later trials could be seen as several neutral benign versions of the object. In this way subliminal exposures, too, might facilitate multiple extinctions. Although this is speculative, some new data support this view (see Snodgrass, Shevrin, Brakel, and Kushwaha, 2013).
25. Note that this chapter is not a polemic for biological versus psychological aspects of treatment. Rather, it describes the discovery of the biological within the very psychological processes that are integral (and perhaps now shown to be essential) parts of classical psychoanalytic technique.

NOTES TO CHAPTER 3

1. Galen Strawson (1994, p. 259) answers the question about psychological distinction in the affirmative: ". . . all of these mental states and occurrences [thoughts, sensations, emotions, beliefs, and desires] can exist without any action or behavior, and without any disposition to action or behavior."
2. *Representational contents* are often called *contents* by philosophers and *representations* by psychologists. In this volume, I consider the three terms—*representations*, *contents*, and *representational contents*—synonymous and use them interchangeably.

3. Note that the question of whether these representations necessitate something external and extant as that which is represented is an important one, but beyond the scope of this chapter.
4. This is a deeply contested view, as will become clear later in this chapter.
5. This is not to deny that intentions and motivations can be very complicated, especially when one considers conflictual and unconscious aspects of motivations and intentions.
6. The terms *physicalism* and *materialism* are essentially synonymous and will be used interchangeably in this chapter.
7. Dualists, even property dualists, must contend with the problem of causal efficacy. If mental properties can only be effects of physical properties, and can themselves cause neither physical nor further mental properties, the mental properties are then mere epiphenomena. If on the other hand, mental properties can be effective causes of mental and physical effects, the characterization problem becomes critical—just what *is* the nature of these non-material, causally active properties? The problem of causal efficacy and the threat of epiphenomenalism will be taken up later in this chapter with respect to non-reductive materialist positions.
8. It may be difficult to imagine that brains identical with human brains, molecule-for-molecule, would be without consciousness—the emergence of conscious awareness from complex neuronal organizations does not seem optional—but for now let us accept Chalmers's zombies as conceivable.
9. Token materialism is a view that I find quite agreeable, as I shall elaborate at length toward the end of this chapter. Hill is a proponent of type materialism. Much more will be said about the pros and cons of both type and token materialism later in this chapter.
10. Indexicals are expressions whose reference changes with changing contexts. This is made much clearer with examples. When I say "I," I am referring to a different person than when you say "I." *Now* changes as time passes, as does *then*, and so do the words *today*, *yesterday*, and *tomorrow*. *Here*, *there*, *this*, and *that* are other examples of indexicals.
11. The brackets within this quotation are mine, not Chalmers's.
12. Full disclosure: I count myself as a physicalist of some stripe, as will be developed throughout this chapter.
13. There is not complete agreement on these categories of impossibility. Nagel (1998, p. 343, footnote 7), for instance, suggests that Levine is too quick to describe certain impossibilities as epistemological *rather* than metaphysical. Thus, for Nagel, at least in some cases—perhaps most importantly in the mind/body problem—the epistemological gap, that is, the impossibility of explanation of the mental in terms of the physical, means there is a metaphysical gap, too. But I must add one final comment on this point. Whereas there does seem to be a genuine disagreement between Nagel and Levine, it should be kept in mind that Levine here is taking up epistemological *possibility* for zombies while acknowledging their metaphysical impossibility; he is not suggesting epistemological *rather* than metaphysical impossibility.
14. Hill's (1997, p. 77) preferred example is "a member of H that is capable of producing intuitions to the effect that heat is separable from molecular motion."
15. In Chalmers's defense, this is not the major thrust of Leuenberger's (2008) notion of blockers at all. Leuenberger does, however, briefly allude to the idea of physical blockers in two footnotes (p. 152, footnote 13; pp. 157–158, footnote 19).
16. Physical blockers—resulting in the absence of normal states of qualitative consciousness arising in (and from) the neural organization of the human

brain—do exist. They range from the normal neuroanatomical and neurochemical occurrence seen in the induction and maintenance of stages of dreamless sleep to the therapeutic administration of anesthetic drugs to the multiple biological causes of pathological states of minimal responsiveness, vegetative state, and coma.

17. Before moving away from dualism and the important Zombie/Conceivability Argument, there is an issue I cannot resist discussing, although admittedly it is not in the form of an argument, and in fact I am not at all certain of its usefulness. This concerns combining the Brain-in-a-Vat Case with the Zombie Case. In its usual form, the Brain-in-a-Vat Case looks something like this: Person X's brain is removed intact and placed in a vat. Many millions of neural/chemical connections are made (by technicians as clever as they are evil) in such a way that X's brain is stimulated to produce qualitative conscious experiences of the external world identical to those he has experienced of the actual external world. (These include X's experience of his own body.) These evil techs are so good that X cannot distinguish his vat experiences of the world from the ordinary world experiences he has had as an embodied person. We philosophical observers are horrified, but amazed at the complex deception and its success. Now take Zombie X and remove his brain, a brain that is physically identical to X's brain. When Zombie X's brain is disconnected and placed in a vat, no connections creating brain stimulations identical to those producing qualitative conscious awareness of the external world are necessary. Zombie X experiences nothing different and nothing unusual because Zombie X in both cases *experiences* nothing. We philosophical observers are still horrified, but this time incredulous (rather than amazed) that no deception was necessary. If this really were to be our reaction, would it not add something of weight to the view that we humans (even philosophical types) really cannot conceive of zombies?
18. It is for this reason I feel happiest as a physicalist of some sort; the precise nature of my physicalism will unfold as the chapter develops.
19. Nonreductive physicalists endorse material monism—there is nothing that *is* not physical; no concrete particulars. However, they allow real nonphysical mental entities (i.e., events, states, properties) and, therefore, should be obliged to specify both how these mental entities are "mental" and how these mental entities are instantiated in a physical world.
20. Weak supervenience, on the other hand, tolerates some autonomy of what supervenes from the supervening base (see Kim, 1993, p. 75). But to the extent that this is the case, weak psychophysical supervenience equivocates on a very hard problem—the question of independent mental causation. (This problem is central and will be explored in both depth and detail in the text to follow.)
21. According to Kim (1993, p. 69), global or world supervenience is "nothing but strong supervenience." The concept of global supervenience, which Kim attributes to Lewis (1983), is described by Kim (1993, p. 69) as follows: ". . . psychophysical supervenience has been explained by saying that worlds that are physically indiscernible are psychologically indiscernible (in fact, such worlds are one and the same)." This necessitates that there can be no change in the psychological world without change(s) in the physical world.
22. In fact there is a version of physical realization—namely, multiple realization—wherein the same type of mental state could in principle be instantiated in different physical structures (silicon, carbon-based, etc.)—which helped nonreductive physicalists argue that the reduction of any particular *type* of mental property to any single *type* of physical property (type-type reduction) would be impossible. (There will be much more discussion of this later in this chapter. Also see Kim, 1993, pp. 341–342.)

23. Those in this section are just a sample. Additional types will be discussed in later sections of this chapter.
24. Strawson's nonreductive token identity view is appealing. However, there are unresolved problems in his nonreductive physicalist solution. If we allow with Strawson that experiential properties are physically fundamental, it is true that the important and vexing question of *how* these mental properties arise from nonmental ones is cleverly blocked. However, there is the problematic issue of an expanding ontology as he posits additional fundamental physical elements. Also we are left with the following dilemma: Just what is the relation of experiential properties to other better understood fundamental physical properties?
25. The exclamation point is bracketed by Strawson.
26. As is will become obvious in the next chapter, particularly in sections on the positive functions of thought experiments, I am quite sympathetic to views demonstrating that the wrong question is being asked. However, as will become equally clear later in this chapter, I do not agree with Searle here—neither on his diagnosis of the "deep mistake" nor on his characterization of his own view.
27. That on Searle's account particular physical states are not causally necessary allows his view to be consistent with multiple realization, in which different physical states can underlie/cause a particular mental state. Multiple realization is quite important, biologically as well as philosophically, and as such will be taken up at length in later sections.
28. Property dualists, for instance, need not embrace even the most basic psychophysical supervenience. This is the case insofar as for some in this group mental properties are only contingently related to physical facts and properties. (These statements are paraphrased from: www.jimpryor.net/teaching/courses/mind/notes/supervenience.html © The President and Fellows of Harvard College. This source was accessed on May 5, 2012.)
29. I admire the spirit of Strawson's attempt to "physicalize" the mental, but on some intuitive level I must admit that I feel Strawson's solution circumvents rather than solves the gappy problems to which I allude in the text to follow immediately.
30. Included in this list but not yet addressed, is the significant problem of autonomous mental causation. Alluded to briefly before, it will be taken up in earnest in later sections of this chapter.
31. Or, to use Kim's comments in the context of the Searle/Chalmers issue: In our search for metaphysical emergence, are we looking for something either that does not exist or that we can never recognize? To what extent do these amount to the same thing, even though they seem importantly different—one having to do with ontological reality and the other our human cognitive epistemic limitations?
32. Unsurprisingly, Kim (1993, 2002, 2005, 2010) holds that emergentism really amounts to one of the following—dualism, mysterianism, incoherence, or reduction.
33. Both essays—one a chapter in a 1989 anthology and the other a 1989 address to the American Philosophical Association, later published in the proceedings of same—are reprinted in the 1993 volume.
34. Kim (1993, pp. 281–282) does admit that there is a possible relationship between a mental and physical cause that would work. It is the identity relation. But he takes up only "type identity," in which mental property types are supposed to be identical with physical property types. Yet, as will be discussed later in this chapter, type identity was for specific reasons already acknowledged by many philosophers at that time (including Kim) as a deeply flawed view. Kim writes

(p. 282) ". . . what is for us at issue is the causal efficacy of mental properties of events vis-a-vis their physical properties. Thus, the items that need to be identified are properties . . . [and] we would need to identify mental properties with physical properties . . . [this] is the heart of 'type reductionism.'" Kim does not address "token identity," in which *this particular* instantiation of a physical property (say, at time *t*) is identical with *that particular* instantiation of a mental property (also at time *t*). Along with the problems type identity faces, the viability of the token identity solution will be taken up at length later in the chapter.

35. And endorsed by Kim (see Kim, 1993, pp. 93, 102).
36. It should be clear that a lateral independent cause, say M causing M*, is also ruled out by the combination of the Exclusion Argument and the principle of causal closure of the physical domain.
37. This subsection is "The Generalization Argument: An Argument Mounted Against the Causal Exclusion Argument."
38. Block (2003, p. 133) has further worries here, that if "there is no bottom level of physics, the Causal Exclusion Argument has the consequence that . . . there wouldn't be any causation anywhere." He feels this second matter is the stronger challenge, but that either one, if true, would be sufficient "to reject the Causal Exclusion Argument."
39. Multiple realizability, an important topic in itself (which will be treated at length at various points in this chapter), was seen as providing a devastating objection to type reductionist physicalism. This is credited to the work of Hilary Putnam (see, for example, Putnam, 1967a/1975, 1967b/1975). Briefly, Putnam suggests that what is arguably the same (or a similar) mental state occurring in various species (and perhaps in computers) can have vastly different physical realizers—biologically based but different among different species, and even nonbiologically based, for example, in silicon machines.
40. In Lewis's (1978/1983) "Mad Pain and Martian Pain," for example, Lewis (playfully but instructively) introduces (p. 123) ". . . a Martian who . . . feels pain just as we do, but whose pain differs greatly from ours in its physical realization. His hydraulic mind contains nothing like our neurons. Rather, there are varying amounts of fluid in many inflatable cavities . . . When you pinch his skin you cause no firings of C-fibers—he has none—but rather, you cause the inflation of many smallish cavities in his feet. When these cavities are inflated, he is in pain . . . he groans and writhes . . ." Similarly, mind/body functionalists allow that silicon-based structures could in principle have states and properties capable of realizing mental states such as pain. Functionalism will be addressed briefly in the section on type identity reductive physicalist views.
41. Yablo's (1992) determinable/determinate account covers both properties and events. Thus, he states (p. 271): "A mental event *m* occurs if some physical determination *p* of *m* occurs."
42. I have not included the eliminative materialists here (or elsewhere in this chapter), because they have "solved" the mind/body problem, basically by eliminating the mind. For the eliminative materialists, mental events/states/properties have neither ontological standing nor causal powers. They are mere "folk" concepts; stand-ins until neuroscience provides concepts better able to pick out the physical (brain processes, etc.) constituents that are the genuine causally active elements.
43. In an area where there is much disagreement (as can be attested in the work reported in this chapter), the fact that the details have not been worked out is accepted by all. It is fairly well established that neurons in brain circuit assemblies are both the causes and constituents of mental events/states/properties.

And while this identity is in some ways not unlike H_2O molecules causing and constituting water, there is an important difference. While there *are* fundamental scientific findings explaining *how* the H_2O molecules and their bonds cause and constitute water, in the physical/mental case, even the most optimistic scientists would have to say it is not yet known *how* brain circuits assemble to constitute and cause mental events, states, and properties.

44. Of course it still looks like a problem on Kim's account, in which he contends that mental events are not physical micro-based macroproperties. But the strongest support for Kim's view comes from those cases most damaging to *type* reduction, wherein pain or other mental states can, in theory, be realized with heterogeneous physical realizers, including silicon-based as well as carbon-based material. More on this must await the discussion of multiple realization to follow in the next section.
45. For Hill (1991), competing theories would include any sort of dualism, and double-aspect theory, which in his description (esp. p. 21) seems like a version of nonreductive physicalism.
46. Not all identity theorists agree. J. J. Smart (1959), an important early contributor, held: "That these [sensations, etc.] should *be correlated* with brain processes does not help, for to say that they are correlated is to say that they are something 'over and above'. You cannot *correlate* something with itself" (p. 142).

    However, Hill goes on to contend (wrongly in my view) that if such positive correlations were found, identity theories would no more need to offer "an explanation of this correlation" (p. 24) than would someone need to explain the correlation of Clark Kent and Superman always turning up in the same place. Hill's putative answer that there is no more to it than "Because . . . Clark *is* Superman" (p. 24) fails to acknowledge that the *how* question—"how is that the case?"—is not pointless, even if there is identity. His very example bears that out. There is, in fact, a complex "how" story regarding the fact that Clark and Superman both always turn up at the same place, but never at exactly the same time. Nonetheless, this problem does not necessarily damage Hill's claim for reductive physicalism and the best explanation principle.
47. The best explanation principle Hill cites is also called "inference to the best explanation" or "inference to the best hypothesis." There is a sizable literature on the topic. See, for example, Harman (1966), who is credited with first explicitly addressing this notion, and Lipton (1991), for his book-length treatment and for references. (I have had occasion to discuss the use of this principle regarding aspects of the placebo effect. See Brakel, 2010, chaps. 5 and 6.)
48. Possibly for Smart, nonreductive materialism would fare no better than dualism on this matter.
49. In Hill's text the word is "larger," but from what follows, it appears that he meant "smaller."
50. The double-aspect theory according to Hill (1991, p. 35) ". . . asserts that there are things that exemplify both qualitative [mental] characteristics and physical characteristics, but because it denies that qualitative characteristics are identical with physical characteristics, it must reject the view that the fact that consists of something's exemplifying a qualitative characteristic is identical with any of the facts that consist of that thing's exemplifying a physical characteristic . . . [Double aspect theory is thereby] committed to the existence of two irreducible categories of fact."
51. This idea is also considered, but summarily dismissed, by Putnam (1967b/1975, p. 437). It was then picked up and taken further by Fodor (1974).

52. Indeed, on my account to be presented soon, a version of token physicalism I term "diachronic conjunctive token physicalism" (or DiCoToP) *does* do better.
53. They are more accurately *almost* identical tokens; they are separate instances, distinguishable because they are uniquely time marked. For more on the view that these are actually separate tokens ontologically, see the section on token physicalism, later in this chapter.
54. Token physicalism can even accommodate both the mad pain (same physical realizers of pain, different pain behavior) and Martian pain (different physical realizers of pain, same pain behavior) made famous by David Lewis (1978/1983).
55. Remember that Kim, as has been discussed above, disagrees, finding that Ms are not to be considered genuine macroproperties, micro-based. Hence, for Kim, proponents for the causal powers of Ms are wrongheaded. These proponents should accept that Ms are either causally otiose or epiphenomena whose putative causal powers are no more than those of magic.
56. Are these gaps related? They appear to be—not as identical twins, but at least as full siblings, if not fraternal twins.
57. Chalmers uses the plural here (philosophers) in referring to a view raised by Dennett (1979) on this matter that Chalmers regards as similar to Jackson's (2003) approach.
58. As is repeatedly discussed in the text, the *how* of this causation is still unknown.
59. More accurately, the M tokens can at best approximate being identical, given, for example, their unique time stamp.
60. Evidence of this comes from the work of Bechtel and Mundale (1999), Edelman and Gally (2001), Figdor (2010), and the several articles of Friston, Price, and colleagues, referenced and discussed in the section on MR and the troubles it brings for type physicalism. See also the very similar discussion above concerning three instances of a "single" belief of my own—the belief that dogs are wonderful.
61. This issue of scale could, of course, go on for many cycles—what would the dead ant's now-dying parasite view as the primary causal agent of its unlucky fate?
62. Granted, the difference may not be humanly perceivable.
63. Ganeri (2011, p. 691) seems to have been getting at something similar in his account of emergence of the mental. He allows downward causation of the mental, but only diachronically, while he sees the synchronic relationship as materially causative and constitutive. On my view, too, mental tokens at a time slice are constituted synchronically by their physical constituents. But diachronically, over time, different multiply realized physical tokens contribute to what is regarded as the same mental event/state/property. (For further elaboration, see the next section on Diachronic Conjunctive Token Physical ism, DiCoToP.)
64. As is probably obvious from the text, my view is also profoundly different from Kim's multiple-type physicalism. The major difference is that, for Kim (1993, pp. 364–366), ". . . an *M*-instance [is not] identified with an instance of the disjunctive property P_1 or $P_2 \ldots [P_n]$"; in fact it is not clear how (or even if) Kim identifies each *M*-instance. Whereas on my account, an *M*-instance at a particular time slice is identified with its unique particular *P*-instance realizer at that time slice.
65. Note that, just like planks in a ship, some neurons and their connections drop out or die but are replaced by others.
66. My account does assume that diachronicity—that is, that existence over time and therefore time itself—has ontologic and not mere epistemic standing. This

is a question beyond the scope of the current volume, but something I shall explore in the future.

NOTES TO CHAPTER 4

1. Bruner and Postman (1949) performed an experiment in which they presented stimulus items in a tachistoscope—an apparatus capable of very brief stimuli delivery—and recorded the speed at which participants could recognize the various stimulus items. The items employed were (1) playing cards with regular/*consistent* suits and colors (e.g., red hearts, black clubs) and (2) cards with incongruous/*inconsistent* suits and colors (e.g., red spades, black diamonds). They found that the average time for recognizing the ordinary cards was significantly shorter (28 millisecond mean) than that for the inconsistent cards (114 millisecond mean), *even after the participants had experience with, and therefore expected, the "trick cards"* (p. 210).

   Although Bruner and Postman's overall conclusion supports the point I am making, this experiment is not without a serious problem. That which is familiar to the point of being "overlearned" is not only more readily recognizable but certainly easier to identify and name. To the extent that this would be true of normal versus trick playing cards, mediating their faster recognition times, the experiment is flawed.
2. Note that I indeed mean "understood as consistent" rather than "restored to consistency," because consistency, while hard to appreciate, was never ontologically absent. This will become clearer in the text to follow.
3. Tangential to the consistency issue at hand, I come to a somewhat different conclusion for the Frankfurt thought experiment. In my view his thought experiment suggests that the principle of alternative possibilities should be changed to one that reflects the moral agent's epistemology: that is, a person is morally responsible only if the person *believes* he/she could have done otherwise. On further reflection, perhaps these are not *two* new replacements for the principle of alternative possibilities but rather two complemental pieces of the same new principle—Frankfurt's statement of the principle applies to those agents who know that they cannot do otherwise; my statement of the principle applies to those who do not yet know that they cannot do otherwise.
4. The therapeutic ratio is calculated on the basis of the quantified effective treatment responses over the quantified toxic effects.
5. Laboratory animals, some even genetically identical, are bred for this type of controlled experiment. Often laboratory animal experiments are followed by tests with human participants. In the human testing, at first researchers might want patients to be of similar age, socioeconomic profile, general health, biologically relevant habits (smoking, drinking), and with the same level of Disease Q. However, it is clear that it is also important to ascertain whether a drug's usefulness is restricted—for example, to one age group or a certain level of the disease. Thus, further testing must use age and level of disease as distinct experimental condition variables.
6. Mikhail cites neither the Spranca et al. (1991) nor the Petrinovich et al. (1993) work.
7. More on the "trolley cases" will follow throughout this chapter.
8. Note that there has been much commentary on this study (see, for instance, Greene, 2003; Greene and Haidt, 2002; and Mikhail, 2007).
9. These brain areas (as reported by Greene et al., 2001, p. 2107) are the medial portion of Brodmann's Areas 9 and 10 (medial frontal gyrus), Brodmann's

Area 31 (posterior cingulate gyrus), and Brodmann's Area 39 (angular gyrus, bilateral).

10. Brodmann's Area 46 (middle frontal gyrus, right) and Broadmann's Area 7/40 (parietal lobe, bilateral) were the areas less activated in the moral/personal condition (see Greene et al., 2001, p. 2107).
11. Despite the impressiveness of this experiment, an additional control condition would have improved it greatly—namely adding a category for personal/emotional nonmoral dilemmas. As it stands, one cannot know whether the effects are carried simply by the fact that the dilemmas in question are emotional and personal simpliciter, with the moral aspect not particularly relevant. Thus, the addition of this control condition would be vitally important, because the point of the study is to investigate differences in moral judgments and intuitions (see Section Three, "Abuses of Consistency," for more on this experiment and this particular criticism).
12. Freud's metapsychology is indeed famous, but not without its detractors, both inside and outside the psychoanalytic world. There is an immense psychoanalytic literature both on the metapsychology as a whole and on several of the particular principles. This topic is, however, quite tangential to the current volume.
13. Here is an example. Patient Q, whose father was a controlling military man, experiences his male analyst as harsh and punishing. This is especially the case whenever the analyst asks why the patient is late, which the analyst does (in a rather neutral way) every time the patient is late. This is a transference manifestation. Later in the treatment, the analyst learns that the patient's father required promptness, punishing any lateness quite severely. If the patient had been even two minutes late to a family meal, the father would insist that the patient receive no food. But since the analyst is not controlling, harsh, or punishing, the transference experience is, in this sense, inappropriate to the current relationship between patient and analyst. And yet the experience is clearly caused insofar as the analyst frequently inquires even about minimal lateness, behaving in this small respect in a fashion actually quite like Patient Q's father.
14. Note that the analyst has transferences to the patient, too. Called countertransferences, these are personal reactions arising in psychoanalysts concerning their patients. The analyst often experiences less organized, but sometimes intense, feelings, thoughts, fantasies, desires, wishes, and so on. These, along with the more structured countertransferences, are usefully examined by the analyst toward understanding the patient (and probably the analyst, too).
15. Patients frequently respond to "good" interpretations ("successful" pilot experiments) with this sense of knowing now what had been known before, but unconsciously so, and therefore unavailable for examination. Remarkably, Kuhn (1964/1977) describes an almost identical phenomenon with successful thought experiments (p. 263): "The outcome of thought experiments can be the same as that of scientific revolutions: they can enable the scientist to use as an integral part of his knowledge what his knowledge had previously made inaccessible to him. That is the sense in which they [thought experiments] change his knowledge of the world."
16. I say "allows" rather than "ensures" consistency because even in large participant pools unequal distribution can occur. When this does happen, however, and a particular variable (say age) is positively correlated with the measure of interest (i.e., the dependent variable—in this case, how much the symptom improves), a statistical process of removing the variability associated with the covariant factor (so-called partialing out) can be usefully applied.

17. Subjects will, of course, have fantasies concerning which medications they are to receive. Experimenters, too, might have hunches as to which medication a particular participant was assigned.
18. Placebos with side effects similar to the drugs with which they are compared are called active placebos. These are much more efficacious in producing therapeutic placebo responses than passive, inert placebos.
19. Within-subject (or within-participant) design experiments are those in which a particular subject participates in all the conditions under study. Each subject's different responses to all the different conditions are registered. Thus, in the Spranca et al. (1991) experiment, Subject A's response to the omission version was compared with Subject A's response to the commission version. In contrast, between-subject (or between-participant) design experiments are those in which different groups of subjects participate in different conditions. Here, differences between the groups of subjects, each having experienced a different condition, are paramount. For example, the drug study discussed just above is a between-subjects experiment, in which each of three different participant groups receives just one of three drugs—either N, E, or P.
20. Unlike Zangwill's seeming neutrality on this matter, Knobe and Doris try to demonstrate the deleterious consequences entailed by "the assumption of invariance," a view compatible with Section Three, "The Abuses of Consistency."
21. In Brakel (2010, chap. 4), I take up at length the question: What is the nature of the "me" I care about, when what I care about is "my" continued survival? Among the various views explored there, Parfit's (1984) thought experiments and the resultant deliberations figure prominently.
22. So, for instance , if a man with one million hairs on his head is not bald, what about a man with 999,999 hairs? Obviously, he is also not bald. But suppose one iterates this question, subtracting one hair at a time until a man has one hair on his head, or no hair at all on his head. This man is certainly bald; but what was the sharp borderline? (Vagueness and the sorites paradox are discussed at length in Brakel, 2010, chap. 3.)
23. For Parfit it is "Relation R," a blend of psychological connectedness and psychological continuity that is distinct conceptually from personal identity. Relation R, unlike personal identity, is not transitive, while personal identity must be transitive (see Parfit, 1984, pp. 199–243, esp. p. 206 for a complete account).
24. Note how well this account fits with the assumptions of psychoanalysis as a general theory of mind discussed previously in the text.
25. See Nagera (1966) for a thorough and enlightening account of the relations between the infantile neurosis and adult psychopathologies.
26. As I reviewed this section concerning Mr A's father transference, I noticed a possible countertransference manifestation of my own. I began to refer to A almost exclusively as Mr. A rather than Patient A. This could reflect a wish on my part to escape the negative father transference by proclaiming: "Hey, I am a better father figure. I am interested in Mr. A, the whole person, not just the poor sick Patient A."
27. See Schlesinger (1995) for additional reasons that analysts too often fail to take note of their patients' responses to interpretations.
28. This is actually a paraphrase of psychoanalyst Jon Myer's words (circa 1985) to a friend of mine who was contemplating psychoanalytic treatment.
29. The work of Chapters Two and Three in this volume are also quite relevant in further addressing the reasons psychoanalysis takes so long. Remember that, although the extinction of aversively conditioned behaviors can only be

approximated, they are best approximated by allowing the development of many transference experiences, which serve over time as the multiple contexts for safe-here/safe-now trials. Now add to this that each neurotic/aversively conditioned symptom, on my view, constitutes a genuine mental macroproperty with many micro-based physical realizers—each realizer needing its own safe-here/safe-now set of extinction trials. Moreover, because neurotic/aversively conditioned behaviors tend to generalize, many situations at various different stages of life become affected. No wonder, then, that psychoanalysis, in which multiple transferences allow extinction trials in many and diverse contexts, becomes both more time-consuming and more essential to deal with problems of this nature.

30. The article discusses two studies, but the first one will suffice, because the results for both studies are comparable and the stimuli for the second study introduce more complexity than is necessary for our purposes.
31. Elegant, but wrongheaded, as I intend to show.
32. In addition, one "but" was changed to an "and."
33. Knobe's (2003) study includes another very similar experiment. Two lieutenants are faced with (a) men who will be killed by being put in direct line of fire or (b) men who will be rescued by being taken out of the direct line of fire. The lieutenant in the (a) case claims not to care about men being killed, his only concern is taking the hill. The lieutenant in the (b) case claims not to care about men being rescued. He only cares about the taking of the hill. Again, the lieutenant in the (a) case is a plausible military man, if somewhat fanatical; the (b) case lieutenant, a man who would not be relieved about men rescued, if only to look better himself, is a fiend, and likely unbelievable to subjects.
34. Note that I have also used "but" and "because," much as Knobe used "and" and "but" in the original, to increase the naturalness of the statements.
35. Another problem with this experiment: the findings may be mediated by a factor not at all relevant to the good or bad nature of the side effect, x. It is possible that the not-caring-at-all attitudes of the chairmen carries much of the effect. To test this specifically, Knobe might want to add two cases that are slightly different from the two proposed in the text: two chairmen who are both really concerned about the environment. Thus: (1) a chairman who knew about the anticipated good side effects, *did care a lot* about the environment, *and* whose program led to good side effects; and (2) a chairman who knew about the anticipated bad side effects, *did care a lot* about the environment, *but* whose program led to bad side effects. Even in a between-subjects design, would these two cases show the greatly significant difference that Knobe's cases did? (I will have more to say about this study and particularly the benefit of adding chairmen who do care in Section Five.)
36. My spinning head gives me an appreciation for those experimental philosophers who claim that any theory developed by any armchair philosopher can gain support from some devised parallel case that will seem to support it. Or, to phrase it from the negative side (Knobe and Doris, 2010, pp. 321–322): "We have been extremely impressed with the ingenuity philosophers have shown in constructing counterexamples to each other's theories . . . The result is a kind of mutual annihilation." Apparently this has driven some philosophers to do empirical research on real attitudes of the real "folk." But other solutions are possible, too; for example, see Section Four of the current chapter.
37. For another example in which the passive/active distinction dissolves, see Rachels (1975, p. 79). Here, Smith stands to gain a large amount of money if his young cousin dies. He drowns him, arranging it to look like an accident. Jones, in a similar situation, plans the same act, but his young cousin happens

to drown all on his own as Jones stands by and does absolutely nothing to save his cousin. Rachels declares Jones as culpable as Smith.

38. She does not, however, cite Tooley's work in her article.
39. The doctrine of double effect holds that misuse of a person directly is not permitted, whereas manipulating the threat, even with the same anticipated outcome for the person, is permitted. Although the doctrine's most famous application can be found in religious proclamations on obstetrical decisions—situations, for example, when it is possible to spare the life of the mother *or* the baby but not both—some find that strictures imposed by the doctrine of double effect can also be used to explain some of the trolley case variations. For instance, in the case just discussed in the text, the doctrine of double effect would allow activating the catapult with the weight properly in place, notwithstanding the fact that the man at the catapult site would surely die. His death would be seen as a side effect, despite its total predictability. While with the weight not in place, the act of catapulting the man down to the track could no longer be regarded as just an incidental effect. It would be a direct misuse of his person and thereby forbidden.
40. The word *agent* introduces another consideration. Is there a difference between agents who violate the rights of persons, on the one hand, and the rights of persons being violated, on the other? For Kamm (1989), these are not just semantic variations. They represent two different strands in moral thinking: agent-focused and victim-focused principles.

    Kamm (1989, pp. 251–252) points out something very intriguing about victim-focused principles. She argues that it would not be acceptable for person X—knowing that person Y is about to violate the rights of two victims, say by throwing both of them off of a footbridge to stop a trolley—to minimize the number of deaths by X himself violating the rights of one victim, throwing just one person off of an adjacent footbridge. On her account, the one person cannot be made a victim, even to spare the two others because, ". . . a moral system . . . that permits minimization of the violation of a certain right by transgression of that very right essentially eliminates that right from the system" (p. 252).

    Then regarding agent-focused principles, the following question occurs to me. Does the composition of firing squads, including several shooters and even one or more with blanks, preserve each agent's belief that no one agent in particular is responsible?
41. Montmarquet indicates that this case originates with Foot. It does indeed (Foot 1967, p. 13), even though Montmarquet has made a few insignificant changes (for example, in Foot's version there are five patients whose lives could be saved).
42. For more on the transference neurosis, see Chapter Two (pp. 29–30; 46) and the current chapter (pp. 107–108; 118–119; and notes 13 and 14). I thank Arthur Brakel for pointing out that the development of the transference neurosis functions as an intermediate stepwise case.
43. Actually, if the subject pool were sufficiently large, it would be of great interest to run and contrast Knobe's original experiment versus replication–with-extension experiments adding each of my two new sets of items—more realistic chairmen; more caring chairmen—in both between-subject and within-subject design versions. Moreover, directly contrasting results of the studies when done in a between-subjects version and a within-subjects version could provide quantitative data potentially indexing the pull for consistency, potentially of great importance. (I longed for something similar for the Medin et al. 1990 study as discussed above.)

44. It is interesting to note that, since each individual is asked about the two endpoint cases as well as each case in between, the intervening steps method approximates a within-subjects design type of study where each subject is exposed to every experimental condition.
45. From here, in fact, Unger (1996, p. 98) heads in a somewhat different direction to make a similar point.
46. In fact, as Unger (1996) develops his thesis—one that offers a grand utilitarian account—his view on this matter more approximates that of Harris (1975) in his survival lottery thought experiment discussed earlier in the chapter.
47. Along these lines, it is of interest that in my own use of intervening stepwise cases in the Transplant Case, I quite unconsciously (i.e., without conscious deliberation) rendered the potential donor "unconscious." Also, as commented on earlier, in note 40, even firing squads are arranged so that the feeling (and burden) of active agency is lessened. It is kept intentionally ambiguous as to who has actually fired the shots that did the killing. First, there are many riflemen. Second, at least one shooter has blanks in his rifle, with the group unaware of how many and which of them have the killing ammunition. In addition, the watchful awareness of the victim is decreased because a blindfold is used.
48. Unger (1996, pp. 88–91) bases his "method of several options" technique on recognizing the human need for consistency. He, in fact, says (p. 92), ". . . the response someone makes to a given example can be greatly influenced by . . . responses made to cases previously encountered. And, since folks want their responses to seem consistent, often the influence is greatest when the present case seems 'essentially the same' as the just previous example."
49. Unger's (1996) interest is moral and ethical. He advocates strongly for us not to ignore the plight of those with whom we are not personally connected, who are in fact so distant that their emotional situation remains invisible to us. Unger urges us not to feel that morality performed at a distance would be hopeless. He, in fact, suggests that, to the extent that we can reduce feelings of hopelessness about these more distant acts, the evaluation of their salience would increase.

NOTES TO CHAPTER 5

1. I thank Arthur Brakel for suggesting this acronym.
2. This is understood to also include whatever other brain factors are contributing to this particular collection of neurons—for example, neurochemicals and supportive nonneuronal brain cells.
3. Singular, in that it is identical in content, affect, type of mental process (it being a thought), and it is mine.
4. Note that this is the case notwithstanding the fact that some of these variations in neuronal assemblies will likely be very small, both for the phobic with a particular fear state and for me and my loving thought(s) about my dog.

Index

Note: page numbers with *n* indicate footnotes.